Political issues in Ireland today

Published in our
centenary year
~ **2004** ~
MANCHESTER
UNIVERSITY
PRESS

Politics Today

Series editor: Bill Jones

Political issues in Ireland today

Third edition

edited by

Neil Collins and Terry Cradden

Manchester University Press
Manchester and New York

distributed exclusively in the USA by Palgrave

First published by Manchester University Press 1994
Second edition published 1999

This edition published by Manchester University Press
Oxford Road, Manchester M13 9NR, UK
and Room 400, 175 Fifth Avenue, New York, NY 10010, USA
www.manchesteruniversitypress.co.uk

Distributed exclusively in the USA by
Palgrave, 175 Fifth Avenue, New York,
NY 10010, USA

Distributed exclusively in Canada by
UBC Press, University of British Columbia, 2029 West Mall,
Vancouver, BC, Canada V6T 1Z2

British Library Cataloguing-in-Publication Data
A catalogue record for this book is available from the British Library

Library of Congress Cataloging-in-Publication Data applied for

ISBN   0 7190 6571 2 *paperback*

This edition first published 2004

13 12 11 10 09 08 07 06 05 04   10 9 8 7 6 5 4 3 2 1

Typeset in Photina
by Servis Filmsetting Ltd, Manchester
Printed in Great Britain
by Biddles Ltd, King's Lynn

Contents

Tables and figures

Tables

Figures

Contributors

Michael Breen is head of Media and Communication Studies at Mary Immaculate College, University of Limerick.

Patrick Butler is a lecturer at Trinity College Dublin. His research covers a wide range of marketing, including politics, music and public services.

Mark Callanan is a lecturer at the Institute of Public Administration in Dublin. He is co-editor of *Local Government in Ireland: Inside Out* (Institute of Public Administration, forthcoming) and has undertaken extensive research in the field of local government reform.

Neil Collins is professor and head of the Department of Government at University College Cork. He is co-author with Terry Cradden of *Irish Politics Today* (Manchester University Press, 2001).

Terry Cradden is presently visiting lecturer at University College Dublin, and was formerly head of the School of Commerce and International Business at Magee College, University of Ulster.

Elizabeth DeBoer-Ashworth is the assistant director of the School of Business and Government, University College Cork. Her doctorate, *The Global Political Economy and Post-1989 Change: The Place of the Central European Transition*, is published in the International Political Economy series (Macmillan, 2000).

Eoin Devereux lectures in sociology at the University of Limerick. His books include *Understanding the Media* (Sage, 2003). He formerly worked for RTE.

Clodagh Harris is a lecturer in politics in the Department of Government at University College Cork, specialising in the European Union and Northern Ireland.

Kathleen Long is director of development at the US–Ireland Alliance, Washington, USA, and lectures on gender issues at University College Cork.

Michelle Millar teaches public policy at the National University of Ireland, Galway. She has undertaken extensive work on health inequality in Ireland.

Gerard Mullally is a lecturer in sociology at University College Cork and a senior research fellow of the Cleaner Production Promotion Unit. He has researched and published widely on environment, sustainability and Local Agenda 21, a programme promoting sustainable economic and social development and greater participation at local level.

Jane O'Mahony is a researcher at the Dublin European Institute, University College Dublin. She specialises in the relationship between Ireland and the European Union.

Séamus Ó Tuama is a lecturer in politics in the Department of Government at University College Cork. His research and teaching interests are focused on citizenship, democracy, human rights and science and technology policy.

Aodh Quinlivan is a lecturer in politics in the Department of Government at University College Cork, specialising in local government studies and public management reforms.

Preface

This third edition of *Political Issues in Ireland Today* draws on the research of political scientists and others in several Irish universities. The topics chosen reflect the editors' wish to revisit some areas but also to redress the neglect of others. Thus the pressure of events at European Union level (Chapter 2), as well as in local government (Chapter 4), are revisited. Similarly, health policy (Chapter 6) continued to demand attention – if anything it has risen up the public's agenda. A further continuing topic of pressing popular and scholarly interest is the search for peace in Northern Ireland (Chapter 3).

By contrast with areas which are being revisited, this edition explores the newly urgent problems associated with environmental policy (Chapter 7) and racism (Chapter 10). Similarly, science and technology policy (Chapter 9), while not enjoying the same level of media coverage, throws up major concerns about future risks and opportunities which will inexorably push their way into the public debate about Ireland's future direction.

Finally, this volume addresses gender (Chapter 11), social partnership (Chapter 5) and the recasting of citizens as consumers (Chapter 8), which are 'slow burners' in the Irish political arena but present significant policy choices. The book begins, however, by examining the underlying determinant of the partnership of the policy debate in Ireland, the health of the much-heralded 'Celtic Tiger' (Chapter 1).

Neil Collins
Terry Cradden

1

The 'Celtic Tiger' in a global context

Elizabeth DeBoer-Ashworth

Introduction

Ireland has attracted global interest since the early 1990s because of its eco-nomic performance. The boom at the beginning of the period saw Ireland acquire the nickname 'the Celtic Tiger', and its export growth, particularly in the high-tech sectors, was widely applauded. However, much of the praise for the country's performance came from those writing from an economic rather than political or sociological perspective. In terms of industrial production and foreign direct investment Ireland's growth was indeed impressive. But while economic development is always eagerly sought after by governments, it does not necessarily simplify the political task of governing a country. In the case of Ireland, development increased the number of long-term unemployed and created an ever-widening gap between the rich and poor. As a result, Ireland's place in the global economy is characterised by paradox: a small former British colony yet a full member of the European Union (EU); possessed of a sophisti-cated, well-educated workforce but with some of the worst poverty in the Organisation for Economic Co-operation and Development (OECD) countries; and a major high-tech exporter with a fifth of its economy still dependent on agriculture.

As Irish industry readjusts to a global slowdown following the September 11 terrorist attacks in the US, it is appropriate to review the place of Ireland in a world economic context. To try to make sense of that, this chapter will examine the historical problems of Ireland's development, the nature of the 1990s boom, and current political issues arising in a post-boom Irish economy.

Ireland's economic legacy

It is important to understand the political and social context in which the devel-opment of Ireland's economy has occurred. Ireland was a British colony, and its

1

development in the nineteenth century was typical of that generated by an extractive colonial economic system. Goods were grown on the periphery to be sold at the centre. Emigration from Ireland after the potato famine of the mid-nineteenth century is well known; however, emigration had been taking place well before the crisis that the famine was to produce. The population of Ireland in 1841 was over 8 million, but over 1.5 million had already left between 1815 and 1840 – half a million to each of Great Britain, Canada and the US (Sweeney 1999: 22). The economy was mainly agricultural and, on the face of it, the Irish peasantry was initially more fortunate than many of its European counter-parts, to the extent that many peasants had access to small plots of land on which to grow crops. However, as the population grew these plots were inevitably subdivided, to the point where smallholdings became tiny and unable to sustain farmers and their families.

Overlaid on this was a problem of underinvestment: the wealthy in Ireland received a better return by putting their money into the growing industrial heartland of Britain rather than investing at home. The result was a slow de-industrialisation of Ireland during the early part of the nineteenth century. For example, at one time Ireland was possessed of very profitable woollen mills, but these were rendered redundant by the huge growth of industrial textile pro-duction in Britain. The potato blight famine of 1845–48, following on the heels of industrial decline, was devastating. One million people emigrated or died and the population was to drop by 1.5 million, to just 6.5 million, by 1871 (Sweeney 1999: 22). The political economy of modern Ireland seems far removed from the influence of famine. However, the legacy of famine was to endure until well after Irish independence in 1922. In particular, the solution to unemployment would remain systematic emigration, right through to the 1970s.

Before independence there was little government interference in the economy, but the new state had a number of economic difficulties to face. World War I had been generally good for Ireland: higher food prices and remittances home from soldiers had proved very beneficial. However, after 1922 there was a decline in agricultural employment; and the Free State also suffered severe economic disadvantage arising directly from partition – not least because it was deprived of the area which became Northern Ireland, the most industrialised part of the country. During the run-up to the Great Depression, economic policy became a matter of great contention, and the free trade versus protec-tionism debate went on in Ireland as much as elsewhere. From the late 1920s until 1932 the Cumann na Gaedheal government followed the free trade route, but this changed when Fianna Fáil came to power in 1932 and instituted high levels of tariff protection against imports from abroad, and in particular from the UK. Though there was also a political purpose behind the duties placed on UK goods (i.e. to extract certain concessions from the British government), the new tariff wall was mainly intended to insulate existing industries from inter-national competition and to encourage the growth of new indigenous indus-tries making goods that would substitute for those previously imported.

However, Fianna Fáils's protectionist policies were themselves to have serious economic repercussions. The British government responded in kind by erecting similar barriers against imports from the Irish Free State, and the resulting 'economic war', as it was called – which lasted until 1938 – actually caused a two-thirds drop in Irish exports, 96 per cent of which had previously gone to the UK (including, of course, Northern Ireland). It deserves to be said that many newly independent colonies in the 1960s and 1970s would echo Irish action and employ economic policies of import substitution and protectionism in a bid to enhance their political independence. Moreover, Ireland was certainly not alone in putting up tariff barriers during the 1930s. Protectionism was widespread, and nations large and small used border tariffs as a key instrument of national economic policy during the Depression.

The trade war with Britain ended with honour preserved on both sides; but while UK markets were once again thrown open to Irish exports, especially agricultural goods, Ireland continued to maintain tariff barriers against foreign goods of all kinds. For what makes Ireland unusual is that after World War II it held onto the same protectionist policies as it had instituted in the 1930s. Tariff protection and policies with a similar purpose, such as forbidding total foreign ownership of companies, did of course keep firms in Irish hands and they did increase employment significantly – though not nearly enough to prevent the continuation of emigration. However, these policies did not increase productivity; manufacturing industry was deeply inefficient; 'protected' goods were often very expensive; and they were sometimes of poor quality. So, when the world economy started to expand during the 1950s, Ireland's industrial development began inevitably to stagnate (Ó Gráda 1995: 433). The end result was that Ireland became more dependent on the UK market than it had been before independence. The volume of its exports that now went to Great Britain and Northern Ireland increased to 99 per cent; and there was an emigration rate of over 36,000 a year (Sweeney 1999: 34).

Many of Ireland's economic problems, such as declining employment (and incomes) in the agriculture sector, did not lend themselves well to free market solutions; but the search for a new economic policy was in any case hampered by the deeply embedded notion that economic development could only be generated by direct government intervention. Independent Ireland had from the beginning a disproportionately large number of state-owned companies. As late as 1987, enterprises such as the Electricity Supply Board and An Post (the postal service) employed over 70,000 (6 per cent of the workforce) and accounted for more than 10 per cent of Ireland's GNP (Dooney and O'Toole 1998: 190–1). However, during the 1950s and 1960s the government set up a number of economic advisory bodies and commissioned a number of policy reports. A Capital Advisory Committee appointed to look into public investment suggested that a programme of economic development was needed. As a result the Department of Finance prepared a paper entitled *Economic Development* in 1957. According to Sweeney this was followed by a government-sponsored

Committee on Industrial Organisation that produced one of the earliest reports on industrial policy, at the beginning of the 1960s (Sweeney 1999: 37). The findings of the research done during this period all pointed to problems arising from unproductive agriculture, a lack of industrial development, small-scale, underfunded production capacity, little research and development work, and population decline. However, despite having requested the advice, it was to prove most difficult for conservative Ireland's government to accept this, still less implement it.

Changes in the global economic system

Ireland's reluctance to change the way it conducted economic policy was mirrored throughout the world. Although the 1950s brought an expanding global economy, most countries had no desire to dismantle the trade barriers that helped protect certain of their industries. It must be understood that the international contraction of the world economy during the 1930s meant that international trade was a shadow of what it had been during the late nineteenth century. When industrial production started to improve during the 1950s most companies relied on local or national markets, not international ones.

Although there was much international co-operation during World War II, there was not the same level of global governance as there is at present. However, this was soon to begin to change. International bodies formed in the 1940s, such as the United Nations (UN) and the Bretton Woods institutions (the International Monetary Fund (IMF), the World Bank and the General Agreement on Tariffs and Trade (GATT)), would have a profound impact in years to come. We might note in passing that during the 'Cold War' between the West and the Soviet bloc, while most Western countries theoretically espoused the virtues of free market capitalism, few enough practised it in its fullest form, and protectionism was rife. The Bretton Woods institutions, however, were created specifically to manage, monitor and facilitate international trade and finance. GATT (the forerunner of the present-day World Trade Organisation (WTO)) was specifically intended to lead to the reduction of international tariff and trade barriers through multilateral negotiation. Before the creation of these bodies, national policies and international policy were often distinctly at variance. How a government protected its industry, what kind of social policies it chose to follow, and what kinds of economic interventionism it engaged in were its own business. Countries, whether large or small, obviously had a high level of autonomy in, and sovereignty over, their domestic affairs. In Europe after the war many countries experimented with different forms of welfare state policies, as a consequence of which a degree of wealth redistribution became an accepted part of government policy.

In gradually moving these countries away from that, the role of the US was crucial. It had emerged as the major superpower after World War II, and it was plainly in its interests that there be a politically and economically stable Europe. With this end in view, the US was prepared to part-finance Europe's recovery through the Marshall Plan – conceived in 1947 and named after the then Secretary of State (or Foreign Minister), George C. Marshall. It was based on the US providing raw materials, goods and capital in the form of credits, or even subsidies, in the hope of stimulating economic growth in Europe (DeBoer-Ashworth 2000: 23). The manner in which the US disbursed its funds was crucial to the creation of the European Economic Community (EEC) (later the European Community, and now the EU – see Chapter 2).

Under the Marshall Plan, countries were required to submit joint proposals for funding and were encouraged to adopt a more American style of economic policy; they were particularly encouraged to liberalise trade and make their currencies convertible – though making these changes was not easy, and the opening up of European markets and the implementation of convertible currencies took from 1946 to 1958. By then Italy, France, Germany and the Benelux countries had signed the 1957 Treaty of Rome creating the EEC, and the Marshall Plan organisation was revamped and renamed the OECD (Cox 1987: 215–16). A new international order based on notions of political and economic liberalism had thus been created; the rules of the global trading game had been rewritten; and by the time Ireland joined the EEC in 1973 it was obliged to play by rules that it had had no part in drawing up.

Ireland's response to increased liberalisation of the global market

The liberalisation and globalisation of markets would force change upon Ireland. The European Commission has defined globalisation as the 'process by which markets and production in different countries are becoming increasingly interdependent due to the dynamics of trade in goods and services and flows of capital and technology' (1997: 45).

The outputs and potential of the current globalised capitalist order are quite different from those of the post-war European welfare state system. McMichael (1996) has pointed out that economic development after the war was associated with the idea of the 'developmental state' – of the state generating national development through economic management. By contrast, the current globalisation project integrates regions into the world market, where decisions are made at a global rather than local level. McMichael sees the 'promises' of these two developmental approaches as being very different: the old-style developmental state promised social entitlements and welfare provision, whereas globalisation promises only the right to participate in the world market. This has forced a major shift of gear as regards Irish economic policy-making. Successive governments have remained concerned about developmental issues, but are not permitted under EU and WTO rules to intervene significantly in the economy, as was so common in the past.

Let us first recall the situation in Ireland in the 1980s. The most recent of a number of economic crises had deepened and unemployment, for example, reached a peak at 17 per cent of the people available for work (Clinch et al. 2002: 27). High unemployment and heavy emigration translated into voter dissatisfaction and a series of collapsing political coalitions. Governments during the 1980s rarely served out their full term, and at one stage three general elections were held within a period of just 18 months. By the mid-1980s both main political parties, Fianna Fáil and Fine Gael, were citing national debt and high public spending as a deterrent to development.

In the UK and North America straightforward, neo-liberal, free market solutions were being canvassed as the way forward, in reaction to the new rigours imposed by the globalised market. What makes Ireland's case unusual is the nature of its response to the same pressures. In 1986 the National Economic and Social Council (NESC) produced a report entitled *Strategy for Development 1986–1990* (NESC 1986). Echoing calls from assorted Irish politicians and the media, this report insisted on the need for public spending cuts. However, it contained one vital suggestion that would mark out future economic policy in Ireland as quite different from that then being applied by the Conservative government in the neighbouring UK. The NESC report suggested that hard public policy decisions should be taken on the basis of a wide consensus or partnership of economic and social interests (Connolly and O'Hagan 2000: 5). Moving the debate on during the 1987 election campaign, the then Labour Party leader Dick Spring was quoted as saying that the partnership in question should be made up of 'trade unions, employers, farmers, and government sitting down . . . to decide what the real priorities were and to agree on what measures were necessary' (*Irish Times*, 26 January 1987). The Irish Congress of Trade Unions (ICTU), a key potential participant, was of the same mind and produced a pre-budget submission offering proposals for job creation, tax reform, social welfare and coping with the national debt (Connolly and O'Hagan 2000: 5). Fine Gael, the main opposition party, and the new Progressive Democrat party were both also advocating severe public spending cuts, and all this seemed to point to the emergence of some kind of neo-liberal consensus on future economic policy. Remarkably, however, throughout the discussions about what needed to be done, all political parties and interest groups assumed that there would be a continuation of Ireland's social welfare system and traditions.

It is important to note that the pulling together of what was to become the social partnership process was also due to a very specific set of political circumstances. All political parties had called for change and Fianna Fáil in particular had made much of the need for consensus. However, having failed to gain an overall electoral majority, and faced with reliance on independent non-party Teachtaí Dála (TDs, or Members of Parliament) to push the party's policy programme through the Oireachtas (parliament), Fianna Fáil's leader, Charles Haughey, opted for consulting with employer organisations and trade unions to achieve consensus on economic policy. The suggestion is that Ireland's foray into social partnership was born out of Fianna Fáil's realisation that the opposition parties would be reluctant to criticise its policies if such powerful interests were agreed on what was needed to stimulate growth in the economy (Connolly and O'Hagan 2000: 6).

Despite assenting to participation in talks, Ireland's employers were initially unhappy about sitting at the same table as the unions. This was because of fears that, as in earlier ventures in national pay bargaining, there would be inflationary effects and further increases in public expenditure. Yet the employers did eventually take part, albeit with some reluctance. Indeed it is likely that none of the social partners fully appreciated what a ground-breaking endeavour they were engaging in. In any case, by 1987 the Programme for National Recovery (PNR) had been successfully negotiated; and by 1989 the Federated Union of Employers (FUE) was happy to acknowledge that the PNR had minimised industrial action and contributed to an upturn in the economy (Connolly and O'Hagan 2000: 7). Turner and Wallace assert that although social partnership was only one factor in a complicated policy mix, there is evidence that since 1987 social partnership and its subsequent agreements have achieved clear economic benefits (2001: 5). Since the PNR, follow-on negotiations have resulted in a succession of three-year comprehensive economic and social policy programmes, culminating most recently in the Sustaining Progress agreement of 2003. The mix of social partners has been widened to include not only employers and unions but also the voluntary sector, the NESC and other sectoral interests. The upshot of all this is that a range of stakeholders has become increasingly involved in the creation of public policy. The cooperation between them does not mean that the participating groups do not continue to hold distinctly different views on political and economic development; but social partnership is ultimately a problem-solving exercise, devoted to reconciling different views (O'Donnell 1999). Although there were other influences, then, it must be acknowledged that Ireland's public policy response to its economic crisis – that of social partnership – contributed signally to its ability to institute a fiscal austerity programme without endangering the business climate, and thus helped lay the groundwork for the Irish economic miracle. (For more detail on the social partnership process, see Chapter 5.)

Positive aspects of the economic boom

The Irish economic boom of the 1990s was nothing short of spectacular. Economic growth throughout the late 1990s held steady, giving Ireland one of the highest growth rates in the world at over 8 per cent per year; Sweeney reports that this was higher than those of twenty-nine other OECD members. Moreover, between 1987 and 1999 the number of people in employment rose by 45 per cent (during the same period employment in the US increased by just 1 per cent); and the traditional spectres of emigration and a poor rate of job creation were virtually eliminated, with over 1,110 new jobs a week being created between 1994 and 2000 (Sweeney 1999). Moreover, Ireland went from having a very high emigration rate to having the highest net immigration rate in the EU (Clinch et al. 2002: 27). All the economic indicators during the late 1990s, from gross domestic product (GDP) through to levels of industrial production, showed Ireland's development as verging on the phenomenal (see Table 1.1).

Table 1.1 *World economy – growth, industrial production and prices: percentage change, 1997–98*

Country	GDP	Industrial production	Consumer prices
Brazil	−7.9	−3.3	2.3
China	8.3	9.4	−1.2
Czech Republic	−2.9	−11.3	2.8
France	3.1	0.6	0.2
Germany	2.5	1.3	0.2
Hong Kong	−5.7	−13.8	−1.1
Israel	1.4	4.2	7.8
Japan	−2.6	−7.5	0.2
Republic of Ireland	9.1	15.0	2.6
Russia	−4.6	−4.9	125.6
Singapore	−0.8	2.8	−0.5
South Korea	−5.7	4.0	0.2
Taiwan	3.7	7.8	2.1
United Kingdom	2.7	−0.4	2.4
United States	3.5	1.7	1.7

Source: OECD *Economic Outlook*, No. 64, December 1998.

Despite its small size, by 1998 Ireland had become the world's second largest exporter of software, after the US (O'Hearn 2000: 75). The increase in well-paid jobs translated into a rapid rise in living standards – which by 2000 had overtaken those of Great Britain (Sweeney 1999: 5). Higher levels of income in turn translated into a retail boom and growing pressure on the housing market. Other major public policy difficulties also began to be relieved. Before the boom Ireland had one of the highest ratios of foreign debt to national income in the world (O'Hearn 2000: 71). By 1999 the national debt had been hugely reduced and the Irish exchequer actually began experiencing a surplus in government revenues (Sweeney 1999: 6).

The co-operation between the social partners meant that Ireland was able to undertake its fiscal austerity programme without creating a spate of industrial disputes. This, combined with low corporate taxes, investment grants and a highly educated workforce, made Ireland an increasingly attractive location for multinational corporations. To add to this mix there was the continued support of the EU. The effective doubling of structural funds for the period 1993–99 (see

Chapter 2) meant receipt of transfers worth approximately 10 per cent of Ireland's growing gross national product (GNP) (Kirby 1997: 127). The truly remarkable aspect of the boom was that despite the high growth rate, inflation remained low, allowing for real gains in development.

In 1991 the Irish government had to offer an incentive of more than Ir£100,000 (approximately €125,000) per job to persuade the US corporation Intel to set up a plant near Dublin. By the mid-1990s Ireland no longer had to court American multinationals, US foreign direct investment (FDI) having already topped $10 billion (O'Hearn 2000: 75). By the late 1990s nearly every major international company in the information technology business had a location in Ireland. These included: PC makers Gateway, Dell, ASST, Apple, Hewlett-Packard and Siemens-Nixdorf; integrated circuit manufacturers Intel, Fujitsu, Xilinx and Analog Devices; disc-drive producers Seagate and Quantum; and software designers Microsoft, Lotus and Oracle (O'Hearn 2000: 74). In addition to these large companies there were also many smaller manufacturers, suppliers and service-providers supporting the high-tech sector. The increase in employment opportunities soon began to exceed the supply in the labour market of the kind of skilled people needed. As a result Ireland's university sector went through a period of major expansion in an attempt to meet the demand for highly qualified men and women, for the computer industry in particular.

During the late 1990s a number of publications and institutions usually quick to criticise fiscal performance began praising Ireland in an unprecedented way. The British weekly *The Economist*, the London dailies *The Times* and the *Financial Times*, and the OECD all noted Ireland's remarkable success. And as Ireland continued to grow at almost three times the rate of the rest of the industrialised world, the 'Celtic Tiger' became an almost magical creature. It seemed as if Ireland alone had discovered the secret of high and sustainable growth.

Negative aspects of Ireland's economic development

The first price of Ireland's success has been an unprecedented dependence on foreign multinationals, especially those from the US. In the wake of the September 11 terrorist attacks and the subsequent economic slowdown, the enormity of Ireland's reliance on this one country for so much of its FDI began to hit home. During 2002/3 a number of high-profile factory closures highlighted the fact that Ireland is one of the world's most vulnerable countries in terms of its reliance on transnational corporations. Having analysed data from the Industrial Development Authority (IDA Ireland), O'Hearn notes that the foreign share of fixed capital investment in industry rose from about 60 per cent in 1988 to 85 per cent in the late 1990s. During the same period, the US share of transnational corporation investments rose from 40 per cent or so to more than 80 per cent (O'Hearn 2000: 73).

Just a few of the foreign-owned computer, electrical engineering and chemical companies can be credited with producing 40–50 per cent of Irish growth in the 1990s. Murphy claims that during 1994 ten American multinationals in computers and chemicals accounted for a third of value-added in Irish manufacturing (1994). O'Hearn makes a similar point: in 1998 the Irish economy grew by 10 per cent, much of this being claimed as the result of a 60 per cent growth in organic chemical exports (2000: 75). The level of dependence is demonstrated by the fact that the increase in organic chemical exports was attributable not just to one plant, but to one product: a factory in County Cork is the main world site for the production of the highly popular anti-impotence drug for men, Viagra.

This overdependence prompted some analysts, even during the height of the economic boom, to point out that Ireland had much more in common with a developing country than with a developed one (Kirby 1997: 133); and there was, and remains, an accompanying concern at the lack of growth of indigenous Irish companies. O'Sullivan (1995) has asserted that the Irish government's response to the need to encourage home-grown industry has been conservative and hesitant. In her comparison of the East Asian 'Tigers' with the Irish economy, she has also criticised Irish industrial policy. This is based, she claims, on an expectation that given the right incentives such indigenous capabilities as local research and development will simply emerge – a hope that reflects, in her view, a lack of understanding of the complexity of the social process underlying industrial development (1995: 395).

Of course the large amount of FDI has certainly created jobs. However, jobs in the technology sector tend to be highly paid only for those with university qualifications. This is particularly manifest in a chasm in the labour market between the long-term unemployed (those who have been out of work for more than a year) and well-qualified high-tech employees who have become Ireland's new economic elite. The term 'social exclusion' has become a commonplace description of this uncomfortable state of affairs. It was already clear in the early 1990s that Ireland's economic growth was leaving behind an entire section of Irish society, the members of which simply could not find their way back into the labour force. Public concern resulted in a government report (Office of the Tánaiste 1995) that indicated a continuing deterioration in the position of the long-term unemployed, despite a host of schemes intended to facilitate the finding of jobs in the new economy. Over half of the long-term unemployed had not been working for more than three years, and 40 per cent had been without work for over five years. Another study confirmed that the number of long-term unemployed rose from 35,000 (2.8 per cent of the workforce) in 1980 to 135,000 (10 per cent) in 1993; and by 1997, 50 per cent of all those unemployed fell into the long-term category (Kirby 1997: 137). Another depressing statistic is that over the period of Ireland's greatest economic growth, suicides increased in line with the increases in GDP; most of those concerned were male – 83 per cent in the year 2000 figures (Clinch et al.

2002: 175). Despair resulting from marginalisation is thought to have contributed to this.

The problem of inequality is not simply to do with those who have work as opposed to those without. There is evidence of a high level of income inequality *among* working people. During the mid-1990s the Economic and Social Research Institute (ESRI) carried out two major household surveys that suggested a large increase in wage dispersion (essentially meaning that the difference between the lowest and highest incomes had increased), and Turner has shown that since 1987 Ireland has continued to experience pronounced income inequality (1999: 36–46). Among OECD countries, Ireland has the third highest level of income inequality. The proportion of low-paid workers (full-time workers earning less than two thirds of the median earnings for that group) increased from 18 per cent in 1987 to 21 per cent by 1994, placing Ireland behind only the US as regards the incidence of low pay (Barrett et al. 1999). There is little nationwide data on income distribution since 1994, but there are strong indications that government tax and welfare changes since 1997 have actually benefited higher-income groups (Nolan and Maitre 2000: 154–5).

In addition to accepting an increase in long-term unemployment and a rise in income inequality, the Irish government has also neglected the public infrastructure. Despite economic growth and declining debt in the 1990s, there continued to be underfunding in crucial areas such as health care. Between 1987 and 1999 there was a 9 per cent decrease (in terms of GDP) in expenditure on public health, and this despite an increase in both population and wealth (Turner and Wallace 2001: 8). As a result, health care became a major issue during the 2002 general election. Ireland's persistent social problems also provide a real challenge for government: in the aggregate Ireland is experiencing a decrease in overall poverty, but upon closer examination the figures reveal it to be a country with growing inequality and an increasingly marginalised underclass. However welcome the boom has been, the issue of social exclusion is a blot on Ireland's economic success.

Current political issues and public policy responses

At present a considerable amount of research effort is being expended in order to understand the Irish economic success of the 1990s. In part, academic interest in the 'Celtic Tiger' era arises from a concern that the boom was an aberration – was it simply a regional phenomenon, or did it represents a convergence with Ireland's European partners (Barry 2002)? Convergence suggests that Ireland has attained a solid level of development – one that cannot be undone. A once-off regional boom, however, would portend the real possibility of a spectacular decline. The fundamental premise of this research, however, is a conviction that the 'Celtic Tiger' era is over. The economic growth of the 1990s had begun to slow even before the September 11 attacks, and areas beyond the high-tech sector also had their share of difficulties. An agricultural crisis in 2001, arising from a fear of the spread of foot-and-mouth disease in cattle, caused an effective ban on tourism in the countryside. This proved devastating for poorer rural areas to which foreign visitors had traditionally brought much needed revenue. Bord Fáilte, the government body with the task of promoting tourism, suggested that the foot-and-mouth crisis represented a loss of over 1 million tourists in a year and a consequent loss to the economy of over Ir£500 million (approximately €625 million).

In tandem with the foot-and-mouth scare there was a general slowdown in the world economy during 2001. Because of Ireland's economic dependence on US multinationals, a contraction in world markets sparked job losses in the summer of 2001, well before the September 11 attacks. In August 2001, for example, the American computer manufacturer Gateway announced the closure of its European headquarters in Dublin, signalling a loss of 900 jobs. Following September 11 both the information and communication technology sectors, as well as the tourist sector, experienced further downturns. Bord Fáilte estimates that there was a reduction of 40 per cent in coach tours for US visitors. Similarly, a survey in the Shannon region in County Clare revealed that eight out of ten tourist businesses experienced a sharp downturn in overseas bookings and sales. As regards the information technology sector, January 2002 began with a series of plant closures in key sectors. Fujitsu Isotec decided against investing in the modernisation of its Irish facilities and closed its entire operation in January 2002, followed shortly by Sanmina-SCI. Plant closures and job losses continued, and by March 2002 the then Minister for Social, Community and Family Affairs announced that the live register of unemployed had risen by 26,367 to 162,252, representing an unemployment rate of 4.3 per cent.

Yet despite recent shocks the Irish economy as a whole has not gone into a much-feared economic free fall. The slowdown of the US economy has had its effect, but most of Ireland's major economic indicators are within reasonable limits as compared to the overall situation of its fellow OECD members. In terms of output growth and price inflation, Ireland is predicted to remain above the EU average until 2004 – but the figures are not disastrous. Indeed, the growth of the Irish economy in 2002 and 2003 has been somewhat greater and inflation has been slightly lower than was predicted by the ESRI (ESRI 2002). There remains some concern about current economic performance, none the less – particularly when comparisons can be made with a mid-boom peak of growth in industrial production of over 15 per cent coupled with a rise in consumer prices of only 2.6 per cent.

Ultimately, the Irish economy will only show strong signs of growth if there is a robust recovery in the global economy. In the meantime the Irish government has to wrestle with a deterioration in the public finances while trying at the same time to maintain its commitment to a number of national development programmes and to the EU Stability and Growth Pact, which dictates a number of economic and fiscal parameters within which members of the euro-zone must operate. Fortunately, the lessons of the 1980s have left an indelible mark on Irish public policy-making. Despite the current downturn, the government remains strongly devoted to the completion of its National Development Plan (NDP), an ambitious programme of investment in the national infrastructure. The government has committed €29 billion to a series of projects in key areas such as roads, public transport, environmental services, health, housing and education. Another important component of the NDP is the search for workable solutions to Ireland's social exclusion problems. It is hoped that sensible public investment, coupled with economic stability during a downturn, will see the Irish economy well placed to take advantage should an upswing occur in the global economy.

References

Barrett, A., Callan, T. and Nolan, B. (1999), 'Rising Wage Inequality Returns to Education and Labour Market Institutions: Evidence from Ireland', *British Journal of Industrial Relations*, Vol. 37, No. 1, pp. 77–100.

Barry, F. (2002), 'The Celtic Tiger Era: Delayed Convergence or Regional Boom?', Policy Discussion Forum, Economic and Social Research Institute, *Quarterly Economic Commentary*, Summer.

Clinch, P., Convery, F. and Walsh, B (2002), *After the Celtic Tiger: Challenges Ahead*, Dublin: O'Brien Press.

Connolly, E. and O'Hagan, E. (2000), 'Employers' Organizations as Political Actors: Between Social Partnership and Internationalization', Paper to the Annual Conference of the Political Studies Association of Ireland, Cork, 13–15 October.

Cox, R.W. (1987), *Production, Power, and World Order: Social Forces in the Making of History*, New York: Columbia University Press.

DeBoer-Ashworth, E. (2000), *The Global Political Economy and Post-1989 Change: The Place of the Central European Transition*, London: Macmillan.

Department of Finance, *Economic Development* (1957), (Pr. 4803), Dublin: Stationery Office.

Dooney, S. and O'Toole, J. (1998), *Irish Government Today*, second edition, Dublin: Gill and Macmillan.

ESRI (Economic and Social Research Institute) (2002), *Irish Economy*, *Quarterly Economic Commentary*, Summer.

European Commission (1997), *European Economy*, Brussels: European Commission.

Kirby, P. (1997), *Poverty amid Plenty: World and Irish Development Reconsidered*, Dublin: Trocáire/Gill and Macmillan.

McMichael, P. (1996), *Development and Social Change: A Global Perspective*, Thousand Oaks, CA: Pine Forge.

Murphy, A. (1994), *The Irish Economy: Celtic Tiger or Tortoise?*, Dublin: Money Markets International.

NESC (National Economic and Social Council) (1986), *Strategy for Development 1986–1990*, Dublin: NESC/Government Publications Office.

Nolan, B. and Maitre, B. (2000), 'Income Inequality', in B. Nolan, J. O'Connell and C. Whelan (eds), *Bust to Boom? The Irish Experience of Growth and Inequality*, Dublin: Institute of Public Administration.

O'Donnell, R. (1999), 'The Development of Enterprise-Level Partnership in Ireland', Paper to the Annual Enterprise Partnership Conference of the National Centre for Partnership, Royal College of Surgeons, Dublin, 28 September.

OECD (Organisation for Economic Co-operation and Development) (1998), *Economic Outlook, No. 64*, December.

Office of the Tánaiste (1995), *Interim Report of the Task Force on Long-Term Unemployment*, Dublin: Office of the Tanáiste.

Ó Gráda, C. (1995), *Ireland: A New Economic History 1780–1939*, Oxford: Oxford University Press.

O'Hearn, D. (2000), 'Globalization, "New Tigers", and the End of the Developmental State? The Case of the Celtic Tiger', *Politics and Society*, Vol. 28, No. 1, pp. 67–92.

O'Sullivan, M. (1995), 'Manufacturing and Global Competition', in J.W. O'Hagan (ed.), *The Economy of Ireland: Policy and Performance of a Small European Country*, Dublin: Gill and Macmillan.

Sweeney, P. (1999), *The Celtic Tiger: Ireland's Continuing Economic Miracle*, Dublin: Oak Tree Press.

Turner, T. (1999), 'Income Equality in the Irish Labour Market: Changes in Earnings and Taxation Levels, 1987 to 1995', *IBAR – Irish Business and Administrative Research*, Vol. 19/20, No. 1, pp. 36–46.

Turner, T. and Wallace, J. (2001), 'The Irish Model of Social Partnership: Achievements and Limitations', Paper to the European Industrial Relations Congress, Oslo, 25–29 June.

Ireland and the European Union: a less certain relationship?

Jane O'Mahony

Membership of the EU has been central to Ireland's interests for the last 30 years. We are seen by many as the shining example of how membership can benefit a small, peripheral, underdeveloped country. We have successfully integrated our economy, our currency and many other aspects of our lives with our European partners. Not being part of Europe is, frankly, unthinkable. (Ahern 2003)

Introduction

In keeping with the Republic of Ireland's membership of the European Union (EU),[1] successive Irish governments have signed up to and participated in the continuing evolution of European integration through the Single European Act, the Treaty on European Union, and the Amsterdam and Nice Treaties. The Irish electorate has shown its positive support for such projects in a number of referendums. It is undeniable that membership of the EU has had a significant impact on Ireland in economic, social and political terms. The Irish economy has benefited considerably from membership of the Single European Market and its ancillary developments. Membership of the EU has also given Ireland the opportunity to play a role on the European and world stages that would have been above and beyond its capacity as a small state. However, on 7 June 2001, Ireland's relationship with Europe and the EU reached a critical juncture following the rejection of the Nice Treaty by referendum. Irish European policy has thus entered a new and uncertain phase – a phase in which the Irish electorate's previous commitment to the European project can no longer be taken for granted. The central purpose of this chapter is to examine Ireland's changing relationship with the EU.

Looking at the period since the early independence of the state, Ireland's relationship with Europe can conveniently be divided into four separate phases. In broad terms, from independence until 1958 Irish foreign or external policy centred on coming to terms with statehood and the pursuit of an independent foreign policy. Movements to integrate in Western Europe through the European Coal and Steel Community (ECSC), the European Political Community (EPC) and the European Economic Community (EEC) were watched closely, but participation was not then envisaged. Irish governments concentrated their diplomatic efforts over the years on participation in the League of Nations, the Council of Europe and the United Nations (UN).

But the publication of the White Paper *Programme for Economic Expansion* in 1958 by the Fianna Fáil government of Sean Lemass marked a new phase in Irish European policy – that of 'coming in from the cold'. The rejection of protectionism as the basis for Irish economic policy was accompanied by the realisation that a more substantial engagement with the European project was needed in order to ensure future Irish prosperity. Membership of the EEC was judged to be the best means to bring this about. Simply put, for Ireland, participation in the then EEC was directly linked to the national project of economic modernisation (Laffan and O'Donnell 1999: 156). The natural ending of this phase of reorientation came with accession to the EEC in 1973.

From 1973 until the late 1990s, then, Irish involvement in European integration seemed wholehearted and committed. Indeed, as we shall see, the benefits of membership have been considerable, particularly in financial terms. In this phase, the Irish executive and electorate slowly but surely adapted to membership of the EU, and Ireland became a full member of the European family by signing up to the developing *acquis communautaire*.[2] However, from the late 1990s onwards, a shift in the emphasis and tenor of Irish European policy can be identified. In 2000 in particular, a change in the attitudes and behaviour of certain parts of the political elite and of the electorate was apparent, prompting speculation as to whether Ireland's 'honeymoon' with the EU is over and a more Eurosceptic attitude to the EU is emerging (Gilland 1999). The indisputable sign of a movement to a new phase of Irish European policy came with the rejection of the Nice Treaty in June 2001 (see Table 2.1).

This chapter will proceed as follows. First it will survey Irish involvement in the EU prior to 2000 – concentrating on the impact of membership on the Irish economic, social and political realms. The second part of the chapter will concentrate on the new phase in Irish European policy, focusing on the Nice Treaty referendum and its aftermath, and will show how Ireland's relationship with the EU is undergoing redefinition. The chapter will conclude with an outline of a number of issues on the European agenda that pose challenges for Ireland in the future.

What has EU membership meant for Ireland?

As stated above, Ireland's EU membership experience can be seen to have been overwhelmingly positive until the late 1990s. Until the Nice referendum in June 2001, on the four previous occasions Irish voters were requested to give their

Table 2.1 *Key dates in Ireland's membership of the European Union and its predecessor bodies*

Year	Date/s	Event
1956	October	Committee of Secretaries established to consider Ireland's position in context of relations between the EEC and the Organisation for European Economic Co-operation
1959	December	Diplomatic relations established with the EEC
1961	July	Ireland's application to join the EEC sent to the European Council
1963	January	Breakdown of negotiations with the UK, Denmark, Ireland and Norway on EEC membership – the 'de Gaulle veto'
1966	January	Irish government decision to accredit a separate diplomatic mission to the then European Communities – EEC, Euratom and ECSC
1967	May	Second application for EEC membership
1970	June	Formal opening of accession negotiations
1972	January	The taoiseach, Jack Lynch and the minister for foreign affairs, P. J. Hillery, sign instruments of accession
1972	May	Referendum on membership (83 per cent in favour, 17 per cent against)
1975	First six months	Ireland holds EC presidency for the first time
1987	May	Ratification of Single European Act (69.9 per cent in favour, 30.1 per cent against)
1990	First six months	Ireland holds EC presidency
1992	June	Ratification of Maastricht Treaty (69.1 per cent in favour, 30.9 per cent against)
1996	Second six months	Ireland holds EU presidency
1998	May	Ratification of Amsterdam Treaty (61.7 per cent in favour, 38.3 per cent against)
2001	June	Referendum on Nice Treaty (46.1 per cent in favour, 53.9 per cent against, failure to ratify treaty)
2002	October	Ratification of Nice Treaty (63 per cent in favour, 37 per cent against)
2004	First six months	Ireland to hold EU presidency

Source: B. Laffan and J. O'Mahony (2003), *Managing Europe from Home: The Europeanisation of the Irish Core Executive*, Dublin: Dublin European Institute.

endorsement to European integration in the various treaty reforms, support for
the European project was not found to be lacking. The first four referendum
results are as shown in Table 2.2.

Table 2.2 *Results of referendums in Ireland on European issues, 1972–98*

Date	Subject	Turnout (%)	Yes (%)	No (%)
10 May 1972	EEC membership	70.3	83.1	16.9
24 May 1987	Ratify Single European Act	43.9	69.9	30.1
18 June 1992	Ratify Maastricht Treaty	57.0	69.1	30.9
22 May 1998	Ratify Amsterdam Treaty	56.3	61.7	38.3

Source: IPA (Institute of Public Administration) (2001), *IPA Yearbook and Diary*, Dublin: Institute
of Public Administration.

The image of Ireland projected by successive Irish governments in the EU
was as *communautaire* – as a constructive and fully committed member. Indeed,
the 1996 government *White Paper on Foreign Policy* went so far as to claim that
'Irish people increasingly see the European Union not simply as an organisation
to which Ireland belongs, but as an integral part of our future. We see our-
selves, increasingly, as Europeans' (Government of Ireland 1996: 59). This
support for the European project had its basis in the convergence between the
EU's programme of treaty reform and policy development with Irish economic,
social and political preferences as espoused by successive governments.

Economic benefits

It is well known that Ireland joined the EEC primarily for economic reasons, and
in this it was no different from a number of other applicant states. With the shift
away from protectionism, EEC membership was the logical outcome of an
outward-looking economic policy, involving a commitment to trade liberalisation and the free movement of capital, and with the attraction of foreign enterprises as the mainspring of growth. Similarly, once Britain indicated an interest
in EEC membership, the Fianna Fáil government held that it became an economic imperative for Ireland to do likewise. Ireland's dependence on the British
market for a large proportion of its external trade meant that Ireland could not
have remained outside without suffering serious economic consequences.
Moreover, membership of the EU offered a way out of the existing excessive economic and political dependence on Britain (Laffan and O'Donnell 1999: 156).
The emphasis in the accession negotiations was primarily on economics, and
subsequent membership of the EU was seen largely in these terms.

Until the early 1990s Ireland's profile in the EU was indeed that of a relatively peripheral, small, poor member state and a major net beneficiary of the
EU budget, with a continuing protectionist orientation in agriculture policy

and an atypical outlook on security matters, due to its policy of neutrality (Laffan 2001: 8). All this meant that Irish strategic preferences within the EU were easily defined and identified. Because of the state's difficult economic situation, a pivotal point of European policy so far as Ireland was concerned was that the benefits of economic integration should be spread evenly, and that political integration should be based on economic solidarity. Arising from this was the suggestion that Ireland was 'conditionally integrationist': 'Ireland accepted financial support – a literal quid pro quo – in return for its abandonment of traditional policies, whether economic, commercial or political' (Scott 1994: 3). The implication is, therefore, that Irish support for further political integration was contingent upon the recognition that poorer, more peripheral countries must not be disadvantaged by moves towards integration – in other words, such countries must be compensated economically for this. This meant that Ireland was strongly supportive of European structural and cohesion policies that were intended to ensure the economic 'catching up' of the smaller and poorer member states; and it also meant maximising receipts in all other areas of the EU budget, most importantly in the Common Agricultural Policy (CAP) – a key focus of Irish policy-makers, given the traditional strength of the farming sector.

The pursuit of such a conditional strategy eventually bore fruit in economic terms. Ireland has greatly outperformed all other Organisation for Economic Cooperation and Development (OECD) economies since the late 1980s. Ireland's gross national product (GNP) expanded by 140 per cent between 1987 and 2000, for example, compared to an expansion of 40 per cent in the US and 35 per cent in the EU as a whole (Barry et al. 2001: 537–52). Inevitably much debate has centred on the question of whether Ireland's super-performing 'Celtic Tiger' economy resulted from the large amount of financial receipts from the EU. According to one expert, the precise timing of the economic turnaround is ascribable to a number of concurrent developments. These included a dramatic increase in foreign direct investment (FDI) inflows, particularly from the US; the stabilisation of the public finances and an associated improvement in cost competitiveness since 1987; and the development of an Irish labour force with higher educational qualifications (FitzGerald 1998). However, in addition to these factors, there is no doubt that the EU's structural funds have had a significant impact on the Irish economy. During the decade from 1989 to 1999, Ireland's receipts from the structural funds averaged about 2.6 per cent of GNP. While the impact of this is hard to quantify, statistical estimates suggest that they increased the level of GNP by 2 percentage points (O'Donnell 2001). More significantly, however, the Economic and Social Research Institute (ESRI) has calculated that the beneficial effect of participating in the European Single Market on the Irish economy has been to add as much as 9 per cent to GNP (FitzGerald 1998). Beneficial EU-derived influences also came in the form of exchange rate stability; low inflation; financial discipline; competitive reorientation; a new regulatory framework for services and utilities; developmental planning, monitoring and evaluation; new standards for consumer protection and social regulation, and agencies to implement them; and support for policy innovation and experimentation (O'Donnell 2001).

Foreign, social and political affairs

Ireland's *communautaire* orientation also bore fruit in foreign policy terms, as successive governments were able to support the EU's efforts to co-ordinate foreign policy, but at the same time ensure that moves towards the formulation of a Common Foreign and Security Policy (CFSP) did not impinge upon Irish neutrality. Through involvement in the CFSP and the emerging European Security and Defence Policy (ESDP), the horizons of the Irish minister for foreign affairs and those of Irish diplomats have been widened hugely. As Tonra points out, Irish diplomats' involvement and influence in global issues today is both substantively wider and deeper than at any time in Irish diplomatic history (2002: 43). Through EU foreign policy working groups and the CFSP Secretariat, through EU presidency activities, and through the mechanisms of the ESDP (with its Political Committee and nascent Rapid Reaction Force), Irish diplomats and military personnel now find themselves with an influence on the world stage far beyond that normally exercised by a small state. Involvement in the Council presidency system has also given Irish governments and officials the opportunity to punch well above their weight politically.

The EU has effected major changes in Irish social policy and services too, many of them unanticipated. The influence of the EU in this respect is difficult to quantify, but it has certainly been significant with regard to the rights of women and of workers generally. Without EU membership it is unlikely that legislation on equality of opportunity, consumer protection and certain labour rights (including matters like health and safety at work) would have been implemented as early as it was.[3] In addition, Ireland benefited significantly from the European Social Fund (ESF). In the five years to the end of 1995, Ireland received Ir£1 billion from the fund, which represented just over one third of all money spent in Ireland in that period on vocational training and employment programmes. A significantly larger percentage of the labour force in Ireland has benefited from the ESF than in any other member state – 18 per cent of women and 13 per cent of men have received ESF assistance in Ireland, while the EU average is 2 per cent (Ó Cinneide 1993: 20). This is at least partly due to the large proportion of the Irish labour force aged under 25, given the emphasis that the rules of the fund place on this age group. The ESF has been used to fund schemes to help the long-term unemployed, early school leavers, handicapped people and women returning to work after raising a family.

Membership of the EU has affected territorial politics within the Irish state as well, albeit in a more limited manner. Ireland joined the EU as a highly centralised state with little or no regional governance structure. Through the structural funds, in particular the European Regional Development Fund and the Cohesion Fund, the European Commission has encouraged the strengthening of the regional government tier in EU member states. However, until 2000 Ireland was designated as one region for the purposes of the dissemination of funds, and therefore the incentive for full-scale regional reform did not exist. Even so, the highly centralised nature of Irish public policy was loosened somewhat and regional structures established in order to maximise receipt of funds. According to Laffan (2002), the original regional structures, established in 1988, were largely an administrative expedient that added a weak regional layer to the implementation of the Community Support Framework and thereby satisfied the Commission. Community initiatives such as Leader, involving area-based economic partnerships, and County Enterprise Boards all reinforced the territorial dimension of development; however, they were not in themselves capable of giving Ireland effective local and regional government. In the original rounds of structural funds negotiations, the management of the funds was dominated by central government and large, state-sponsored bodies. The policy formation process has now been widened to include an input from diffuse interests such as local authorities, community groups, environmental groups and the social partners. This new, multi-levelled policy-making also exposed local and subregional actors to Continental European practices, which fed into the programmes of social partnership from the late 1980s onwards. The obligation to produce development plans and evaluate projects has encouraged more formalised policy-making at the national level over the medium to longer term.

Strong on support, but weak on information

EU membership has had a more limited impact the central political arena. A broad political consensus on Ireland's involvement in the EU has meant little contention about European issues in the media or in the houses (Dáil and Seanad) which make up the Oireachtas (parliament), although there have been a few party political differences on issues of particular sensitivity, like security policy at the time of the Single European Act negotiation. Until the critical juncture of the first Nice Treaty referendum defeat in June 2001, the relationship between the Oireachtas and the core executive of the Irish system of government, the Cabinet, seems to have been weak. And relations between the Oireachtas and the EU have been characterised as a combination of neglect and ignorance (O'Halpin 1996: 124). On accession to the EEC in 1973, a Joint Oireachtas Committee on the Secondary Legislation of the European Communities was established as a 'watchdog committee'. However, its performance was modest, hampered as it was by limited resources and lack of interest by parliamentary deputies and the media. In 1993, it was reconstituted as the Joint Oireachtas Committee on European Affairs, with the primary role of informing Teachtaí Dála (TDs: deputies, members of parliament) and Senators of EU policy developments, rather than scrutinising EU legislation as such.

The broad support of the electorate for Irish membership of the EU, and their conviction that it was a good thing and of benefit to the country, was unequivocally clear until very recently. Since they began, the EU's *Eurobarometer* surveys have consistently shown the Irish people to give a high level of approval to Ireland's membership (Sinnott 2001), yet this positive perception was accompanied by relatively low levels of knowledge about the EU. In a study carried out in 1995, Sinnott found that 'there is very considerable room for improvement in levels of knowledge' about the EU. Ireland ranked just above the EU average in knowledge of European affairs, and 59 per cent of Irish respondents to *Eurobarometer* surveys displayed 'low' or 'very low knowledge' of the EU (Sinnott 1995: 34).

Although Irish ministers and civil servants were actively and successfully engaged in EU policy-making in the Brussels arena, the impact of the EU on the governance of Ireland was not significant. The period between January 1973 and the end of Ireland's first presidency in December 1975 was Ireland's apprenticeship in the EU system. During this period the Irish governmental system put in place structures and processes for managing the relationship with Brussels. Overall, there was very little institution building, in the form of new structures; rather there was a reliance on the adaptation of existing structures within the broad parameters of collective responsibility and ministerial responsibility. Responsibility for day-to-day co-ordination of EU matters was assigned to the Department of Foreign Affairs, and the principle of the responsibility of the 'lead department' was firmly established. Individual departments were responsible from the outset for co-ordinating preparations for Council meetings falling within their policy domain. Interdepartmental EU co-ordinating committees were also established over the years, but were not permanent fixtures on the institutional landscape. They were simply formed on an *ad hoc* basis to deal with pressing cross-cutting EU issues (Laffan and O'Mahony 2003: 19).

In the period from 1973 to 2000, then, Irish support for European integration was strong, yet conditional.[4] Support for the European project was, on the whole, contingent upon the complementarity of Irish governmental preferences with developments at the EU level. The benefits of membership were clearly in evidence. But Ireland's European policy has now entered a new stage – a stage of seeming uncertainty. This found its clearest expression in the Nice referendum result, which provided obvious evidence of doubt among voters. The 2001 referendum, together with a number of public opinion surveys undertaken in the run-up to it and after the result was known, hint at a shift in public attitudes both to the EU and to the perception of Ireland's place within it – in effect, the strong support for European integration of the past has signally weakened.[5] This development, together with a governmental strategy that seems less coherent than heretofore, means that Ireland's relationship with the EU is undergoing a period of redefinition.

Entering a new phase?

It is perfectly natural for Irish voters' attitudes to the EU to vary in accordance with our status as a net recipient or net contributor ... I presume that Ireland, like every other member state, predicates its European policies and actions on what is termed 'enlightened self interest'. That is not to be equated with cynicism or greed. We have a collective interest in the success of the European project and as Irish per capita income approaches and exceeds the European average, we have all the more reason to re-evaluate where our enlightened self interest really lies. (Michael McDowell, former attorney general, 18 June 2001, quoted in the *Irish Times*, 19 June 2001)

Perhaps the most obvious mark of a new phase in the relationship with the EU is the fact that economic success means Ireland will soon move from being a net beneficiary of EU funds to being a net contributor to the EU budget. Ireland is manifestly no longer part of the poorer EU member state cohort – the so-called cohesion countries – and it is no longer classed as an Objective 1 Region for the purpose of the dissemination of structural funds. In 2001, according to the European Commission, Irish GNP per person relative to the EU average (100 per cent) was 102 per cent, compared to 103 in the UK, 121.2 per cent in Denmark, 104.2 per cent in Germany, 101 per cent in Finland, 83.2 per cent in Spain, 72.6 per cent in Greece and 72 per cent in Portugal.[6] With the enlargement of the EU to include the accession countries of Central and Eastern Europe together with Cyprus, Malta and Turkey in 2004, Ireland's position on the EU's economic league table will rise even higher. As McDowell's comments above demonstrate, a reconsideration of strategy at this juncture would not be unexpected, given Ireland's previous policy preferences, discussed above.

The Nice I referendum

The most tangible indication of a change in Ireland's relationship with the EU can be seen in the rejection of the Nice referendum in June 2001 – what we shall call Nice I. Ireland was the only member state obliged to submit the Nice Treaty to a popular vote, for constitutional reasons. Turnout at 34.79 per cent was the lowest level ever recorded for a European Integration referendum in the country. Spoiled votes came from over 1.5 per cent of those who actually voted, and the referendum was rejected by 53.87 per cent (see Table 2.3).[7] Was the Nice I result just a temporary blip, or was it a sign of a developing anti-European undercurrent in Ireland?

While many politicians and commentators expressed surprise and shock at the referendum result, there were signs of a possible upset even before the results were revealed. In 2000 in particular, a serious divergence of views on the EU emerged in the coalition government of Fianna Fáil and the Progressive Democrats – one that undermined the previously positive attitude of government

Table 2.3 *Result of the Nice I referendum, 7 June 2001*

Category	Number	Percentage
Electorate	2,867,960	100.00
Total poll	997,826	34.79
Yes	453,461	46.13
No	529,478	53.87
Spoiled votes:	14,887	

Source: IPA (Institute of Public Administration) (2001), *IPA Yearbook and Diary*, Dublin: Institute of Public Administration.

elites towards EU membership. Indeed, the reaction of a number of Fianna Fáil ministers, both before and in the aftermath of the referendum, seemed to suggest that a more questioning attitude to the EU and Ireland's place within it was emerging in the party. The Minister for Finance, Charlie McCreevy, Minister Síle de Valera and Junior Ministers Eamon O'Cuiv and Willie O'Dea all made clear in the public arena that their enthusiasm for the EU was far from total.[8] Then in early 2001, McCreevy challenged the right of EU Economic and Finance Ministers to censure his budgetary policy, and held that the censure had been a contributing factor in the Nice 'No' vote. During the Gothenburg EU Summit in June 2001, he said:

> Here we had all the political parties, all of the media, both in broadcast and print, all of the organisations – IBEC [the Irish Business and Employers' Confederation], ICTU [the Irish Congress of Trade Unions], the IFA [the Irish Farmers' Association] and everybody else [in support of Nice] – yet the plain people of Ireland in their wisdom have decided to vote No. I think that's a very healthy sign. (Quoted in the *Irish Times*, 18 June 2001)

Both de Valera and the Progressive Democrat Tánaiste (Deputy Prime Minister), Mary Harney, also expressed resistance to being moved further, as they put it, 'towards Berlin rather than Boston'. The Boston–Berlin dichotomy involves a simplistic comparison between the general European belief in good levels of social provision and public services (and consequently higher taxation) and the US preference for free markets, low taxation and restricted social provision – the direction in which Harney and McCreevy would prefer to lean. In July 2000, Harney, in an address to the American Bar Association in Dublin, endorsed a vision of a neo-liberal Europe and ended by saying 'I believe in a Europe of independent states, not a United States of Europe.' The speech was followed later by an opinion piece in the *Irish Times* in September 2000 in which she outlined her enthusiasm for enlargement but not further integration: 'Enlargement is perhaps the best protection against excessive integration ... We in Ireland should be enthusiastic about enlargement, but cautious about further integration' (quoted in the *Irish Times*, 20 September 2000).

Síle de Valera, in an address in Boston College in the United States, also in September 2000, adopted an obviously 'Eurosceptic' tone when she questioned the erosion of Irish culture by European directives and called for a more vigilant, questioning attitude towards the EU and for more diligence in protecting Irish interests. This was in sharp contrast to the more pro-European pronouncements of the Taoiseach, Bertie Ahern, and the Minister for Foreign Affairs, Brian Cowen, during the referendum campaign. In the wake of the referendum, both were careful to acknowledge the anxieties and concerns of those who opposed the Nice Treaty, but declared themselves to be deeply disappointed with the result, as it now represented an additional obstacle for enlargement. According to Cowen:

> Nice is necessary for enlargement; and a failure to ratify Nice, therefore, would leave a fundamental dimension of the enlargement process in limbo. It would without question impede the accession of States with which we have much in common and which see us as a model of how a small state should operate within the Union. (Institute of European Affairs, 19 December 2001, quoted in the *Irish Times*, 20 December 2001)

A *Eurobarometer* report (No. 54, April 2001) also provided some indication of changing attitudes among the electorate in advance of the referendum result. While more than seven in ten people surveyed in Ireland continued to feel that membership of the EU was a good thing (Ireland was second highest in this ranking) and people in Ireland continued to be by far the most likely to feel that their country had benefited from EU membership (86 per cent), 52 per cent of those surveyed felt 'very' or 'fairly' attached to Europe, whereas 43 per cent felt 'not very' or 'not at all' attached (the remainder were 'don't knows'). What seemed significant about this figure is that the 'feeling attached' percentage had dropped from 57 per cent in spring 1999 to 52 per cent in spring 2001. Denmark and Ireland were the only two countries where a significant negative shift was recorded, the former also showing a 5 percentage point drop. In an opinion poll conducted in Ireland a week before the Nice I referendum vote, 45 per cent of those surveyed indicated that they would vote yes, 28 per cent that they would vote no, and 27 per cent that they had no opinion (MRBI/*Irish Times*, 29–30 May 2001), showing a narrowing in the gap between the 'Yes' and 'No' votes over the course of the campaign. Perhaps more importantly, however, when asked how well they understood what the Treaty was about, 15 per cent felt they had a 'good understanding' 32 per cent 'understood some of the issues' but not all, 31 per cent were only 'vaguely aware' of the issues involved, 19 per cent 'did not know' at all, and 2 per cent had no opinion.

In Nice I, the 'No' side included the Green Party, the National Platform (which saw the Treaty as portending a further loss of Irish national sovereignty), and the No to Nice Grouping (which feared erosion of Irish family values, especially as regards the availability of abortion, through closer integration with the EU). They clearly conducted the most effective campaign; by

contrast, the 'Yes' campaign, which included the government and main opposition parties, seemed to lack vision and enthusiasm and did not succeed in
mobilising the electorate. According to Laffan, 'the yes supporters were successfully portrayed as part of a tired establishment out of touch with the Irish
public' (Laffan 2002: 12).

In terms of the perception of Ireland by its European partners, the result of
the referendum meant the image of Ireland as *communautaire* was seriously
undermined. Amidst widespread disappointment across the rest of the EU
member states, political reaction came from the Commission President,
Romano Prodi, the Swedish President of the EU, Goran Persson, and the Dutch
Prime Minister, Wim Kok. They stressed that while the EU was ready to take on
board the concerns of the Irish electorate, there was no question of a renegotiation of the Nice Treaty; they emphasised, moreover, that negotiations concerning the enlargement of the EU by the accession of new members must not
be delayed by the vote. European press reaction was not so muted, with the
French daily *Le Monde* referring to Ireland as 'l'enfant terrible' (9 June 2001),
and the Italian daily *Corriere della Sera* saying that Ireland was now suffering
from the syndrome of the selfish 'full stomach' (*Le Soir en Ligne*, 11 June 2001).

In the aftermath, questions abounded as to why so few people turned out to
vote and why the majority of those who did vote said 'No'. Was the result
prompted by the claimed threat of the Rapid Reaction Force to Irish neutrality?
Was it led by fear of the institutional changes and the diminution of Irish voting
power? Was it a fear of the economic consequences of enlargement now that
Ireland would be a net contributor to the EU? Was it a more general fear of
increased European integration in a federal direction? Or was it because people
felt that they were not informed of the issues? 'No' campaigner Dana Rosemary
Scallon declared that the result reflected the defence of Irish sovereignty and
independence by the Irish people, as was their constitutional right (quoted in
the *Irish Times*, 9 June 2001). John Gormley of the Green Party was sure that
some people did indeed vote against Nice for selfish reasons, because they were
not in favour of enlargement (Institute of European Affairs, 15 October 2001,
quoted in the *Irish Times*, 16 October 2001). According to Michael McDowell,
a possible reason was 'a general perception that the European project is being
energetically driven towards the creation of a European State with a much
greater pooling of political sovereignty and with major implications for the
independence of member states – particularly smaller nation states such as
Ireland' (Institute of European Affairs, 18 June 2001, quoted in the *Irish Times*,
19 June 2001). Journalist Fintan O'Toole pointed to the possibility that voters
were alienated from the whole political system:

> there is a big, largely unmapped, terrain of resentment, suspicion and anger.
> Those who occupy it are more cynical than apathetic. They have been disillu-
> sioned by the endless tales of corruption in politics. They are haunted by a vague
> but powerful feeling that their Republic has been stolen from them, that the State

is no longer theirs ... Best of all, for the broad constituency of anti-establishment resentment, [the Nice Treaty] has the inestimable advantage of being supported by virtually the entire establishment: the four big political parties, the trade unions, the employers, even the bishops. The chance to bloody all their noses with a single swipe was far too good to miss. (*Irish Times*, 9 June 2001)

The key to whether a more Eurosceptical Irish electorate is emerging lies in the answers to these questions. As Sinnott has pointed out in the survey by the European Commission Representation (ECR) after Nice I, the fact is that compared to the result of the 1998 Amsterdam referendum, the 'No' vote actually *declined* in 2001 (Sinnott 2001). In overall terms, the 'No' vote in European referendums, as a proportion of the whole Irish electorate, has indeed grown over time – but only from 11.9 per cent in 1972 to 21 per cent in 1998. In Nice I the 'No' vote, again as a proportion of the electorate, actually fell back to 18.5 per cent. But Sinnott's analysis of the pattern of change in voting and in abstention at constituency level since the Amsterdam referendum indicates that more than half of those who had voted 'Yes' to Amsterdam must have abstained in Nice I. Thus, instead of just asking why people voted 'No', we must also ask what the reasons were behind the widespread abstention.

According to the results of the ECR survey, by far the most frequent explanation given for abstention was lack of information and lack of understanding of the issues; 44 per cent of Nice abstainers explained their non-voting in these terms.[9] The predominant characteristics of those surveyed who voted 'No' were a feeling of not being adequately on top of the issues and a tendency to follow a maxim which had also been prominent in the 'No' campaign in the Amsterdam referendum: 'if you don't know, vote no'. Thirty-nine per cent of those asked the open-ended question as to why they had voted 'No' said it was because of lack of information, compared to some 16 per cent who mentioned concerns about loss of sovereignty or a federalist Europe; neutrality was mentioned by 12 per cent; fear of more refugees by 3 per cent; and concerns about abortion by 2 per cent. In the responses to this question, there was no direct mention of opposition to enlargement, yet this may have been an influence which people were reluctant to admit in order to avoid appearing selfish. Nevertheless, as extrapolated by Garrett FitzGerald, it appeared from these figures that almost 1 million people either opposed the treaty or failed to vote because of lack of information, lack of understanding, or confusion (*Irish Times*, 5 January 2002).

The Nice II referendum

The implications of these results were clear for the second referendum on Nice – Nice II. The political elite was no longer able to rely on the electorate's unquestioning support for Ireland's continued participation in moves to further EU integration. The permissive consensus that existed from accession to the late

1990s, when membership of the EU was supported unquestioningly and European integration issues were not generally discussed, had ceased to be. The government established a National Forum on Europe in the immediate aftermath of Nice I in order to ascertain the electorate's views on the EU and Ireland's engagement within it. The Forum consisted of representatives of the political parties from both houses of the Oireachtas and a number of observers from a range of interest groups. It met regularly in public, both in Dublin and throughout the country, inviting guest speakers such as ministers, officials, Members of the European Parliament (MEPs) and national parliamentarians, as well as academics from the other member states and the 'accession' countries. While its deliberations received only sporadic attention in the country's media, it provided a forum for a debate on all aspects of the EU and the Nice Treaty.

Nice II took place in October 2002 following the successful re-election of the Fianna Fáil–Progressive Democrat coalition in May. The referendum was very different to the first, both in its conduct and in its outcome. In contrast to Nice I, 49.47 per cent of the electorate turned out, with 62.89 per cent of those voting 'Yes' and 37.11 per cent voting 'No'. With turnout up by 14 per cent, instead of two out of every three electors abstaining, only one in every two did so this time round. The Nice II campaign was characterised by far higher, more committed and engaged mobilisation on the part of the government parties, the pro-EU opposition parties, and business and other miscellaneous interest groups such as the Irish Alliance for Europe. This latter was composed of a diversity of organisations seeking a 'Yes' vote, including the Disability Alliance, Women for a Yes Vote, the IFA, IBEC, Ireland for Europe, and Lawyers for a Yes Vote; and the Irish President of the European Parliament, Pat Cox, also played a major role in the campaign. The success of the 'Yes' campaign was confirmed by the evidence of an *Irish Times*/MRBI series of polls; these showed that the electorate's confidence in its overall grasp of the issues raised by the Nice Treaty went from 37 per cent at the beginning of the Nice I campaign to 47 per cent at the end of it, then to 53 per cent at the beginning of the Nice II campaign, and finally to 64 per cent just a few days before the vote.[10]

The consequences of Nice I and Nice II for the Irish political system

As we have noted, the most immediate consequence of the Nice I defeat was a more widespread engagement with and debate on European issues on the part of the political elites and of society as a whole. The defeat also had important consequences for the management of EU business at home. Following Nice I, the efforts of the Irish government and the central administration to co-ordinate EU affairs have become more coherent and structured. The Oireachtas committee system is finally beginning to become embedded in Irish political structures. A cabinet subcommittee on European affairs now meets every second week to discuss EU matters, aided by the Interdepartmental Co-ordinating Committee on European Affairs (formerly known as the Senior Officials Group), which is chaired by a new Minister of State (junior minister) for European affairs. Senior civil servants from every government department attend the Committee, and entitled to be there also is the Irish permanent representative based in Brussels. From December 2002, the Interdepartmental Committee has also met every second week and is used as an early warning system for potentially problematic issues arising out of EU business, as well as a forum to facilitate strategic thinking across government departments (Laffan and O'Mahony 2003: 19). A number of other interdepartmental committees with smaller memberships have also been created to handle specific and/or pressing issues on the EU horizon.

Thus in the immediate aftermath of the September 11 tragedies in the United States, it became clear that the negotiation of the EU response, namely the European Arrest Warrant and the Framework Decision on Terrorism, necessitated more intensive co-ordination mechanisms within the Irish system. An interdepartmental committee was set up to deal with the European Arrest Warrant negotiations, chaired by the Department of Justice and serviced by the Department of the Taoiseach. On the conclusion of these negotiations, this committee became the Interdepartmental Committee on Justice and Home Affairs, which meets before every European Justice and Home Affairs Council meeting. The ongoing Lisbon Agenda (with its goal of making the EU the most competitive knowledge-based economy in the world by 2010) poses a fundamental challenge to the Irish system as regards the structures necessary to handle cross-cutting issues. The primary reason behind this is the development of the open method of co-ordination as a policy mechanism within the EU.[11] The diverse and broad range of policy areas that is gathered under the Lisbon umbrella necessitates some kind of central co-ordination. To this end, an interdepartmental Lisbon Group has been set up and is chaired and serviced by the Department of the Taoiseach.

The weakness or perceived absence of parliamentary scrutiny of EU business was highlighted as a serious problem during the Nice I referendum. In response to this, the government developed a new system of enhanced Oireachtas scrutiny of EU affairs. The parliamentary link for the new procedures is the Select Committee on European Affairs. All EU-related documents are deposited in the EU Co-ordination Unit of the Department of Foreign Affairs and passed on by the Unit to the Select Committee. A subcommittee of the Select Committee, informally described as the 'sifting committee', goes through them on a regular basis and identifies EU proposals that are significant enough, according to certain agreed criteria, to merit parliamentary scrutiny. If the sifting committee sees a need, a request is made for the drafting within one month of an explanatory memorandum or 'note' concerning the EU proposal from the relevant government department. These memoranda are then passed to the relevant sectoral or departmental Oireachtas committees, which will eventually produce reports on their deliberations on the matters concerned; these are in turn laid before the Oireachtas. While provision is made for extensive engagement between the Oireachtas, ministers and officials, ministers are not obliged to accept the opinion of the Oireachtas on EU proposals (a position similar, incidentally, to that which prevails in Denmark). Instead, ministers are simply honour bound to take the opinion of the relative committee into account when negotiating at the Council of Ministers in Brussels.[12] This fairly elaborate system of scrutiny means that management within each department will have a far better idea of just how much EU business they must handle, and how best to deploy their resources: 'following the original circular on the management of EU business in 1973, the guidelines on Oireachtas scrutiny are the next most significant formalisation of the management of EU business in Ireland' (Laffan and O'Mahony 2003: 29–30).

Contentious issues for Ireland in the future

It is O'Donnell's contention that Ireland's European policy has reached a crisis (2001). While some may feel this claim is a little strong, it is clear that European policy currently appears to lack a clear direction and vision. The long-standing strategy of 'reaction' to EU policy developments of the first twenty-five years of membership is plainly unsuited to this new EU policy phase. In her recent study of Irish central government's management of EU policy, Laffan found that among the Irish officials she interviewed there was a sense that the signposts or route map for Ireland's EU policy were less clear than in the past (Laffan 2001: 8). A number of important items are now on the EU's agenda – items involving the pursuit of objectives that may prove problematic for Irish negotiators unless some coherent strategy is put in place in advance of negotiations. The new structures and co-ordinating processes outlined above should facilitate this.

The debate on the future of Europe that took place at the European Convention in Brussels between 2002 and 2003 brought into sharper focus a number of tough issues for the Irish government.[13] The Declaration signed at the Nice Summit in December 2000 flagged up four matters to be clarified by the Convention:

- the division of competences between the EU and the member states;
- the future status of the Charter of Fundamental Rights;
- the simplification of the treaties;
- the role of national parliaments vis-à-vis the EU.

At the Nice summit, the Irish government had strongly resisted the proposal to give the Charter of Fundamental Rights 'treaty status'; it also resisted the subsequent proposal to incorporate the Charter by reference in Article 6 of the Treaty.[14] However, the Draft Constitution published on 6 February 2003 by the Convention President, Valery Giscard d'Estaing of France, does contain a reference to the Charter, and has clearly proven that this issue will not go away. The role of the Irish Parliament vis-à-vis the EU will also require more attention in the future. Other difficult issues on the horizon for Irish negotiators will include the reform of the CAP, state aids to industry, the equalising of corporation taxes across member states, Ireland's contribution to the EU budget, and matters of security and defence. Irish strategic preferences on these issues have begun to diverge from those of many other of the EU member states. For example, any renationalisation of the CAP – the devolution to member states themselves of responsibility for financial supports for agriculture – will certainly be vehemently opposed by Irish negotiators in the mid-term review of the agricultural elements of the 2000–6 EU budgetary package. A mooted move by the EU to determine fiscal and taxation policies for application to all member states – as opposed to allowing these matters to remain mostly in the hands of national parliaments – has been pre-emptively criticised by the Irish minister for finance. Moves to strengthen the EU's security and defence identity through the Rapid Reaction Force will also be a tough issue for Ireland. In short, instead of positioning itself, by and large, in the majority grouping as in the past, Ireland may find itself increasingly in a minority, with more Eurosceptical member states as allies in negotiations.

Conclusion

Ireland has gone from being one of the poorest and least developed members of the EU to one of the most economically dynamic. In any circumstances, this would make it necessary to reflect on priorities and objectives. What has hopefully become clear from the analysis in this chapter, however, is that Ireland's relationship with the EU is less certain than heretofore. In future EU negotiations Irish governments will no longer able to project and maintain the image of being everyone's friend. Indeed, it is quite possible that Irish negotiators could increasingly find themselves marginalised. Irish policy preferences are no longer like those of its southern Mediterranean member state allies. The next few years will significantly redefine Ireland's relationship with the EU.

Notes

1 The Republic of Ireland will hereafter be termed 'Ireland'. The EU was formerly known as the European Economic Community (EEC) and then as the European Community (EC).
2 Treaties and secondary legislation of the EU.
3 Although the Fine Gael–Labour coalition government and employers' organisations actually lobbied for derogation from implementation of the EU Equal Pay Directive in 1974, it was implemented none the less. Until April 1991, workers' rights

(including rights of part-time workers, that is, employees who worked for less than 18 hours a week) were, generally speaking, excluded from social insurance coverage and from protective labour legislation. A number of cases before the European Court of Justice suggested that such exclusion could be contrary to the Equal Pay and Opportunities Directives. This then prompted changes in Irish legislation.

4 This argument is not new. See Scott (1994) and Laffin (2001).

5 See also O'Mahony (2002).

6 With regard to the Maastricht European Monetary Union (EMU) criteria indicators – the standards required in order to conform to the rules of the EMU – Ireland is still at the upper end among the euro-zone countries.

7 Only two constituencies accepted the Nice Treaty: Dun Laoghaire (53.28 per cent 'Yes') and Dublin South (51.88 per cent 'Yes'). There was little regional variation in the vote, with the lowest 'No' vote recorded in the Rest of Leinster (52.37 per cent) and the highest 'No' vote in the Ulster counties that are part of the Republic – Donegal, Monaghan and Cavan (56.13 per cent).

8 O'Cuiv announced soon after the referendum result that he had voted 'No', in spite of campaigning for a 'Yes' vote. O'Dea is on record as saying that the referendum result 'showed that Irish people are stubborn, and if they want to make a decision, they will. It shows a certain robust independence which I admire' (*Irish Times*, 18 June 2001).

9 The ECR and Irish Marketing Surveys (IMS) Poll fieldwork was conducted between 20 August and 10 September 2001 among a quota sample of 1,245 adults. Although post-election and post-referendum surveys tend substantially to overestimate turnout and quite often overestimate support for the winning side, the reported turnout in the survey (42 per cent) was quite close to the actual turnout of just under 35 per cent, and the survey estimates of the 'Yes' and 'No' votes (42 and 58 per cent respectively) are also quite close to the actual result.

10 R. Sinnott, 'No Vote Stagnated while Yes Side Gained Hugely' (*Irish Times*, 21 October 2002).

11 The Lisbon Agenda/Process makes use of new modes of governance, such as the open method of co-ordination, that do not necessitate legislation in the form of directives and regulations, but rely on adherence to targets and benchmarks.

12 At the same time, committees are obliged to give an opinion on a proposal within a tight deadline and in advance of negotiation at EU Council of Ministers' level, otherwise approval of the proposal is taken as given. Ministers must be able to give oral briefings and reports of EU meetings on an agreed basis, and the committees deliberating on proposals may meet in private if a proposal is of a particularly sensitive nature. If the Committee concerned so desires, the chief whips of the political parties are in agreement, and the parliamentary timetable permits, proposals may be debated on the floor of the Oireachtas.

13 The Convention of the Future of Europe was a year-long deliberation by parliamentary members of EU states, and countries soon to become members, on the future shape of the EU. Its report on a proposed new EU Constitution will form the basis for negotiations on the way ahead.

14 The reason the government was reluctant to cede legal competence over the kind of rights enshrined in the Charter of the EU was because this would have implied a weakening of the role of Ireland's own Constitution with regard to citizen rights.

References

Ahern, B. (2003), Radio Telefís Éireann Radio 1, Thomas Davis Lecture, 27 January.

Barry, F., Bradley, J. and Hannan, A. (2001), 'The Single Market, the Structural Funds and Ireland's Recent Economic Growth', *Journal of Common Market Studies*, Vol. 39, No. 3, pp. 537–52.

FitzGerald, J. (1998), *An Irish Perspective on the Structural Funds*, Dublin: Economic and Social Research Institute.

Gilland, K. (1999), 'Referenda in the Republic of Ireland', *Electoral Studies*, Vol. 18, No. 3, pp. 430–8.

Government of Ireland (1996), *Challenges and Opportunities Abroad: White Paper on Foreign Policy*, Dublin: Stationery Office.

IPA (Institute of Public Administration) (2001), *IPA Yearbook and Diary*, Dublin: Institute of Public Administration.

Irish Business Bureau (2001), *European Monthly Newsletter*, December, No. 151.

Laffan, B. (2001), *Organising for a Changing Europe: Irish Central Government and the European Union*, Dublin: Policy Institute.

Laffan, B. (2002), 'Irish Politics and European Politics', Radio Telefís Éireann Radio 1, Thomas Davis Lecture, November.

Laffan, B. and O'Donnell, R. (1999), 'Ireland and the Growth of International Governance', in W. Crotty and D. E. Schmitt (eds), *Ireland and the Politics of Change*, London: Longman.

Laffan, B. and O'Mahony, J. (2003), *Managing Europe from Home: The Europeanisation of the Irish Core Executive*, Dublin: Dublin European Institute.

Ó Cinneide, S. (ed.) (1993), *EC Social Policy and Ireland*, Dublin: Institute of European Affairs.

O'Donnell, R. (2001), 'To be a Member State: The Experience of Ireland', Public Lecture, Dublin European Institute, University College Dublin, 26 September.

O'Halpin, E. (1996), 'Irish Parliamentary Culture and the EU: Formalities to be Observed', in P. Norton (ed.), *National Parliaments and the European Union*, London: Frank Cass.

O'Mahony, J. (2002), 'Ireland at the European Crossroads', in *Österreichisches Jahrbuch für Internationale Politik 2001*, Vienna: Braumüller.

Scott, D. (1994), *Ireland's Contribution to the European Union*, Dublin: Institute of European Affairs.

Sinnott, R. (1995), *Irish Voters Decide*, Manchester: Manchester University Press.

Sinnott, R. (2001), *Attitudes and Behaviour of the Irish Electorate in the Referendum on the Treaty of Nice*, results of a survey of public opinion carried out for the European Commission Representation in Ireland, carried out by Irish Marketing Surveys Ltd, in association with EOS Gallup Europe, 31 October.

Tonra, B. (2002), 'Irish Foreign Policy: Small States in a Big World', in W. Crotty and D. E. Schmitt (eds), *Ireland on the World Stage*, London: Longman.

3

The Northern Ireland peace process: obstacles remain

Clodagh Harris

Introduction

The conflict in Northern Ireland, which has lasted since the end of the 1960s, is one of the most researched in the world.[1] In more recent years, terms such as 'historic', 'in crisis', 'stalled' and 'derailed' have all been used to describe the ongoing peace process – a process intended to resolve the conflict once and for all. But what exactly is a peace process? This chapter analyses the various developments that led to the Belfast Good Friday Agreement of 1998, as well as its implementation, by reference to the five criteria for a peace process to exist offered by MacGinty and Darby (2000). They are:

- the protagonists are willing to negotiate in good faith;
- the key actors are included in the process;
- the negotiators address the central issues in the dispute;
- the negotiators do not use force to achieve their objectives; and
- the negotiators are committed to a sustained process.

The chapter concludes with an examination of the current obstacles in the path of peace.

'The protagonists are willing to negotiate in good faith'

The first of the criteria (or tests) is that the protagonists make a conscientious choice to negotiate and that they do so in good faith. So to whom can the term protagonist be applied? MacGinty and Darby adopt a broad definition which includes the British and Irish governments and Northern Ireland's 'constitutional' political parties (those opposed to the use of violence) as well as those parties that politically represent, or offer 'political advice' to, paramilitaries –

more contentiously described as terrorist groups. As for the protagonists themselves, these authors also recognise that the conscientious decision to participate in negotiations is often made at the leadership level (MacGinty and Darby
2000: 7)

Both Lijphart and Nordlinger argue that only political elites can make a
significant contribution to the management of conflict in deeply divided
societies (Lijphart 1977; Nordlinger 1972). However, it would be erroneous to
assume that the non-elite are without influence. The major role that the
Northern Ireland Civil Rights Association played in winning electoral and
security reforms in the late 1960s highlights the impact of mass popular movements. Furthermore political leaders, keen to maintain electoral support,
attempt to anticipate their voters' reactions to proposed changes. Finally, the
influence of the wider society in policy formulation – in the form of think-tanks,
community groups and support groups – cannot be overlooked. None the less
the negotiations that resulted in the Good Friday Agreement took place at the
'top' elite level, often in regular consultation with the 'middle' level elite, but
with less frequent involvement of the 'grassroots'. It is for this reason that this
study focuses almost entirely on the role of the leaders in assessing the behaviour of the protagonists.

So did these protagonists act in good faith? This question lies at the heart not
so much of the negotiations themselves as of the difficulties in implementing
the Good Friday Agreement. However, there were some initial problems. Sinn
Féin, the Progressive Unionist Party (PUP) and the Ulster Democratic Party
(UDP) were all included in the all-party talks after their associated paramilitary
organisations, respectively the Irish Republican Army (IRA), the Ulster
Volunteer Force/Red Hand Commandoes (UVF/RHC) and the Ulster Defence
Association/Ulster Freedom Fighters (UDA/UFF), declared ceasefires. But
when the IRA and the UDA/UFF broke the terms of their ceasefires in early
1998, their respective political parties were expelled, albeit temporarily, from
the talks.

On the other hand, the Ulster Unionist Party (UUP), the Social Democratic
and Labour Party (SDLP), the Alliance Party of Northern Ireland (APNI) and
the Northern Ireland Women's Coalition (NIWC), whatever their differences,
always acted in good political faith – none of them having any connections with
paramilitary organisations. The only negotiators who refused in the end to act
at all – whether in good faith or not – were the Democratic Unionist Party (DUP)
and the tiny United Kingdom Unionist Party (UKUP). Their representatives
walked out of the talks when Sinn Féin was permitted entry.[2]

Why enter the process?

What motivated unionists and (ultra-unionist) loyalists, and nationalists and
(ultra-nationalist) republicans, with diametrically opposing political and constitutional ambitions, to engage in negotiations? Nordlinger outlines four

possible elite motivations and argues that elites need to be influenced by at least one of these to engage in accommodation. The four motivations are: the need to retain/acquire power; the wish to end/avoid bloodshed; the desire to eliminate the economic costs of the conflict; and external threat (1972: 42). All, with the exception of the last, were felt by each of the protagonists. They were not, however, of equal saliency. The wish to end bloodshed, or the 'Troubles' – the popular euphemism for the violent conflict – was common to all the parties. Yet it was probably of greater importance to republicans and loyalists, who, by virtue of their overlapping political and paramilitary memberships, had greater first-hand experience of bloodshed. Moreover communal violence in Northern Ireland has tended to be concentrated in urban working-class areas, which are more likely to be either loyalist or republican. Over 40 per cent of deaths resulting from political violence have occurred in Belfast, which contains 20 per cent of Northern Ireland's population. Within Belfast, over 75 per cent of the deaths from sectarian violence have happened in the north and west of the city, areas with high levels of social and economic deprivation (Morrissey and Smith 2002). Some within the leadership cadres of loyalism and republicanism, having sacrificed their own youth to their respective struggles, had become war-weary and had no desire to bequeath a similar lifestyle to their children and grandchildren. More significantly the 'war' between the IRA and the British forces had been in stalemate for some considerable time, with neither side going to achieve 'victory' but neither side likely to be defeated either. As a consequence, the Sinn Féin leadership seized upon the 'kite' flown by the British Secretary of State for Northern Ireland, Peter Brooke, to justify to its supporters a reorientation of their efforts to achieve their political goal of a united socialist Ireland by non-violent means.[3]

The desire to acquire power was also a strong motivation for political elites that had enjoyed little political influence after Northern Ireland's Parliament in Belfast was suspended in 1972, and direct rule from the ultimately sovereign UK Parliament at Westminster was imposed instead. Northern Ireland sent only seventeen Members of Parliament (MPs) to London, where they had a very marginal role.[4] Not belonging to either of the two main parties in the House of Commons, they were never going to become members of a government, and thus tended to play a reactive rather than proactive role in the British Parliament. Paradoxically, direct rule from London actually became attractive to some unionists, who began to see the very existence of the devolved Parliament at Stormont as having contributed significantly to the troubles. Indeed, in the late 1970s and early 1980s, those in the UUP advocating the even fuller integration of Northern Ireland into the rest of the UK, as opposed to being an awkward appendage with its own distinctive characteristics, were in the ascendancy. But direct rule began to lose its shine in the mid-1980s. The Anglo-Irish Agreement of 1985 gave the government of the Republic of Ireland a formal role in the affairs of Northern Ireland for the first time, for although it stopped short of joint British–Irish authority it clearly did erode

British sovereignty. Not surprisingly, this tarnished the integrationist project in unionist eyes, for it was Westminster that had betrayed their trust and sold the pass to the Irish government. The prospect of a new agreement to replace the reviled Anglo-Irish Agreement served as a further strong incentive for the UUP to participate in the all-party talks. There was also real concern that a new governmental arrangement for Northern Ireland could simply be foisted upon them if they chose not to take part.

As for the SDLP, local institutions of government – which seemed the most likely outcome of multi-party talks – were not its favoured constitutional solution to the Northern Ireland problem, but they were infinitely preferable to direct rule, which was essentially unitary and central and had done little to redress the peripheral region's disadvantaged socio-economic status. So participation in the talks which held out the possibility of the SDLP having a share of governmental power and responsibility was never in the slightest way problematic for that party. Indeed, the desire to acquire power was a potent incentive to accommodation even for the DUP, for despite its refusal to participate in the talks beyond the very early stages and its virulent anti-Good Friday Agreement stance subsequently, the party took up its place in the governing structures created under the Agreement's terms.

The economic cost of the conflict perhaps also enticed the protagonists to negotiate, and eventually to accommodate. Yet it was not as strong as the other motivations, since the Northern Ireland economy was significantly subvented or subsidised by the UK Treasury, which also bore all the heavy security costs of the Troubles. Furthermore, although it would be wrong to describe it as representing an 'external threat' in Nordlinger's terms, pressure to compromise was also brought to bear from 'outside' on the Northern Ireland protagonists. As well as the obvious push on the parties by the British and Irish governments, accommodation was also facilitated by the Irish-American lobby in the US, which put particular pressure on Sinn Féin. The Clinton administration, and the President himself, were also a very effective influence on the parties at the eleventh hour.

Sustaining motivations

Sustaining elite motivations during the implementation of the Good Friday Agreement has proven difficult, however. This prompts the question of whether it is sufficient to negotiate in good faith. Acceptance on the part of all participants that each is acting in good faith is required. Neither the DUP nor the UKUP believed that Sinn Féin could negotiate in good faith; in particular they doubted Sinn Féin's sincerity with regard to the decommissioning of IRA armaments. The same issue divided the UUP too at a senior level on the day the accord was finalised (three of its negotiators walked out of the talks). It has also been seriously eroding support for the Agreement within the party since the 1998 referendum, which provided the required public endorsement for the

Agreement. For their part, Darby and MacGinty assert that trust is not a pre-condition for negotiation but may be a consequence of it. But trust is certainly required for implementation. Each side must be assured that the other will deliver its side of the bargain – the protagonists 'may not trust one another, but they need to trust the process' (McGinty and Darby 2002: 3). This partly explains the recurring crises caused by the decommissioning issue.

Opposition to the Agreement from the DUP and from senior people within the UUP has placed UUP leader David Trimble and the pro-Agreement members within his party in a dilemma, and left him little if any room for manoeuvre. The unionist community may be content to have acquired a measure of power though UUP and DUP membership of the Northern Ireland Executive. Yet having initially agreed to share power by accepting Sinn Féin as members of the Executive, the UUP has become more and more unhappy about this because of the failure of Sinn Féin's fellow members of the Republican Movement in the IRA to engage in more than token acts of decommissioning. The DUP took the 'moral high ground' regarding Sinn Féin from the beginning, and the UUP's policy of accommodation with republicans has certainly not paid electoral divi-dends. By the 2001 local government elections (for city and district councils) the gap in support between the two parties, having previously been significant, became negligible: the UUP won 22.9 per cent of the votes and 154 seats, while the DUP increased its number of seats and percentage of the votes to 131 and 21.4 per cent. This was in stark contrast to the 1997 elections, in which the UUP won 27.9 per cent of the votes and 188 seats while the DUP received 15.8 per cent of the votes and 91 seats.[5]

Furthermore, the UUP's pro-Agreement stance has not garnered it electoral support across the community divide. It has received few if any transfers under the proportional representation (single transferable vote) (PR[STV]) electoral system from SDLP voters.[6] Likewise, UUP voters have been slow to transfer pref-erences to SDLP candidates. An analysis of the pattern of vote transfers in the 1998 Assembly elections indicated they showed possibly the most 'communal' (meaning staying entirely with one's 'own side') voting pattern since the re-introduction of PR(STV) into Northern Ireland in 1973. An examination of the constituency results indicated that no UUP candidate was elected as a conse-quence of SDLP vote transfers – though an SDLP candidate in East Antrim was successful as a result of transfers from a UUP candidate. An exit poll for Radio Telefis Éireann (RTÉ), the main Irish radio and TV provider, by Ulster Marketing Surveys showed that only 1 per cent of UUP voters would give their second pref-erence vote to another party, and only 3 per cent of those that gave a second preference would opt to give a third preference. The SDLP figures, which were 1 per cent and 4 per cent respectively, mirrored this. Overall, the transfer pattern 'revealed the election to be highly communal with little sense of the new political cleavage of pro- and anti-Agreement'.[7] This is of great concern for both both the UUP and the SDLP as they face Assembly elections (now promised for the autumn of 2003, having been deferred from May); for while presently the two largest parties in terms of votes, there is real danger that they may be overtaken by the DUP and Sinn Féin respectively.

The need for political security

In his analysis of the role of elites in conflict regulation, Nordlinger refers to the need for elite political security – that is, the need for what has been called here the 'top' elite to enjoy the support of the 'middle' level elite of their party (1972: 67) For the most part, SDLP and Sinn Féin leaders have been successful in protecting their party positions, enjoying support not only within their parties but also at grassroots level. The exception to this, involving Sinn Féin, occurred when in May 1998 a section of the IRA broke away under the leadership of its quartermaster general to form the 'Real' IRA and its alleged political wing, the Thirty-Two County Sovereignty Committee. The UUP leader, David Trimble, has had a different experience, facing pressures on his leadership not only from the anti-Agreement unionist parties but also from dissidents within his own party. His increasingly shaky position has restricted his ability to take risks in defending the Agreement. This has hindered, and continues to hinder, the impetus of the peace process. Having given ground on the issue of the decommissioning of paramilitary weapons several times during the negotiation of the Good Friday Agreement, once the Executive was set up Trimble was inevitably dogged by his internal party opponents constantly reminding him of the Agreement's provisions on decommissioning.

In particular, he was taunted with the phrase coined by one of his own aides: 'no guns, no government' – by which was meant that for so long as the IRA continued to refuse to decommission its weapons, Sinn Féin should not hold ministerial posts in the executive. Although UUP attachment to this notion that decommissioning was a prerequisite for a continuation of the Executive was dismissed by some republicans as simply a unionist desire to get out of sharing power with Catholics, a temporary way round the impasse was found in October 2001: the International Independent Commission on Decommissioning (IICD) set up under the Agreement confirmed that the IRA had put a quantity of arms (amount unspecified) beyond use. This let Trimble temporarily off the hook. However, several other developments made the unionists call even further into question the sincerity of the commitment of Sinn Féin and the IRA to use only peaceful methods to achieve their political objectives. A known IRA member was jailed in Florida in the US for attempting to smuggle weapons to Ireland; three people alleged to have Sinn Féin connections were arrested in Colombia in South America and charged with training anti-government terrorists; then there was the suspected involvement of the IRA in a raid to steal intelligence files stored in police headquarters in Belfast; finally, in October 2002 the police raided Sinn Féin's offices in Parliament buildings at Stormont, seized documents and computer records, and arrested the party's administration manager, the suggestion being that an IRA spy-ring was operating on the premises.

The result was suspension of the Executive and the Assembly. At the time of writing, neither of the two leading unionist parties believes that Sinn Féin is acting in good faith, and the patience of the SDLP is also being severely tested in this regard. However, the British and Irish Governments have put a huge amount of effort into breaking the log jam, placing particular pressure on Sinn Féin to accept that unless there is major movement from the IRA on the arms issue it will be impossible for there to be a return to a devolved power-sharing government at Stormont under the Good Friday Agreement. Yet there is every reason to believe that the IRA has been persuaded that 'acts of completion' are needed. The expectation, therefore, is that in one way or another the IRA will declare its war with the unionists and the British to have ended, and will make that manifest in a tangible, even visible way. In arguably at least as momentous a move, Sinn Féin will declare its intention to join the board overseeing the activities of the Police Service of Northern Ireland, a reformed replacement for that special object of republican hatred, the Royal Ulster Constabulary (RUC). In response, the UUP will accept again the good faith of Sinn Féin; the British government will 'demilitarise', also in a visible way, by removing the remaining army installations and taking troops off the streets; and the institutions of devolved government will be restored. The only problem with this scenario is that all parties are worried about overcommitting themselves in advance of the Assembly elections promised for the autumn of 2003. For example, Sinn Féin has already made it clear that it is unlikely to have received the endorsement of the party faithful for any of the movement described above in advance of an election. Put another way, acceptance of good faith all round is being temporarily put on hold.

'The key actors are included in the process'

In their definition of the key actors, MacGinty and Darby include the existing government in the area, the paramilitary groupings and 'all elements which have power to bring about the downfall of an agreement' (2000: 8) In the context of the Northern Ireland conflict the key actors include the British and Irish governments and the political parties in Northern Ireland, all of which were invited to take part in the all-party talks. The IRA, UVF and UDA were represented by their political wings, although Sinn Féin insisted that it did not act for the IRA and relied instead for its authority on its political mandate from the voters. The small dissident organisations, such as the Real IRA, the Continuity IRA and the Loyalist Volunteer Force (a breakaway from the UVF), were not involved at any stage. Other potentially key actors included those 'outsiders' who had played a crucial role in brokering the beginning of the talks: the independent chairman of the negotiations, former US Senator George Mitchell, the Irish-American lobby and the Clinton administration. Yet they were not veto holders in the conflict. The veto holders were the British and Irish governments, the main nationalist and unionist political parties, and the larger republican and loyalist paramilitary groups.

The road to Sunningdale

The influence of the paramilitaries is what mainly differentiates the Sunningdale Agreement – the outcome of what Dixon (2001) calls the 'first peace process' – from the process which led to the Good Friday Agreement. The introduction of direct rule after the prorogation (effectively the suspension) of the Northern Ireland Parliament in March 1972 was seen as a purely temporary measure by the British government. As in the early 1920s, anxious to distance itself once again from the Irish problem, the government in London wanted to restore devolution in Northern Ireland. It thus attempted to construct an accommodation on the 'moderate, centre ground of Northern Irish politics', where it assumed there was a 'moderate silent majority for peace' (Dixon 2001: 129). With this end in view the evidently 'moderate centre' parties of Northern Ireland politics were invited to attend a conference on the political options for Northern Ireland, held in Darlington in England in September 1972. Participating in the round-table talks on the political future were the APNI (essentially a non-sectarian, liberal, middle-class party, formed in April 1970), the UUP, and the slowly fading Northern Ireland Labour Party (NILP). The SDLP, the roots of which lay in the civil rights movement of the late 1960s and early 1970s, was also invited; but it boycotted the proceedings in protest at the continuation of the internment in prison without trial or judicial process of people suspected of engaging in violence.[8] As a result of talks, the British government published a Green Paper, *The Future of Northern Ireland: A Paper for Discussion* (NIO 1972), which set out what were seen as some of the fundamental conditions on which any settlement must rest. These were in turn reflected in the White Paper, *Northern Ireland Constitutional Proposals*, published in March 1973 (NIO 1973).

The White Paper proposed the establishment of a Northern Ireland Assembly, whose members would be elected using PR(STV). It also contained provisions for the creation of Northern Ireland's first power-sharing executive, which would be made up of the chairmen of Assembly departmental committees, whose members would in turn reflect the balance of parties associated with each department. Like the Green Paper that preceded it, the White Paper made a novel concession by a sovereign government in recognising that there was a serious and legitimate interest in a peaceful outcome in Northern Ireland by a foreign state, the Republic of Ireland. This was the so-called 'Irish dimension', and it was to be recognised in the form of a 'Council of Ireland'.[9] That this was a significant departure for the British government in policy terms can be seen by setting it against its first 'Downing Street Declaration', made soon after the Troubles erupted on the streets in 1969, which insisted that 'responsibility for affairs in Northern Ireland is entirely a matter of domestic consideration' (Arthur 1985: 36).

For ardent unionists the prescribed power-sharing with 'disloyal' nationalists was as distasteful as the creation of a Council of Ireland. The Green and
White Papers were rejected by the Orange Order (an organisation devoted to the
defence of the Protestant religion, and which is represented on the UUP's ruling
body), the UDA, Ulster Vanguard (a UUP ginger group) and the DUP. Within the
UUP the Papers' proposals proved too bitter a pill for some to swallow, but at a
meeting of the UUC, in late March 1973, the White Paper was accepted by 381
votes to 231 (Dixon 2001: 138). A few days later the Vanguard faction gave
shape to their rejectionism by forming the Vanguard Unionist Parliamentary
Party (VUPP). For the more moderate wing of UUP, however, the promise of an
end to direct rule and the possibility of acquiring governmental power, albeit in
a power-sharing arrangement, was the sweetener that helped the medicine go
down. For the nationalists of the SDLP, the prospect of participation in government – having been left in the political wilderness for over half a century – was
also a strong incentive for co-operation, as was the inclusion of an Irish dimension, which they hoped would lead to joint sovereignty and perhaps eventually
to a united Ireland.

The rate at which things were changing proved particularly difficult for
many within the UUP. Accustomed to unchallenged power under the majori-
tarian first-past-the-post voting system that had prevailed since 1929, some
Ulster Unionists felt seriously threatened.[10] Their wholly Protestant part-time
auxiliary constabulary, the 'B Specials' – often pejoratively described as the
'armed wing of Unionism' – had been disbanded; the police force, the RUC, had
been disarmed,[11] and their parliament had been prorogued. Yet now they were
expected to share government with people who had no loyalty to the state, and
to develop a cross-border institutional structure with their irridentist neighbour in the Republic. That this unionist identity crisis occurred against a background of intense activity by the IRA and reactive violence by loyalist
paramilitaries only served to exacerbate the situation. The distance that the
UUP had had to travel in this short space of time proved too much for many
within its ranks. The leaders of the DUP and VUPP, waiting on the sidelines,
'rescued' the stragglers who could not keep pace.

Electoral influences

In the run-up to the June 1973 elections for a proposed new assembly, the UUP,
led by Brian Faulkner, faced competition not only from the VUPP and the DUP,
but also from people within the ranks of his own previous supporters, campaigning on a 'no surrender' manifesto. Within the UUP, the power-sharing
issue was proving particularly divisive. The party fielded fifty candidates, but a
number of these refused to take Faulkner's so-called 'pledge', which bound
them to official party policy. In early June, the *Irish Times* reported that Faulkner
had forty-one loyal candidates. A week later this number had fallen to thirty-
nine (Bew and Gillespie 1996: 65). The outcome of the election contrasted

sharply with opinion poll and unofficial British predictions. A poll commissioned jointly by the London *Sunday Times* and the Belfast magazine *Fortnight* had forecast 'a clear shift to the centre parties and almost total support for making the White Paper proposals work'. But though the predictions were for nine NILP, eleven APNI and twelve SDLP seats, the NILP managed to only one while the APNI secured eight. The SDLP, on the other hand, emerged from the election with nineteen seats. The true surprise lay in the level of support for anti-White Paper parties. They succeed in winning a total of twenty-six seats and 'dashed British hopes of a moderate power-sharing executive composed of the NILP, APNI and liberal unionists' (Dixon 2001: 137–8) (see Table 3.1).

Table 3.1 *Assembly election results, June 1973*

Party	Percentage of the vote	Number of seats
Pro-White Paper UUP	29.3	24
SDLP	22.1	19
APNI	9.2	8
NILP	2.6	1
'Pro' total	63.2	52
Anti-White Paper UUP	8.5	8
DUP	10.8	8
VUPP	10.5	7
West Belfast Loyalists	2.3	3
'Anti' total	32.1	26

Source: P. Dixon (2001), *Northern Ireland: The Politics of War and Peace*, Basingstoke: Palgrave.

The failure of the adamantly non-sectarian APNI and NILP to poll as well as had been predicted left Faulkner in an extremely precarious position. As they were cross-community parties it would have been possible, under the terms of the White Paper, for him to form a power-sharing executive with them. Their poor electoral performances, however, dictated that any coalition would have to include the SDLP. But Faulkner did not have a mandate for power sharing, still less power-sharing with the SDLP. Yet by a small majority of 132 against 105, he managed to win a UUP standing committee vote to allow UUP members of the Assembly to take part in any future power-sharing executive. At a 750-strong meeting of the UUC in late November, some days before the Executive was announced, an anti-power-sharing motion was defeated, but only by the tiny margin of ten votes (Farrell 1976: 310). Faulkner's position was further weakened by the formation, on the eve of the Sunningdale Conference in December, of the United Ulster Unionist Council (UUUC); this included anti-White Paper Members from his own party, together with the VUPP and the DUP.
At the Sunningdale Conference, Faulkner took another dangerous step,

when he agreed to an all-Ireland body with 'executive and harmonising functions and a consultative role', to be called the Council of Ireland (Hennessey 2000: 14). He did manage to secure a unionist veto on a range of issues, but failed to win the restoration of policing powers to the new Executive, a key demand of the UUP. He also failed to convince the Irish government to amend or drop Articles 2 and 3 of Bunreacht na hÉireann, the Irish Constitution (the articles which laid formal claim by the Republic to the territory of Northern Ireland). None the less, a power-sharing Executive was duly set up, made up of UUP, SDLP and APNI ministers.

Sunningdale: a peace process?

For a variety of reasons, to describe Sunningdale as a peace process is arguably wide of the mark. The Green and White Papers were drafted at a time of intense sectarian violence, for, unlike the case with the Good Friday process, there were no associated paramilitary ceasefires. In addition several key actors/veto holders were missing, as many of the protagonists were either unwilling, or not invited, to take part in negotiations. Compromise with one another, even with the moderates in their respective communities, was at complete variance with hard-line unionist, loyalist and republican traditions. By being outside the process these parties and factions challenged the moderates' political security and the Executive's stability. The fact that the Sunningdale Agreement did not have majority unionist support gravely undermined its legitimacy. And it was not resisted only by the 'ultras' of the new UUUC; at a meeting of the UUP's Ulster Unionist Council in early January 1974, the Agreement was rejected by a majority of eighty. Then action on the part of one of the key veto holders led to the rapid demise of the power-sharing institutions. When the Sunningdale Agreement was ratified in the Assembly in May 1974, the loyalist Ulster Workers' Council (UWC) – an *ad hoc* body set up for the purpose – announced a 'constitutional stoppage' (Farrell 1976: 315). What was effectively a strike, but which active trade unionists denounced as a distortion of working-class militant traditions, lasted just two weeks and was particularly effective as regards cutting electricity and petrol (gasoline) supplies. The stoppage only ended when the Faulknerite unionists felt obliged to resign, and brought down the power-sharing Executive.

One of the reasons why the Good Friday process succeeded where the Sunningdale quasi-process failed was the shift from a zero-sum to a positive-sum approach in the all-party negotiations. Although Bleakley argues that a calm reading of the Sunningdale communiqué indicates that there were 'no winners or losers', this was clearly not the case (Bleakley 1995: 125). The Irish Minister for Foreign Affairs at the Conference, Dr Garret FitzGerald, noted at the time that 'on any objective assessment the Irish Government and the SDLP have gained most and the Unionists least' (1991: 220). The unionists agreed to a Council of Ireland with executive powers and the prospect of policing, an issue which had been instrumental in the fall of the Stormont regime, coming under the remit of what opponents saw as an embryonic all-Ireland government. Moreover, the failure on Faulkner's part to persuade the Irish government to drop or amend Articles 2 and 3 of the Irish Constitution further weakened the Sunningdale Agreement in unionist eyes. The Irish Fine Gael–Labour coalition government was not prepared to make such a move and was 'handicapped by [its] concern lest any formulation [it] agreed be struck down as unconstitutional by [Irish] courts' (FitzGerald 1991: 222). Neither could it support the British interpretation of Northern Ireland's status, as this would have directly conflicted with the Constitution. Instead the Irish government declared that 'there would be no change in the status of Northern Ireland until a majority of the people of Northern Ireland desired a change in that status'. This was obviously short of declaring that Northern Ireland was part of the UK, but it did have all the force of an international agreement. That it was described by some unionists to be 'worthless' was more a polemical than a constitutional point.

Faulkner did not take this view, and dismissed the Council of Ireland's executive functions as being in the 'necessary nonsense category' required to ensure the co-operation of the Irish government and the SDLP; in the end he was 'more than satisfied that the constitutional integrity of Northern Ireland was secure' (Bleakley 1995: 125). He clearly failed to calculate correctly the political ramifications for himself and his party of being placed in an apparently losing position. Each leader had entered the conference prepared to defend his corner and had expected the others to do likewise. Faulkner was, by this measure, the least competent of them. In hindsight the Agreement itself was the loser, as it was only as strong as its weakest link; and the UUC lost no time in bidding Faulkner goodbye. Failure on the part of the other participants at the conference to take account of the difficulty of Faulkner's position, coupled with their eagerness to celebrate their spoils, tainted the Agreement from the beginning. Although APNI and SDLP negotiators were concerned that Faulkner was being pushed too far, and toned down the list of executive powers for the Council of Ireland as a result, the British and Irish governments both 'assumed that if Faulkner accepted something then he could sell it' (Hennessey 2000: 14). Their misplaced confidence, or perhaps lack of concern, was fatal to the Agreement. The zero-sum approach, which left clear winners and losers, served neither the agreement nor the Troubles well (Harris 2002: 213). Yet it must be acknowledged that the period in which the Sunningdale Agreement was negotiated and implemented was marred by serious violence perpetrated by the IRA. Bolstered in confidence by the fact that the 'Brits' had actually taken the decisive step of dissolving the Stormont Parliament, the IRA was convinced that one more push on its part would finally force them out of Ireland. It dismissed the 1973 elections and the Sunningdale Conference as a cunning British trick to lure nationalists into accepting continued British presence on the island, and stepped up its violence. The absence of a peace dividend gravely undermined Faulkner's ability to sell the Sunningdale Agreement to his fellow unionists.

The positive-sum approach evident at the all-party talks that initiated the present peace process in September 1997 can be attributed to a number of factors: the role of the independent chairman from the US, Senator George Mitchell, the overarching desire for peace and power, and the lessons learnt from Sunningdale (Harris 2002: 262). Trimble was not alone in wishing to avoid the mistakes made at Sunningdale. Efforts, often heroic, were made by the British and Irish governments and their officials to keep their respective 'clients', in all their varying hues, on board. The 'clients' – unionists, loyalists, nationalists and republicans – were also aware that the success of any political settlement hinged not only on their readiness to accommodate, but on the ability of each of them to sell an agreement to their supporters. This mutual interdependency underpinned the positive-sum approach.

'The negotiators address the central issues in the dispute'

The constitutional status of Northern Ireland lies at the core of the conflict. According to MacGinty and Darby, a peace process may opt to defer discussing constitutional matters until peace building, or confidence building as it was termed in the Northern Ireland context, had taken place (2000: 8). The negotiators in the Northern Ireland peace process could not afford to follow such a line, however, since constitutional compromises were required to bring, and keep, some of the key actors on board from the beginning. In the Joint Declaration on Peace (Downing Street Declaration 'number two') of December 1993, the British government recognised 'that it is for the people of the island of Ireland alone, by agreement between the two parts respectively, to exercise their right of self-determination on the basis of consent, freely and concurrently given'. It also declared that the British had no selfish, strategic or economic interest in maintaining Northern Ireland as part of the United Kingdom. These were essential constitutional prerequisites for Sinn Féin to participate. For its part the Irish government confirmed that 'in the event of an overall settlement' it would, 'as part of a balanced constitutional accommodation, put forward and support proposals for change in the Irish Constitution which would fully reflect the principle of consent in Northern Ireland'.[12] Clearly intended to facilitate DUP and UUP inclusion in the negotiations, this meant that the Irish government was now fully and formally prepared to accept that Northern Ireland would remain constitutionally part of the United Kingdom for so long as that was the wish of its citizens.[13]

Institutional arrangements

Other key requirements included the necessity of devising three sets of institutional arrangements: within Northern Ireland, for the whole island of Ireland, and between the islands of Great Britain and Ireland. These structures and their interlinking relationships formed the so-called three-standard approach of the Good Friday Agreement. A summary of the main institutional provisions of the Agreement will be found in the appendix at the end of this chapter.[14] Some further issues dealt with included the decommissioning of paramilitary arms, the release of convicted paramilitary prisoners, reform of the police and the justice system, and a bill of rights. Decommissioning and police reform have been the two most difficult provisions to implement in practice. Interestingly, the Agreement itself is not specific on these matters. Regarding decommissioning (on which see more below), the participants agreed to do little more than use to 'use any influence they may have' to achieve it. In the area of police reform, the Agreement simply called for a Commission to make recommendations on the future of policing in Northern Ireland.[15]

'Maximalist and risky'

The Good Friday Agreement is described by Horowitz (2001) as 'maximalist and risky'. He views it as maximalist to the extent that it is very explicit about the conditional character of sovereignty, and he is critical of this approach being applied to the constitutional issue because it leaves little room for fudge, and restricts the space for manoeuvre (2001: 89–92). Yet the constitutional question lies at the crux of the Northern Ireland conflict. A lack of clarification on this matter would have meant there was no agreement. Furthermore, it was a piece of fudge in the form of a letter from Tony Blair to David Trimble on the day the Agreement was completed that has led to a number of subsequent problems. This fudge (outlined in the next section) was to do with decommissioning, and was required on the day to ensure that the UUP would sign up to the Agreement.

'The negotiators do not use force to achieve their objectives' and 'the negotiators are committed to a sustained process'

The last two of McGinty and Darby's criteria can be examined together, as they are inextricably linked in the case of the Northern Ireland conflict. Some of the negotiators had, and indeed have, the ability and the potential to resort to force. However, the fact that force had failed to deliver their goals was one of the primary motivations for these groups taking part in the peace process. None the less, decommissioning and the threat of force, either real or perceived, remain the most contentious issues in the Northern Ireland peace process.

Decommissioning looms again

Decommissioning was on the political agenda from before the first IRA ceasefire, having been laid down as a precondition for any movement whatever by several of the parties. John Major, the British Prime Minister, refused Sinn Féin entry into the peace talks because the IRA refused to declare its 1994 cessation of violence to be permanent. Completing the circle, the IRA in turn put the blame on the British government for the massive bomb that IRA volunteers were responsible for planting at Canary Wharf in London, which broke the first ceasefire and killed two uninvolved bystanders. The IRA said that it was in retaliation for Major refusing to budge on the matter of Sinn Féin's participation in the talks. In an effort to broker an agreement on the 'guns and talks' issues, an independent triumvirate under the leadership of Senator Mitchell drafted a set of standards of democracy and non-violence, often referred to as the 'Mitchell Principles', to be assented to by participating parties. All parties eventually did this, thus permitting the negotiations to begin with all of the key actors taking part.

As to the effect of the Mitchell Principles on actual behaviour, the IRA and UVF ceasefires are, at the time of writing, tenuously intact. But in late 2002 the UDA was declared to be in breach, because of its clear association with organised street violence and a number of sectarian killings of innocent Catholics. Furthermore, there remains a sustained level of violence in some localities, and the number of so-called punishment beatings has increased: in 2001 there were 331 paramilitary 'punishment' attacks, an increase of over 25 per cent on the 2000 figure. Loyalist paramilitaries were responsible for 121 shootings and 91 beatings while republicans were responsible for 66 shootings and 53 beatings.[16]

But, perhaps surprisingly, continuing day-to-day violence has not been the rock upon which so many hopes have perished; rather, decommissioning is the issue which still haunts progress. In its reference to this matter, the Good Friday Agreement contains the following provision:

> all participants ... reaffirm their commitment to the total disarmament of all paramilitary organisations. They also confirm their intention to continue to work constructively and in good faith with the Independent Commission [the IICD], and to use any influence they may have to achieve the decommissioning of all paramilitary arms within two years following endorsement in referendums North and South of the agreement and in the context of the implementation of the overall settlement.

While there was a certain linkage between decommissioning and assuming office, one was not dependent on the other (Mallie and McKittrick 2001: 146, 245). On the morning of the day that the Agreement was finalised, the UUP's delegates said they were concerned about the 'way in which the linkage was going to operate'. In response, a letter from the British Prime Minister, Tony Blair, to the UUP confirmed his view that the decommissioning section of the Agreement meant that 'with decommissioning schemes coming into effect in June ... the process of decommissioning should start right away'. This piece of fudge reassured the UUP and enabled it finally to accept the document that became the Good Friday Agreement – though not without a dramatic last-minute rebellion within its ranks, as noted earlier (McDonald 2001: 209).[17]

The euphoria that followed the results of the simultaneous referendums in Northern Ireland and the Republic in favour of the Agreement and the June Assembly elections was quickly dampened when, in October, David Trimble told his party conference that Sinn Féin could not join the proposed Executive without IRA decommissioning. The process totally stalled when Sinn Féin countered with the insistence that no IRA guns would be surrendered before it took its seats in the Executive. In September 1999, Senator Mitchell was recalled by the two governments to find a way through the difficulty. Some time later the IRA intimated it was ready to discuss decommissioning, and would appoint a representative to the IICD. This led Mitchell to conclude that the basis existed for both decommissioning *and* the formation of a multi-party Executive. Soon afterwards, arguably as a direct result, the UUC accepted a leadership compromise that would allow the Assembly and the Executive to begin to operate. This compromise entailed a promise from Trimble that he would return to the UUC to seek its renewed support in February 2000. Furthermore, he handed a post-dated letter of resignation as first minister to a senior party official, to be delivered to the British government in the event of inadequate movement on arms. The path was now open for the restoration of devolution, which occurred on 1 December. In accordance with what came to be called the 'choreography', the next day the IRA appointed an interlocutor to the IICD.

A divided UUP

In February 2000, when a report from the IICD stated it had received no information from the IRA as to when decommissioning would start, the British secretary of state for Northern Ireland, Peter Mandelson, suspended the 72-day-old power-sharing Executive and restored the direct rule of Northern Ireland from Westminster. A month later, clearly on the basis of assurances received, Trimble announced that the Executive might be re-formed without prior IRA decommissioning, but only so as long as there would be firm guarantees that decommissioning would indeed take place. Careful choreography once more produced a sequence of co-ordinated activities. First an IRA statement said that if the Good Friday Agreement was 'fully implemented' they would 'completely and verifiably put IRA weapons beyond use' (Mallie and McKittrick 2001: 296). The IRA also agreed to a number of arms dumps being inspected and sealed by international figures. UUC approval for the UUP rejoining the Executive then paved the way for the restoration of devolved government at the end of May 2000. Finally, between June and October that year there were two agreed inspections of IRA arms dumps.

Yet these gestures were simply not enough for the sceptics within the UUP. At a meeting of the UUC in October 2000, Jeffrey Donaldson, a Westminster MP, put forward a motion calling on Trimble to leave the Executive if the IRA failed to move towards final decommissioning. Trimble, however, proposed a counter-motion that would commit him to preventing Sinn Féin ministers in the Executive from taking part in meetings of the cross-border bodies established under Strand 2 of the Agreement until the IRA had fully engaged with the IICD. Trimble won by 445 votes to 374. In December, however, the head of the Commission produced another pessimistic report on the decommissioning process. The following May, coming under almost unendurable pressure from the anti-Agreement forces within his party, Trimble wrote a letter of resignation for the second time. This letter came into effect on 1 July 2001, as there had still not been significant progress on the decommissioning of IRA weapons. Two one-day suspensions of the institutions were announced during the summer of 2001 in an effort to broker a compromise on the decommissioning question. But in mid-October three UUP and two DUP ministers formally resigned from the Northern Ireland Executive.

But was rescue at hand? At the end of the same month the IRA issued a statement that it had begun to decommission its weapons. Later in the day the Decommissioning Commission announced that it had now witnessed an event, which it regarded as significant, in which the IRA had put a quantity of arms completely beyond use, including arms, ammunition and explosives. No indication was given of the kind and amount of arms destroyed and, possibly as a consequence, this did not resolve the crisis. In early November 2001, Trimble and Mark Durkan (the new SDLP leader, who succeeded John Hume) did not secure sufficient unionist support to be elected as First Minister and Deputy First Minister respectively. Trimble needed thirty unionist-designated votes, but only managed to obtain twenty-nine after two UUP Members of the Legislative Assembly (MLAs) decided not to support him. The temporary redesignation of the two Womens' Coalition MLAs from 'other' to 'unionist' and 'nationalist' respectively was not enough to win the required unionist consent – although the voting of MLAs of all parties produced a call of seventy-two in favour as opposed to thirty against. A day or so later, however, Trimble and Durkan were elected when a number of the Alliance Party MLAs also redesignated themselves as 'unionist' and 'nationalist'. On the day ninety-nine MLAs cast their votes, of whom seventy were in favour of the motion and twenty-nine against. Of the sixty ostensibly 'unionist' MLAs who voted, there were thirty-one in favour and twenty-nine against. Unionist support for the Agreement had reached a new low. In contrast all thirty-eight nationalist members voted in favour.

Obstacles to peace

Decommissioning, or rather the lack of it, is still impeding the full implementation of the Agreement. At the time of writing the most recent crisis in the process stems from unionist fears that the IRA is still active. The institutions were again suspended in October 2002, when the DUP pulled its two ministers out of the Executive a week after the police raid on Sinn Féin's Stormont offices. As already noted, this latest crisis has not been helped by the prospect of Assembly elections, however long deferred. The UUP is keenly aware that the DUP might eclipse it as the largest unionist party in Northern Ireland after the elections. Indeed the SDLP members are similarly fearful of Sinn Féin doing the same to them. Since signing the Agreement, Trimble, facing increasing pressure from anti-Agreement unionists both within the party and among the electorate, has steadily progressed towards what is to all intents and purposes an anti-Agreement stance (McKay 2003). Electioneering has also played a part in the recent decision of the PUP to break off contact with Sinn Féin until it has 'clarified republican intentions towards the loyalist community and the peace process' (Breen 2003). On the same day the paramilitary group with which the PUP is linked, the UVF, suspended its contact with the IICD.

Yet cracks are even beginning to emerge in that great monolith of anti-Agreement unionism, the DUP, where leader Ian Paisley's 'No' seems to be being replaced with 'Maybe' from his two most senior colleagues. As the tension increases between the resulting blocs, a distinguished political commentator has observed that 'there are undeniable signs from the ... pragmatists in the DUP that they are defusing part of their hard-line stance on the Belfast Agreement' (Moriarty 2003). In late 2002 and early 2003, senior DUP politicians appeared on TV discussion programmes together with Sinn Féin representatives, something that they had previously refused to do. Moreover in early January 2003, although he seems later to have received a rap on the knuckles from the Leader for it, a DUP MLA stated that his party could 'sit down and do business' with Sinn Féin once there was 'a clear message from paramilitaries that their war is over and especially from the republican movement that there is a clear timetable for dismantling the IRA'. This contrasts with Ian Paisley's remark in October 2002: 'There will be no negotiations with Sinn Féin. Full stop. Period' (Keenan 2003).

Despite the huge cleavages of opinion between the predominant political parties, they are all committed to at least some degree to sustaining progress already made. Even though the UUP has become more and more unhappy with the Agreement since signing it, the Ulster Unionists have not called for its abolition. In the meantime, while the SDLP is preoccupied with the possibility of declining electoral fortunes, the pressure has been increasing on Sinn Féin and the IRA from all quarters – but especially the British and Irish governments – to show in a conclusive way that their war is over. Finally, it seems fair to describe the DUP's position as anti-Agreement, but not really anti-process – as its demands for an all-party (except, at this stage, Sinn Féin) renegotiation would indicate.

Conclusion

As the Good Friday Agreement faces moves towards its sixth birthday the process is struggling with another crisis. Yet its sheer longevity invites optimism.

For the first time in a generation Northern Ireland politicians have experienced devolved power. Even DUP MLAs have clearly enjoyed both being in office, and the trappings that go with that. The desire to retain power thus remains a strong motivation for further compromise. This is in turn strengthened by a widespread, overarching loyalty in the region to peace. The need for consensus, as enshrined in both the letter and the spirit of the Agreement, means that when progress is made, it is made incrementally. Indeed, the process, together with the Agreement itself, have set important precedents for accommodation, and have provided frameworks for future compromise. These features, coupled with protagonist commitment to a sustained process – despite diverging views – mean the current crisis is arguably but another detour on the long path to peace.

Appendix: summary of the main institutional provisions of the Good Friday Agreement

Constitutional Issues

1 The principle of consent: any change in the constitutional status of Northern Ireland requires the consent of the majority of its people.
2 Agreement by the two governments that it is for the people of the island of Ireland alone, through agreement in both parts, to exercise their right to self-determination on the basis of consent. If this consent is given both North and South, then there is a binding obligation on both governments to introduce and support the necessary legislation in their respective parliaments to give effect to this.
3 Repeal of the Government of Ireland Act 1920, which effectively claimed British jurisdiction over the whole island of Ireland.
4 Amendments to Articles 2 and 3 of Bunreacht na hÉireann, following endorsement in a referendum in the Irish Republic, to remove the Republic's 'territorial claim' over Northern Ireland and to permit the creation of North–South executive bodies (see Strand 2).

Strand 1: Northern Ireland internal

1 Provision for a democratically elected Assembly of 108 members elected by PR(STV).
2 The Assembly to have administrative and legislative powers.
3 Substantial powers to reside in the cross-party Executive authority or Cabinet, which consists of a First Minister, a Deputy First Minister and ten other ministers.
4 Ministerial posts, committee chairs and committee places to be allocated proportionately.
5 Members to register themselves 'unionist', 'nationalist' or 'other'. Key decisions in the Assembly must be taken on a cross-community basis.
6 Key decisions to include the election of the Assembly chairperson, the First Minister and the Deputy First Minister, confirmation of standing orders for the conduct of Assembly business, and budget allocations.
7 The Assembly to deal with areas of legislation specifically devolved to it by Westminster. Responsibility for the areas of defence, security, foreign relations and taxation to remain with Westminster.

Strand 2: North–South

1 A North–South Ministerial Council to be established to 'develop consultation, co-operation and action within the island of Ireland ... on matters of mutual interest'.

2 The North–South Ministerial Council to be composed of ministers from the Northern Ireland Executive and the Irish government.

3 The Assembly and North–South Ministerial Council to be 'mutually interdependent' – one cannot function without the other. The purpose of this is to prevent a unionist boycott of all-Ireland institutions.

Strand 3: East–West

1 The British–Irish Intergovernmental Conference to subsume existing intergovernmental arrangements established under the 1985 Anglo-Irish Agreement. It is a vehicle for summit meetings between the Taoiseach (Irish Prime Minister) and the British Prime Minister and/or other ministers from both sides, to deal with bilateral matters.

2 The British–Irish Council (or 'Council of the Isles') to be a forum for meetings of elected representatives from Dáil Eireann (the Irish Parliament), the British Houses of Parliament, and the representative assemblies of Northern Ireland, Wales, Scotland, the Isle of Man and Channel Islands.

Notes

1 For a short account of the background to the problem, see Chapter 7, 'Northern Ireland', in Collins and Cradden (2001).

2 Fuller information on the Northern Ireland political parties and paramilitary organisations can be found in Chapter 7 of Collins and Cradden (2001); see also n. 10 below.

3 In 1990, Peter Brooke, the then Secretary of State for Northern Ireland, stated that it was 'difficult to envisage a military defeat of the IRA'. This gave the IRA and Sinn Féin room to manoeuvre politically without being accused of surrendering.

4 In the Westminster elections of 1974 and 1979 Northern Ireland had twelve MPs in Westminster. Its level of representation increased to seventeen seats at the 1983 Westminster election. For the June 2001 British general election, Northern Ireland was divided into eighteen Westminster constituencies.

5 Election results have been drawn from http://cain.ulst.ac.uk; this invaluable site is also the source of much of the background information on the peace process provided later in this narrative.

6 For an explanation of the STV system, see Collins and Cradden (2001: 23–31).

7 Election information and quotations in this paragraph are drawn from Elliot (1999: 147–9).

8 In the early stages of internment many of those incarcerated had no connection with paramilitary activity whatever; and serious mistakes, based on poor intelligence and informers with malign intent, continued to be made.

9 Something originally provided for in the 1920 Government of Ireland Act, but never implemented.

10 STV was the electoral system prescribed in the 1920 Government of Ireland Act,

and was intended mainly to ensure adequate Nationalist representation in the Northern Ireland House of Commons. However, voters often used the system to give their second and later preferences to candidates on the left. As a consequence the Unionists were threatened much more by the growth of the Protestant vote for the Northern Ireland Labour Party than by the Nationalists; so they replaced PR with the more traditional 'first-past-the-post' system in 1929 – with precisely the intended result of diminishing the influence of the main party of the left.

11   Unlike the police elsewhere in the UK, the RUC were a permanently armed force, and its officers carried hand guns as a matter of routine.
12   Drawn from http://cain.ulst.ac.uk.
13   The DUP participated in the multi-party talks until Sinn Féin's entry in August 1997.
14   For more information on the Good Friday Agreement, see Collins and Cradden (2001: 131–3).
15   For more detail, see http://cain.ulst.ac.uk.
16   For more on this, see http://cain.ulst.ac.uk.
17   This was the day when three members of the UUP negotiating team walked out in protest.

References

Arthur, P. (1985), 'Anglo-Irish Relations and the Northern Ireland Problem', *Irish Studies in International Affairs*, Vol. 2, No. 36, pp. 37–50.

Bew, P. and Gillespie, G. (1996), *The Northern Ireland Peace Process 1993–1996*, London: Sherif.

Bleakley, D. (1995), *Peace in Ireland: Two States, One People*, London: Mowbray.

Breen, S. (2003), 'Army Body Hopes Contact with UVF Can Be Restored', *Irish Times*, 18 January.

Collins, N. and Cradden, T. (2001), *Irish Politics Today*, Manchester: Manchester University Press.

Dixon, P. (2001), *Northern Ireland: The Politics of War and Peace*, Basingstoke: Palgrave.

Elliot, S. (1999), 'The Referendum and the Assembly Elections in Northern Ireland', *Irish Political Studies*, Vol. 14, pp. 147–9.

Farrell, M. (1976), *Northern Ireland: The Orange State*, London: Pluto.

FitzGerald, G. (1991), *All in a Life: An Autobiography*, Dublin: Gill and Macmillan.

Harris, C. (2002), 'The Evolution of Consociationalism in Northern Ireland', PhD thesis, University College Cork.

Hennessey, T. (2000), *The Northern Ireland Peace Process: Ending the Troubles?*, Dublin: Gill and Macmillan.

Horowitz, D. (2001), 'The Northern Ireland Agreement: Clear, Consociational, and Risky', in J. McGarry (ed.), *Northern Ireland and the Divided World*, Oxford: Oxford University Press.

http://cain.ulst.ac.uk.

Keenan, D. (2003), 'DUP Hints it Could Do Business with Sinn Fein', *Irish Times*, 8 January.

Lijphart, A. (1977), *Democracy in Plural Societies*, New Haven, CT: Yale University Press.

MacGinty, R. and Darby, J. (2000), *Management of Peace Processes*, Basingstoke: Macmillan.

MacGinty, R. and Darby, J. (2002), *Guns and Government: The Management of the Northern Ireland Peace Process*, Basingstoke: Palgrave.

Mallie, E. and McKittrick, D. (2001), *Endgame in Ireland*, London: Hodder and Stoughton.

McDonald, H. (2001), *Trimble*, Dublin: Gill and Macmillan.

McKay, S. (2003), 'Disaffected Loyalists Warn on Peace Process', *Sunday Tribune*, 9 January.

Moriarty, G. (2003), 'Is Robinson Going Down the Path to Compromise?', *Irish Times*, 18 January.

Morrissey, M. and Smyth, M. (2002), *Northern Ireland after the Good Friday Agreement*, London: Pluto.

NIO (Northern Ireland Office) (1972), *The Future of Northern Ireland: A Paper for Discussion*, London: NIO/HMSO, SBN 11 700498 7.

NIO (Northern Ireland Office) (1973), Northern Ireland Constitutional Proposals, London: NIO/HMSO, SBN 10 152590 7, Cmnd 5259.

Nordlinger, E. (1972) *Conflict Regulation in Divided Societies*, Harvard University Center for International Affairs, Occasional Paper No. 29.

4

Local and regional government in transition

Mark Callanan

Introduction

Local government everywhere is based upon the simple premise that local communities should, through democratic structures, have the right to make decisions based upon their own needs and priorities. Local government also fulfils a number of other functions: to provide local physical and social services; to carry out certain activities on behalf of central government; and to act as a local regulator.

The history of local government in Ireland, particularly since the 1970s, is cluttered by a number attempts to reform the system in both Northern Ireland and the Republic. This chapter looks at the common origins of local government in Ireland as a whole, and how the two parts of Ireland took different paths after partition. In particular, it looks at local government structures, the functions assigned to local authorities, and how local government is financed. It concludes with a short overview of how relationships have evolved between local authorities on both sides of the border, and of some of the trends that have been common to local government North and South.

Before partition: a common heritage

The earliest form of local government in Ireland was the Tuath, which was to become the basis for the establishment under King John in the twelfth century of the system of territorial counties with which we are still familiar. Each county had a sheriff who was appointed by the king, and each held all power for and under the king. The forerunners of the county councils were called grand juries, introduced under the aegis of the county sheriff system. Members of grand juries were selected by the sheriff and consisted of the biggest landowners in each county and the richest merchants in the few urban centres. The grand jury only met twice a year, to deal mainly with the administration of justice and tax collection for the king. From the seventeenth century onwards, the juries began to be allocated other administrative functions, such as court-house provision. In the eighteenth century they were given responsibility for the provision of roads, police and jails and, subsequently, the power to provide for 'local development' such as harbours and fishing piers, hospitals and work-houses (the last were a punitive system of accommodation for the destitute unemployed and their families, made intentionally harsh to ensure that they did not stay too long). In the nineteenth century, in addition to all this, the poor law system was introduced. This divided Ireland into poor law unions adminis-tered by 'guardians' appointed by government, whose task was to establish in rudimentary form what we would now describe as public health structures.

Different paths

This system of grand juries and poor law unions was radically reformed by the adoption by the United Kingdom Parliament at Westminster of the Local Government (Ireland) Bill, 1898, which provided for the establishment of elected county councils. It also reinforced the county borough system already in place for designated cities, which had undergone earlier reforms under the Municipal Corporations (Ireland) Act, 1840. County Tipperary was considered too large to be administered by one council and, following the pattern estab-lished in the local government of Yorkshire in England, it was divided into North and South Ridings. Thus the Act created thirty-three new county coun-cils, to add to the six existing county boroughs of Belfast, Cork, Dublin, Limerick, Londonderry and Waterford (Galway City was not established as a county borough until 1985). In addition, a second tier of rural district councils and urban district councils was established. Bodies known as town commis-sioners (originally established under the Towns Improvement [Ireland] Act, 1854) also continued in existence under the 1898 Act. However, the primary units of local government throughout Ireland were to be the county councils and county borough councils.

Keeping control of twenty-six counties

Following partition, the new government of the Irish Free State moved quickly to curtail the power of local authorities. One illustration of this was the adop-tion by the Dáil (the Irish Parliament) in 1923 of legislation which gave the gov-ernment the power to remove the elected members of local authorities on a number of grounds – such as when they refused to adopt a sufficient budget, or where they declined to comply with an express requirement under the law. Members of a number of local authorities were 'removed' during the 1920s, and were temporarily replaced by government-appointed commissioners who carried out the tasks normally allotted to the councils in question. The power of central government to remove elected members from office remains intact, although it has been used only sporadically since the 1920s, and has not been called into play since 1985.

Why this opposition from the centre to the institution of local government, which seems to have persisted, to at least some degree, to the present day? Commentators have noted that Irish nationalist leaders in the early twentieth century were entirely focused on achieving independence. Once that was achieved, the drive was for efficiency and uniformity, with small units of administration being regarded as 'extravagant' (Barrington 1991b). Hence the sometimes tiny rural district councils established under the 1898 Act were abolished in 1925. As Garvin has put it, the perception of many Irish nationalists was that 'local government was a British invention, expensive and anti-national' (2001: 33). It must be acknowledged, however, that some of the changes were absolutely essential. Favouritism in the recruitment of officials to jobs in local authorities had always been in evidence. For example, there was an obvious tendency for local politicians to favour natives of their own area for such jobs, or to try to ensure the appointment of people with a record of devotion to the nationalist cause; and there were also clear instances of corruption and nepotism. Appointment to paid positions in local government was finally taken out of the hands of elected members in 1926 and, in the case of the more senior appointments, was made the responsibility of a central agency, the Local Appointments Commission.

A further major change in local government in the Free State was the introduction of a distinctive management system. It found its first expression in the appointment of a city manager (effectively a chief executive) to Cork Corporation in 1929, and was eventually extended to all county and city authorities following the adoption of the County Management Act, 1940. Further reform seemed to be on its way in 1971, arising from the then government's White Paper on local government reorganisation. It proposed the creation of a single tier of local government along the lines of the European model of municipality or district councils; but this was not followed through due to a change in government.

Extensive reforms did follow in the wake of the 1991 report of the government-commissioned Advisory Expert Committee on Local Government Reorganisation and Reform (Barrington 1991a). It recommended devolution of some functions from central government, and a three-tier system of subnational government, consisting of regional authorities, county/city councils and district councils. The Committee also proposed the introduction of a 'general competence' for local authorities, previously denied to them, to engage in any activities they considered would promote the interests of the local community. Although not all of the Barrington recommendations were accepted, this latter was given effect. However, in practice the exercise of such an apparently broad power is somewhat restricted by the limited local sources of revenue and financial discretion available to local authorities (on which see more below).

Other important landmarks were the publication of the 1996 policy document, *Better Local Government* (DoE 1996), the 1998 *Report of the Task Force on the Integration of Local Government and Local Development Systems* (DELG 1998), the insertion of a specific provision for local government (Article 28A) into the Irish constitution in 1999,[1] and the adoption of the Local Government Act 2001 (which replaced the 1898 and earlier Acts to create a single legislative code applying to all local authorities in the Republic).

Keeping control of six counties

In the case of Northern Ireland, the 1898 system remained largely intact until a major reorganisation in 1972, save that county and county borough councils became health and welfare authorities responsible for providing a number of social services in 1946. By the 1960s, however, the local government system had fallen into considerable disrepute for a number of reasons. Most significantly objectionable were the requirements for eligibility to vote in local government elections. As in the rest of the United Kingdom until the late 1940s, the electorate for local councils in Northern Ireland was made up of two groups. First there were the occupiers (owners or tenants) of domestic property and their spouses. This effectively excluded from voting those children of normal voting age living at home and anyone else not directly paying local rates, that is, the property-based tax intended to fund local council services. The second group consisted of business ratepayers, who were entitled to a number of additional votes related to the valuation of the property that their businesses occupied. However, despite the introduction by the Labour government in Britain in 1947 of a common franchise for both parliamentary and local elections in England, Scotland and Wales, consisting of everyone aged 21 and over, the unionist government in Belfast rejected this fundamental reform, on the rather specious grounds that 'he who pays the piper calls the tune'.

The result by 1967 was that while there were 909,842 voters on the parliamentary electoral register, there were only 694,483 on the local government register. There is a popular impression that this antiquated franchise was generally disadvantageous to Roman Catholics, and Jackson correctly argues that it helped to stimulate the 'one man, one vote' campaign of the Northern Ireland Civil Rights Association (NICRA) (Jackson 2001). There is indeed some truth in the claim of Catholic disadvantage, but only in (fairly insignificant) proportional terms, mainly because of the relatively higher class profile of Protestants and the slightly lower Protestant birth rate. However, the fact that there were then roughly twice as many Protestants as Catholics in Northern Ireland overall meant that in absolute terms a considerably larger number of Protestants were disenfranchised by the unionists' failure to follow the reform of the local government franchise in the rest of the UK.

As well as 'one man, one vote' being a key demand of NICRA, there were two other complaints about local government that were arguably of more practical

significance for the civil rights movement. In order to ensure continued unionist dominance in council areas with a substantial Catholic population, constituency boundaries were manipulated – 'gerrymandered' – to prevent an
increase in the number of nationalist/Catholic candidates elected. The most
notorious case involved the city of Derry, where the electoral boundaries were
deliberately drawn to make sure that an area with an approximately 60 per cent
nationalist/Catholic population always returned a unionist/Protestant majority to Londonderry Corporation. Just as objectionable was the fact that some
local authorities deliberately discriminated against minorities in the allocation
of jobs, publicly provided housing and the location of social facilities (Birrell
and Hayes 1999).[2] In most cases these latter allegations were made against
unionist-controlled local authorities, but it has also been suggested that some
of the very few nationalist-controlled councils at the time displayed a similar
tendency (see Jackson 2001: 62).

A flurry of White Papers, Green Papers and other reform proposals were
published in the 1967–69 period, but the basis for the eventual reform of the
system proved to be the 1970 report of the Review Body on Local Government
in Northern Ireland, known as the Macrory report. It divided public services
into those that could best be provided on a regional basis, and those that ought
to be provided locally. While the report considered the possibility of establishing
three to five larger local authorities to administer regional services, this was
rejected in favour of investing the then Northern Ireland Parliament at
Stormont with responsibility for such functions. The report said that bearing in
mind the size, population and resources of Northern Ireland it could not afford
two levels of local authorities below Stormont 'without running the risk of
being as seriously over-administered as we consider it now to be' (Macrory
1970: 29). So a single tier of local government, the district council, was recommended, with each having responsibility for a town and its hinterland. The
Macrory report recommended a continuation of (property valuation) rating as
the local taxation system, but with two separately determined rates, one to be
calculated (or 'struck') centrally in respect of the provision of regional services,
the other by each district council for local services (see more on this below).

The subsequent Local Government Act (Northern Ireland), 1972, abolished all pre-existing local authorities and replaced them with twenty-six
district councils. An important but often underrated influence on the deliberations of the Macrory Committee was the argument that in view of the contentious record of local authorities down through the years, they should have
only a bare minimum of responsibilities under any new structure. As a result
the 1972 reform left local authorities with a very limited range of functions,
despite the fact that during the period of direct rule from Westminster after
1972, local authorities constituted the only elected representative bodies
within Northern Ireland. The 1972 Act also gave the Northern Ireland
Department of the Environment the power to direct a local authority to take
certain action(s) and if necessary, to authorise employed officials to exercise

the functions of the local authority. An amended version of this provision was passed in 1986, which provided for the possibility of appointing a commissioner to carry out the duties of the council. This amendment arose as a result of a campaign by unionist-dominated councils against the 1985 Anglo-Irish Agreement (which gave the Irish government a formal input into the government of Northern Ireland). The campaign included refusing to hold council meetings and to strike district rates.

The wisdom of keeping local authority powers to a minimum was arguably confirmed by the blatantly partisan conduct of many councils subsequently. To take just one example, at times of high political tension councillors frequently insisted on debating controversial matters that lay well outside their established functions. However, in the hoped-for calmer times arising from the Good Friday Agreement, there are likely to be further reforms in local government (a point pursued further below).

Local government structures in the Republic

Before 2002, local authorities in the Republic had a confusing variety of titles, including 'urban district council', 'boards of town commissioners' and 'borough corporations'. The Local Government Act, 2001, renamed urban district councils and boards of town commissioners 'town councils', and renamed borough corporations 'borough councils'. The present system of local government consists essentially of two tiers. The land area of the state is divided into thirty-four local government areas, consisting of twenty-nine counties and five cities; and within the counties there is a further tier based on towns. Local government therefore now consists of:

- *city councils*. There are five city councils, in Cork, Dublin, Galway, Limerick and Waterford. They have equal standing with the county councils and a similar range of functions. (Before 2002, they were known as county borough councils.) Together with the county councils they also form the primary units of local government in Ireland.
- *county councils*. The twenty-six historic counties which make up the Republic of Ireland actually accommodate twenty-nine county councils, for two reasons. First, as we have already noted, County Tipperary has two separate councils, for the north and south of the county. Secondly, following reforms in the early 1990s, the area of County Dublin outside Dublin City was divided in three, effectively producing three new counties in the most densely populated area of the country; they are Fingal, South Dublin and Dún Laoghaire-Rathdown.
- *town councils and borough councils*. Some borough councils can trace their historical lineage back to the earliest origins of urban government in the twelfth century. There are presently seventy-five town councils and five

borough councils in Ireland. Most town councils and all borough councils have more limited functions than county and city councils.

The basis for the existence of most town councils is largely historic. In the late nineteenth century they would have covered what were then the larger urban centres, but today the towns involved range from significant ones such as Dundalk, Athlone and Sligo to places that are little more than large villages, like Kinsale. Thus they do not all have the economic weight to deliver the kind of services that citizens have come to expect. As a consequence, many of the smaller town councils have increasingly tended to pass their main functions up to the county councils. Indeed, about one third of town councils – those known formerly as 'town commissioners' – have fewer functions than other town councils. For example, they are not responsible for planning, and are not rating authorities.

The members of all these local authorities are elected on an 'all-those-aged-18-and-over' franchise and on the basis of a division of the area concerned into an appropriate number of constituencies. Elections are by secret ballot, using the single transferable vote proportional representation system (PR[STV]).[3] Theoretically, such elections ought to have taken place every five years; but practice during the 1980s and 1990s was for governments to exercise their legal power to postpone them, leading in some cases to intervals of six or seven years. However, in 1999, the 'local government' amendment to the Constitution referred to above provided that local elections now *must* take place every five years. The results of local elections since 1967 are summarised in Table 4.1.

Table 4.1 *Republic of Ireland local government elections: percentage of first preference votes by political party, 1967–99*

	Fianna Fáil	Fine Gael	Labour	Workers' Party[a]	Progressive Democrats	Sinn Féin	Green Party	Others
1967	40.2	32.5	14.8	–	–	–	–	12.5
1974	40.1	33.7	12.8	1.5	–	–	–	11.9
1979	39.2	34.9	11.8	2.3	–	2.2	–	9.6
1985	45.5	29.8	7.7	3.0	–	3.3	–	10.7
1991	37.9	26.4	10.6	3.7	5.0	1.7	2.0	12.7
1999[b]	37.4	27.7	10.6	–	2.6	3.5	2.4	15.7

Source: Department of the Environment and Local Government, www.environ.ie/electindex.html.
Notes: [a] 'Workers' Party' includes Sinn Féin (1974) and Sinn Féin the Workers' Party (1979).
[b] Figures for 1967–91 relate to county and city councils only; 1999 figures also include borough councils.

Membership of councils is open to all persons aged 18 years and over, except government ministers and Members of the European Parliament (MEPs). But efforts to abolish the 'dual mandate', whereby the same person can serve as a

member of both the Oireachtas (parliament) and a local authority, proved fruit-
less until recently. Membership of a local authority is an important marker on
the road to a parliamentary seat in Ireland, and backbench Teachtaí Dála (TDs,
or members of parliament) in particular wanted to preserve the right to be a
member of a council and of the Dáil or Seanad (the upper house) at the same
time, generally citing the need to 'keep in touch' with local issues. However,
during 2003 new local government legislation was passed prohibiting such
dual membership. Somewhat controversially, financial incentives are being
provided by central government to those stepping down from membership of
local authorities.

A lord mayor is elected annually by council members in Cork and Dublin, a
mayor is elected in the other city councils and in borough councils, and a chairperson or cathaoirleach is elected to the county councils and town councils.
The Local Government Act, 2001, allowed counties and towns to adopt the title
'mayor' for their chairperson, and a number of them did so during 2002. Until
2001, elected council members were not paid, being entitled only to reim-
bursement of expenses incurred in carrying out their duties. In a significant
departure, the same Act provided for modest 'representational payments' to be
paid to elected members – in other words salary-type payments which are liable
to income tax. The 2001 Act also provided for the direct, popular election of
chairpersons/mayors in county and city councils for the full five-year life of the
councils, but this provision was repealed in 2003. The main reason seems to
have been a fear among many TDs that popular and colourful local characters
or protest candidates would defeat party political nominees.

As we have already noted, each county and city council also has a manager,
who broadly speaking acts as chief executive of the organisation; but she or he
also has important decision-making powers that make this role in Ireland distinctly different to that of her or his counterparts in other systems of local government. A position of manager is filled following a public national competition
organised by the Local Appointments Commission. Appointment is for a standard contracted period of seven years, although this can be extended up to ten
years. Managers have responsibilities in respect of the county or city in question, and county managers have responsibilities also with regard to the other
elected authorities within county areas, including town councils and borough
councils.

In law there is a clear division between the powers of the elected members and
those of the county manager or city manager. The functions of elected members
are known as reserved functions, and all other functions are described as executive functions. Reserved functions generally involve matters of policy, and they
set the policy framework within which the manager and other local authority
officials must work. For example, the adoption of a local authority development
plan is a reserved function – that is, it must be adopted by resolution of the
members of the council. Other reserved functions include the power to borrow
money, to adopt the council budget, and to make or revoke by-laws. However, any

function not specified in legislation to be a reserved function is deemed to be an executive function, and all executive functions are the responsibility of the manager and/or nominees of the manager. In practice many day-to-day executive functions are devolved to officials known as directors of services.

Although the manager cannot vote on council business, she or he has a right to attend all council meetings; and the fact that the manager also has a role in advising council members in the exercise of their functions clearly makes her or him potentially a very powerful figure. On the other hand, council members have the right to *require* the manager to carry out a specific function. This power is generally known as a 'Section 4' – a reference to the City and County Management (Amendment) Act of 1955, which has since been replaced by Section 140 of the Local Government Act, 2001. It has to be said, however, that there has been considerable blurring of the legal distinction between executive and reserved functions, and in most aspects of a local authority's work, conflict between councillors and the manager and her or his staff tends to be minimal.

A new committee system was introduced to local government to give effect to proposals contained in the *Better Local Government* policy document (DoE 1996). Under this new system, county and city councils have established a number of strategic policy committees (SPCs), with a view to ensuring a community input into the delivery of local authority policies, functions and services. The chairperson of each SPC must be an elected member of the council, and two thirds of the membership of the committees is made up of council members, with the remainder consisting of 'sectoral interests', including social, business, trade union, farming, development and environmental ones. Some sectoral representatives are nominated by national interest group organisations and others through a process involving a local 'community forum'. The formal purpose of SPCs is 'to consider matters connected with the formulation, development, monitoring, and review of policy' and to advise the local authority on these matters.[4] However, the final decision with regard to reserved functions remains with the full council. Another interesting innovation has been the corporate policy group (CPG). The chairpersons of the SPCs, as well as the mayor or chairperson of the council, together make up the CPG, which is intended to introduce a central government 'Cabinet-style' structure into councils. The CPG is consulted on the preparation of the council's key corporate plan and the draft local authority budget, and has a co-ordinating role in respect of the various SPCs. Many county and city councils also have area committees to discuss operational issues pertaining to particular electoral areas or a combination of electoral areas.

In addition to the local authority structures described above, the Republic has eight regional authorities. These were established under the Local Government Act, 1991, following recommendations in the Barrington report. They were a response also to the rules of the European Union (EU) with regard to the disbursement of EU structural funds, which required regional inputs into the overall development plans submitted to Brussels, and in the monitoring of expenditure. The membership of the regional authorities consists of nominees from the constituent local authorities. They have been given a dual role: to monitor the implementation of EU structural fund spending in their area, and to co-ordinate public service policies at regional level. Their activity has been relatively limited, although there are prospects that this may expand with the option open to them to adopt regional planning guidelines under the Planning and Development Act, 2000; they may also become involved in the co-ordination of activities under the Local Agenda 21 programme.[5]

A second super-regional tier consisting of two assemblies was established in 1999.[6] These – the Border, Midland and Western Regional Assembly, and the Southern and Eastern Regional Assembly – are tasked with specific management responsibilities. These include reporting, evaluation, financial control and monitoring of spending under the two regional operational programmes of the 2000–6 National Development Plan (NDP).[7]

Local government structures in Northern Ireland

Northern Ireland was divided into twenty-six district council areas under the Local Government (Northern Ireland) Act, 1972, and the Act also provided for the granting of city or borough status to particular district councils. For many years Belfast and Derry/Londonderry were the only urban areas to have formal city status. However, they were joined in 2000 by Armagh, which was simply having a former position restored, and eventually by Lisburn and Newry, which were awarded the status of city to mark the Jubilee of Queen Elizabeth in 2002. A number of other councils have been granted borough status and can use the title 'borough council'; they are Carrickfergus, Castlereagh, Newtonabbey and North Down, which all lie on the outskirts of Belfast, together with the rural towns of Ballymena, Ballymoney, Coleraine, Craigavon and Limavady. Local elections take place every four years, and since 1972 have been conducted by a secret ballot under the PR(STV) system. The results of local elections held since 1973 are reported in Table 4.2.

Sinn Féin only began to contest local elections in 1985. Their entry into council chambers around Northern Ireland was not at all well received by the various unionist parties, which attempted to exclude Sinn Féin councillors from committees, and insisted that council members sign a declaration against the use of violence for political purposes. Both actions were challenged by Sinn Féin in the courts, and were found to be unlawful.

The election of the lord mayor, mayor or chairperson, together with a deputy, is an annual event, and is often surrounded by controversy. The use of PR(STV) has meant that in the majority of local councils, no one political party has overall control; however, some councils still consistently have either a unionist or a nationalist majority; and in a few councils the majority has changed from unionist to nationalist, and vice versa. A notable event was the

Table 4.2 *Northern Ireland local government elections: percentage share of first preference votes by political party, 1973–2001*

	Ulster Unionist Party	Democratic Unionist Party	Alliance Party	Social Democratic and Labour Party	Sinn Féin	Independent Unionists	Others
1973	41.4	4.3	13.7	13.4	–	10.9	16.3
1977	29.6	12.7	14.4	20.6	–	8.5	14.2
1981	26.5	26.6	8.9	17.5	–	4.2	16.3
1985	29.5	24.3	7.1	13.4	11.8	3.1	10.8
1989	31.4	17.7	6.8	21.2	11.2	3.9	7.8
1993	29.3	17.2	7.7	21.9	12.5	2.7	8.7
1997	27.8	15.6	6.6	20.7	16.9	2.5	9.9
2001	23.0	21.5	5.0	20.7	19.4	–	10.4

Source: C. Knox (forthcoming), 'Northern Ireland local Government', in M. Callanan and J. F. Keogan (eds), *Local Government in Ireland*, Dublin: Institute of Public Administration.

loss of unionist control of Belfast City Council after the elections of 1997; this resulted in the election of the first nationalist lord mayor of Belfast (Alban Maginness of the Social Democratic and Labour Party (SDLP)) in 1997, and the first republican lord mayor of Belfast (Alex Maskey of Sinn Féin) in 2002.

Against this background, perhaps the most remarkable development in many local authorities during the late 1980s and throughout the 1990s was 'power-sharing' between the two political traditions (though many unionists prefer to use the term 'responsibility-sharing'). Essentially, this tends to involve the rotation of the positions of chairperson and vice-chairperson of councils (or mayors and deputy mayors where appropriate) between the nationalist and unionist traditions, and the distribution of positions on council committees and subcommittees in proportion to party strength. Dungannon District Council, which introduced a power-sharing arrangement in 1988, is usually credited with setting the precedent, although others claimed to have been power-sharing for years, albeit with a lower profile (Knox 1998: 12). Following the elections in 2001, the majority of councils were operating some form of power-sharing arrangement, but a few have insisted on maintaining a 'winner-takes-all' regime.

Much of the work of elected members is conducted through council committees and subcommittees, which deal with the work of the different service areas of the local authority. Typically, each council also has a key committee dealing with finance and budgetary issues. Each local authority has a chief executive (sometimes also described as town clerk), who is responsible for the day-to-day management of council services and the implementation of policies, and whose duties have come more and more to resemble those of county and city managers in the Republic. There is no intermediate tier between district councils and the Northern Ireland Assembly and Executive, although the latter could of course be considered a purely regional form of government.

Local government functions in the Republic

Local authorities in the Republic of Ireland possess a relatively limited range of functions as compared to local authorities in most other countries of the EU, where many are responsible for education, health care and social welfare services. Notwithstanding this, local authorities are still responsible for the delivery of a number of vital services to the public, and they employ over 35,000 people for this purpose.

Local government functions are traditionally listed according to eight programme groups, and county and city councils are generally responsible for all of these services. Town and borough councils may be responsible for some services, but increasingly these are being provided by county councils on their behalf. Table 4.3 provides an overview of local government functions.

Some of these groups deserve special mention. Ireland has one of the highest levels in Europe of owner-occupied housing. Yet programme group 1, 'Housing and building', includes the building by local authorities of houses and apartments for rent, intended to provide good-standard accommodation for people who cannot afford to buy their own homes. This is a function that local authorities in many other countries outside the UK and Ireland would be neither familiar nor comfortable with, the renting of property being seen as an entirely private-sector prerogative. Programme group 4, 'Planning and development', is arguably the most controversial of local government powers, and is central to the current enquiries into political and financial corruption. It should also be noted that the responsibilities under programme group 7 are much less weighty than might on the face of it seem to be the case. There is no significant expenditure by local authorities on the matters concerned, nor are they providers of any important educational, health or agricultural services. Local government involvement is purely administrative in character – all the more so since the transfer of health and welfare services to newly established Health Boards in 1970. Finally, although not officially a programme group, an additional function can effectively be added to the list, with the title 'Community and enterprise'. In 1998, the government established a Task Force on the Integration of Local Government and Local Development Systems. Their initial report, followed by two subsequent reports, laid the ground for the establishment of county/city development boards (CDBs) in each county and city council area (see DELG 1998, 1999, 2000).

The Task Force recommended movement towards a more integrated system of local delivery of public services through the preparation and implementation of integrated socio-economic strategies for each county and city. This demanded, in

Table 4.3 *Summary of local government functions in the Republic of Ireland*

Programme group	Title	Summary of activities/services
1	Housing and building	Provision of social housing, assessment of housing needs, housing strategies, dealing with homelessness, housing loans and grants, accommodation for the traveller ethnic group, voluntary housing
2	Roads and transportation	Road construction and maintenance, traffic management, public lighting, collection of motor taxes, taxi licensing
3	Water and sewerage	Water supply, waste water treatment, group water schemes
4	Planning and development	Adoption of development plan for the area, granting or refusing planning permissions, undertaking urban or village renewal works and plans
5	Environmental protection	Waste collection and disposal, waste management planning, litter prevention, the fire service and fire prevention, civil defence, pollution control, burial grounds, building safety
6	Recreation and amenity	Public libraries, parks and open spaces, swimming pools, recreation centres, the arts, culture, museums, galleries and other amenities
7	Agriculture, education, health and welfare	Making nominations to Vocational Education Committees and Regional Health Boards, processing higher education grants, veterinary services
8	Miscellaneous services	Maintaining the register of electors for elections, financial management, rate collection, provision of animal pounds

Source: T. P. Golden (1977), *Local Authority Accounting in Ireland*, Dublin: Institute of Public Administration.

turn, the involvement of a wide range of organisations in membership of the CDB. The local authority is represented by its mayor/chairperson, the chairpersons of each local authority SPC (see above), and the county/city manager. The chairperson of the CDB is also a nominee of the local authority. Included in the representation on each Board are the traditional social partners (business and employers' bodies, representative agricultural organisations and the trade unions); the community and voluntary sectors; various development agencies – county/city enterprise boards and local officers of state agencies such as FÁS (Foras Áiseanna Saothar), the state industrial training agency; Health Boards; the Department of Social and Family Affairs; the Industrial Development Authority (IDA Ireland, responsible for encouraging inward investment from abroad); Enterprise Ireland (the local economic development body); and regional tourism bodies. Each county and city council also appointed a director of service for community and enterprise, to co-ordinate the activities of the different agencies in the local authority area.

During the period 2001–2 each CDB was required, after extensive consultation, to draw up a strategy for the economic, social and cultural development of its area; and at the time of writing, following endorsement by the relevant city or county council, they are working towards the implementation of these. Each strategy sets out a broad framework, with a ten-year vision and three- to five-year manageable targets. The agencies represented on the Board are expected to closely track the individual operational plans and activities that directly affect them, and to ensure they accord with the strategy as adopted. This move to a partnership approach between local government and local development bodies was an attempt to resolve the sometimes strained relationship between the two in some areas.[8] Although the CDB structures do not involve the formal transfer of functions to local government, it can be argued that given the key role allocated to local authorities in driving the CDB process, it does at least offer the opportunity for local authorities to influence the way various public bodies deliver services in their area.

Local government functions in Northern Ireland

The 1972 reform of local government in Northern Ireland left local authorities with very few functions even as compared to councils in the Republic, and certainly many fewer than their counterparts elsewhere in the United Kingdom. Local authorities in Northern Ireland employ some 9,000 people to provide the services summarised in Table 4.4.

With the exception of Belfast City Council, building control and environmental health are provided collectively by groups of neighbouring local authorities, which pool their resources to employ the necessary personnel.

As in the Republic, local councillors have an influence on matters beyond those listed, by reason of their nomination to a range of statutory bodies and

Table 4.4 *Summary of local government functions in Northern Ireland*

Title	Summary of activities/services
Refuse and technical services	Refuse collection and disposal, waste disposal licences, recycling facilities, street cleaning, litter prevention, public conveniences, dog licensing
Community services	Provision of community centres and recreational amenities, financial assistance and facilities for voluntary and community groups, cultural bodies, youth groups, senior citizens, and groups representing women, the disabled, etc.
Leisure and recreation	Provision of recreational amenities such as leisure and sports centres, swimming pools, playing fields, golf courses, etc.
Parks	Provision and maintenance of parks, cemeteries
Building control	Site inspections, examination of plans for new buildings, licensing of public entertainment venues such as dance halls and cinemas, licensing of street trading
Environmental health	Enforcement of public health standards, air, water and noise pollution, food safety and hygiene, health and safety
Economic development	Promotion of inward investment, assisting local businesses, providing information on local resources
Tourism	Local tourist information offices and publications, visitor centres, local museums and other facilities
Other	Registration of births, marriages and deaths

Source: Based on information drawn from D. Birrell and A. Hayes (1999), *The Local Government System in Northern Ireland*, Dublin: Institute of Public Administration.

quasi non-governmental organisations (quangos) responsible for administering services in their areas, such as Education and Library Boards. Moreover, public agencies dealing with issues such as planning, roads and housing are obliged to consult district councils regarding decisions having an impact or potential impact on a particular council area. For example, the Department of the Environment, which is responsible for planning for the whole of Northern Ireland, must consult district councils on the preparation of overall development plans as well as on individual planning applications. However, the final decisions on such matters remain with the Department.

In terms of responding to local demand, the provision by councils of financial and other support to community and voluntary groups developed considerably during the 1980s and 1990s, although there have been occasional tensions between elected members and community groups, some of latter having been under the influence of paramilitary groups. Specific schemes have been developed through local authorities to promote cross-community (joint Protestant/Catholic) projects. Knox argues that 'an active involvement in this area, given their chequered history of discrimination and sectarianism, has added to the emerging climate of cross-party co-operation and stability, within which local authorities have demonstrated a more responsible approach to an incremental increase in devolved powers' (Knox 1998: 7).

District partnerships were established in each council area under the EU Special Support Programme for Peace and Reconciliation (usually called PEACE I). One third of the members of the partnerships are local councillors, a further third are drawn from the community and voluntary sector, and the final third is made up of business people, trade union nominees and other appropriate local interests. Local strategy partnerships have been established as the successor to district partnerships to administer a second round of funding, under PEACE II. Each partnership has drawn up an action plan for its area, and on the basis of the quality of the submission, they are allocated a maximum budget for implementation of the plan. Local authorities have played an important and constructive role in helping to broker and support these partnerships (Birrell and Hayes 1999; Knox 1998) An even more interesting development is that local authorities and elected members have been given a role in the District Policing Partnerships (DPPs) set up under the police reforms flowing from the Good Friday Agreement; the DPPs are intended to oversee the work of the replacement for the Royal Ulster Constabulary (RUC), the Police Service of Northern Ireland.

Financing local government in the Republic

Local government sources of revenue in the Republic of Ireland include:

- rates on commercial properties;
- the Local Government Fund;
- central government grants; and
- charges for specific services.

The rating taxation system as it applied to domestic properties was abolished in 1978, and rates on agricultural land were declared by the courts to be unconstitutional in 1982. The loss of the funding provided to local authorities by domestic rates was to have been covered by an 'equivalent' central government allocation, but successive governments have failed fully to carry through this commitment. The level of the rate on commercial properties is determined each year by the local authority as part of its annual budgetary process. But maximum permissible increases in rates (called 'capping') can be set by central government; this has been common practice in recent years, and significantly limits the ability of local authorities to increase their revenues. Nor can local authorities circumvent capping by increasing the nominal value of the properties concerned, since the valuation of commercial property for rating purposes is determined by a central agency, the Valuation Office.

The adoption of the Local Government Act, 1998, resulted in the establishment of a Local Government Fund made up of government grants and motor tax receipts, the latter being the annual amount motorists pay for the right to use their cars on the public roads. Allocations are then made to local authorities; and most of this money can be spent on any matter within the discretion of the council. However, some central government grants are allocated to specific projects, such as waste water treatment installations or higher education grants, and must be used for these purposes alone. Further sources of revenue for local authorities are the charges they levy for the provision of certain services: housing rents, commercial water charges, planning application fees, development levies, refuse and landfill charges, library fees, and fire prevention and control charges. The most significant thing that needs to be said about local government finance, however, is that the abolition of domestic and agricultural rates, together with the government tendency to cap increases in commercial rates, served to limit local authority discretion in raising revenue, and severely increased local government's dependence on central government for funding. The decision in 1997 to abolish domestic water charges was but a further blow to the independence of local authorities.

Financing local government in Northern Ireland

Local authorities in Northern Ireland too have a number of sources of revenue:

- rates on property;
- general grant;
- specific grants; and
- charges for services.

The system of rates in Northern Ireland remains the same as first proposed by the Macrory report in 1970. Valuation of property for rating purposes rests with an independent valuation office and, as we have already had reason to note, the rating system is divided into two parts:

- the Regional Rate, which is set centrally and applied at the same level across Northern Ireland to pay for services administered by regional government departments and agencies, such as education, social services, roads, housing and water; and
- the District Rate, determined by each district council for those services administered by them at local level.

Because of the concentration of service provision at the regional level, the Regional Rate usually makes up about 85 per cent of the total amount levied. The District Rate remains, none the less, a major source of funding for local authority expenditure. As it happens, the difference between the two rates is largely invisible to the ratepayer, as both are levied as a single financial demand by the central Rate Collection Agency.

The General Grant is allocated by central government. As well as the basic core of funding that it provides, it is also used for equalisation purposes – that is, to compensate disadvantaged local authorities with a low rates base, so as to ensure they can provide an adequate level of services. Local authorities may avail themselves too of specific grants for expenditure in areas such as community and recreational amenities, tourist facilities, energy efficiency, food safety; and they may recoup finances associated with the provision of services on behalf of government departments. As in the Republic, revenue is also collected through charges for the use of things like landfill waste disposal sites, leisure centres and the other facilities provided by local authorities.

Local government in Ireland in the new millennium: sharing experience

Although it has sometimes been a matter of controversy, local authorities in Northern Ireland and the Republic have increasingly sought contacts with each other across the border, have engaged in greater co-operation, and have begun to work on common projects. In some cases this has been encouraged by EU programmes such as INTERREG (an initiative aimed at stimulating interregional co-operation) and PEACE I and II. The INTERREG programme has supported the establishment of three standing cross-border networks. They are: the East Border Region Committee (EBRC), consisting of the Down and Newry and Mourne District Councils (the latter recently upgraded to city council status) together with the Louth and Monaghan County Councils; the Irish Central Border Area Network (ICBAN), consisting of the Cavan, Donegal, Leitrim, Monaghan and Sligo County Councils, and Dungannon, Fermanagh and Omagh District Councils together with Armagh City Council; and the North West Region Cross-Border Group (NWRCBG), consisting of Donegal County Council together with the Derry City, Limavady Borough and Strabane District Councils

The three networks have all established committee structures and a small secretariat, and seek to identify common economic and social needs in their respective cross-border areas, and to work on common projects covering themes such as tourism promotion, economic development and infrastructural co-ordination. They have also clearly helped to establish good working relationships between the local authorities concerned (for examples, see Birrell 1999; Greer 2000; Laffan and Payne 2001). Apart from these formal partnerships, other EU initiatives have facilitated the development of links between individual local authorities from the two parts of Ireland for the purpose of common working on specific projects, often in partnership with local authorities from a number of other EU states. A successful Local Authority Linkages programme is run by the voluntary body, Cooperation Ireland, to assist local authorities to make contacts with their counterparts on the other side of the border. As the level of contact between local authorities North and South increases, so too have the opportunities for exchanging experience on developments that have occurred in both jurisdictions. Despite the fact that they possess a different range of functions and a different lineage, these local authorities have found that they have much in common, and much to learn from each other.

Another common experience has been the process of radical change focused on the development of the notion of the customer/citizen – on providing value for money in services, openness and transparency, and effective corporate and business planning. Compulsory competitive tendering (CCT) was introduced to local authorities in Northern Ireland in 1992, meaning local councils had to compete with private contractors in bidding to run council services. Gratifyingly from their point of view, in the great majority of cases contracts were awarded to the local authority's own team of service providers. The 'Best Value' initiative was subsequently introduced to establish real measures of service quality and to promote continuing improvement in performance. In the Republic there have been similar initiatives, and local authorities have been obliged to publish formal corporate plans and customer action plans; in addition, a set of indicators has been developed for a range of local authority services to allow comparison between the performance of one council and another (for more on the 'citizen as consumer', see Chapter 8).

Many local authorities in both jurisdictions operate their own complaints schemes, whereby individuals can raise issues of concern or criticism about council services. Local government in the Republic is also subject to the 1997 Freedom of Information Act, designed to increase openness and accountability in decision-making, and to allow public access to central and local authority records, subject to a number of exemptions. Local authorities are subject as well to investigation by the Ombudsman (whose responsibilities also include dealing with complaints of maladministration against central government departments and health boards). Similarly, complaints against local authorities north of the border can be investigated by the Northern Ireland Ombudsman, more formally described as the Commissioner for Complaints. Thus local government on both sides of the border, like much of the public service, is under constant scrutiny to ensure that it treats citizens fairly and impartially. Another common thread is the impact that EU legislation has had on local authorities on both sides of the border in fields such as waste management, recycling and public procurement.

Some future challenges

A number of challenges lie ahead for local authorities in Ireland. In the Republic, the major process of reform during the 1990s is currently being consolidated. The abandoned provision for the direct election of the chairperson or mayor of county and city councils may well resurface, possibly resulting in the election of high-profile candidates with a direct mandate from the local population. Certainly the trend in local government internationally has been to strengthen political executive structures, whether that be through directly elected mayors or by setting up 'Cabinet-style' models. Such a development has the potential, however, to disturb the delicate balance between elected members and manager that has evolved since the 1930s. As to other possible changes, the end of the dual mandate might arguably have the effect of obliging TDs to apply themselves more attentively to their role as national legislators, while leaving local government issues to locally elected representatives. Whether this will happen in practice is debatable, however, given the clientelist nature of Irish politics and the apparent expectations of voters that members of the Oireachtas will maintain close touch with local issues. It is also distinctly possible, given the expedient approach taken in the past, that the new EU structural funds regime from 2007 until 2013 will prompt yet further change in regional structures – perhaps even their abandonment.

In Northern Ireland the new political and institutional environment established on the footing of the Good Friday Agreement in 1998 is expected to lead to further changes in local government structures (Knox 1999). In 2002, a commission was established to make recommendations on a restructuring of public administration in Northern Ireland, including local government, in the light of the formation of the Northern Ireland Assembly and Executive.[9] The Northern Ireland Executive has itself stated that 'there is a need for different structures under devolution, taking account of new relationships between local and regional government, as well as the full range of other bodies that function within the wider public sector' (2001: 89). The terms of reference of the review identify a number of values and characteristics concerning public administration in Northern Ireland of which it should take due account. Among these are democratic accountability (including ensuring that local and regional elected representatives can play a full role), community responsiveness, cross-community concerns, quality services, integrated services, and efficiency and effectiveness. Although the commission will address the question of how many layers of government are required in Northern Ireland, it will not necessarily lead to root-and-branch reform.

However, there are a number of important issues on the agenda. Firstly, it is considered essential that the review clarify the relationship between the different tiers of government, in the context of the devolution of such substantial governmental powers to the Executive and Assembly. Secondly, it has been mooted that some major responsibilities removed from local authorities following the Macrory report could be returned to them. Although opposition to this may have softened somewhat since 1999, Birrell and Hayes reported then that there were likely to be major objections to any such change from the nationalist parties, unless accompanied by safeguards to protect against a return to the abuses of local authority power that had occurred in the past. Thirdly, Birrell and Hayes also record some expectation that the number of local government bodies could be reduced to ten, involving the amalgamation of several existing authorities. In this case there appears to be political support for such a reduction from both the Ulster Unionist Party (UUP) and the SDLP (Birrell and Hayes 1999: 143–4). Fourthly, among other suggestions being put forward is one that Northern Ireland local authorities should be granted the power of 'general competence' that has applied south of the border since 1991 (Knox 1998: 11). What is certainly clear, therefore, is that local government reform in Northern Ireland will remain on the political agenda for the foreseeable future.

What we can also say is that despite the rather different functions exercised by local government in the two jurisdictions, there has been much common ground. Local authorities North and South have substantially changed the way they deliver services, and because of shared experiences in many areas have been able to exchange best practice and to learn from each other. This process of functional co-operation between local authorities in Northern Ireland and the Republic has also helped to cement good working relationships between communities in different parts of Ireland.

Notes

The author is indebted to Adrian McCreesh for helpful comments on a draft of this chapter.

1 There were two reasons for this: first, to ensure council elections did take place every five years; secondly, and more importantly, to provide a formal constitutional basis for local government because there was previously no reference whatever to it in Bunreacht na hÉireann – the Irish Constitution.
2 For further testimony to the level of discriminatory practice by local authorities, see the government-commissioned report Cameron (1969).
3 For an explanation of the STV electoral system see Chapter 2 in Collins and Cradden (2001).
4 Local Government Act, 2001, Section 48.
5 Local Agenda 21 provides for the promotion of sustainable economic and social development and greater participation at local level.
6 The Republic of Ireland as a whole had always been in the highest ('Objective 1') category for the award of EU structural funds, which were intended, among other things, to assist the development of infrastructure to the levels prevailing in the more wealthy EU member states. Economic success seemed to portend loss of that status, however, so the Irish government began to argue that while there were parts of the

country which were now 'up to standard', there were still areas of deprivation. The creation of two new regional assemblies was a way of ensuring that the most under-developed area would remain separately eligible for Objective 1 treatment.

7   The NDP provides for an investment of €52 billion in health services, social housing, education, roads, public transport, rural development, industry, water and waste ser-vices, child care and local development during the period 2000–6.

8   The tensions between local authorities and local development groups in some areas are described in Walsh (1998).

9   As of mid-2003, despite the suspension of the Northern Ireland Executive and Assembly, this was still being conducted. However, the final decisions on the outcome of the review are expected to be left to the devolved administration should the Executive and Assembly be restored.

References

Barrington, T. J. (1991a), *Local Government Reorganisation and Reform*, report of the Advisory Expert Committee (Chairman: T. J. Barrington), Dublin: Advisory Expert Committee on Local Government Reorganisation and Reform/Government Publications Office.

Barrington, T. J. (1991b), 'The Crisis of Irish Local Government', in J. J. Hesse (ed.), *Local Government and Urban Affairs in International Perspective*, Baden-Baden: Nomos Verlagsgesellschaft.

Birrell, D. (1999), 'Cross-Border Co-operation Between Local Authorities in Ireland', *Local Governance*, Vol. 25, No. 2, pp. 109–18.

Birrell, D. and Hayes, A. (1999), *The Local Government System in Northern Ireland*, Dublin: Institute of Public Administration.

Cameron (1969), *Disturbances in Northern Ireland: Report of the Commission Appointed by the Governor of Northern Ireland* (Chairman: Lord Cameron), Belfast: HMSO, Cmd 532.

Collins, N. and Cradden, T. (2001), *Irish Politics Today*, fourth edition, Manchester: Manchester University Press.

DELG (Department of the Environment and Local Government) (1998), *Report of the Task Force on the Integration of Local Government and Local Development Systems*, Dublin: Department of the Environment and Local Government/Government Publications Office.

DELG (Department of the Environment and Local Government) (1999), *Preparing the Ground: Guidelines for the Progress from Strategy Groups to County/City Development Boards*, Dublin: Department of the Environment and Local Government/Govern-ment Publications Office.

DELG (Department of the Environment and Local Government) (2000), *A Shared Vision for County/City Development Boards: Guidelines on the CDB Strategies for Economic, Social and Cultural Development*, Dublin: Department of the Environment and Local Government/Government Publications Office.

DoE (Department of the Environment) (1996), *Better Local Government: A Programme for Change*, Dublin: Department of the Environment/Government Publications Office.

Garvin, T. (2001), 'The Dáil Government and Irish Local Democracy 1919–23', in M. E.

Daly (ed.), *County and Town: One Hundred Years of Local Government in Ireland*, Dublin: Institute of Public Administration.

Golden, T. P. (1977), *Local Authority Accounting in Ireland*, Dublin: Institute of Public Administration.

Greer, J. (2000), 'Local Authority Cross-Border Networks: Lessons in Partnership and North–South Cooperation in Ireland', *Administration*, Vol. 48, No. 1, pp. 52–68.

Jackson, A. (2001), 'Local Government in Northern Ireland, 1920–73', in M. E. Daly (ed.), *County and Town: One Hundred Years of Local Government in Ireland*, Dublin: Institute of Public Administration.

Knox, C. (1998), 'Local Government in Northern Ireland: Emerging from the Bearpit of Sectarianism?', *Local Government Studies*, Vol. 24, No. 3, pp. 1–13.

Knox, C. (1999), 'Northern Ireland: At the Crossroads of Political and Administrative Reform', *Governance: An International Journal of Policy and Administration*, Vol. 12, No. 3, pp. 324–5.

Knox, C. (forthcoming), 'Northern Ireland Local Government', in M. Callanan and J. F. Keogan (eds), *Local Government in Ireland*, Dublin: Institute of Public Administration.

Laffan, B. and Payne, D. (2001), *Creating Living Institutions: EU Cross-Border Cooperation after the Good Friday Agreement*, Dublin: Centre for Cross-Border Studies/Institute for British–Irish Studies/UCD.

Macrory, P. A. (1970), *Review Body on Local Government in Northern Ireland*, Cmd 546 (Chairman: Patrick A. Macrory), Belfast: HMSO.

NIE (Northern Ireland Executive) (2001), *Programme for Government: Making a Difference, 2002–2004*, Belfast: Northern Ireland Executive/HMSO.

Walsh, J. (1998), 'Local Development and Local Government in the Republic of Ireland: From Fragmentation to Integration?', *Local Economy*, Vol. 12, No. 4, pp. 329–41.

Further reading

Barrington, T. J. (1991), 'Local Government in Ireland', in R. Batley and G. Stoker (eds), *Local Government in Europe: Trends and Developments*, London: Macmillan.

Callanan, M. and Keogan, J. F. (eds) (forthcoming), *Local Government in Ireland*, Dublin: Institute of Public Administration.

5

Social partnership:
'a rising tide lifts all boats?'

Terry Cradden

Introduction

Sean Lemass, arguably the political progenitor of the great turnaround in Ireland's economic fortunes over the last thirty years or so, was fond of the adage that 'a rising tide lifts all boats'. At the time of writing (mid-2003) the Republic of Ireland is emerging from a period during which it has enjoyed the highest growth rate and one of the lowest inflation rates in the European Union (EU), and attracted to itself the label 'Celtic Tiger' (see Chapter 1), intended to mark its similarity with the booming Asian 'Tiger' economies of the 1970s and 1980s. Moreover, overall unemployment in Ireland has fallen to its lowest levels ever – at present standing at just over 4 per cent.

But there are some 'blackspots', especially outside the main urban areas, where the number of jobless remains stubbornly high – sometimes as many as 18 per cent of the registered employable population – and where long-term unemployment is an intractable problem. It is clear then that the fruits of the recently rising tide of economic progress have not been fully enjoyed by a substantial minority of Irish citizens. What is important for us to note here is that this inequity has persisted even though the development of the economy since the late 1980s has been underpinned by a series of comprehensive 'social partnership' agreements between government, employers and trade unions designed to ensure, among other things, that everyone would benefit from the rising tide of economic advance.

Before attempting to account for the emergence of these tripartite agreements, it is important to examine the available range of policy choices as regards state involvement in industrial relations, in pay determination in particular; secondly, we need to look at the historical record on this score in independent Ireland, a process that Roche has so precisely described as one of 'identifying the changing boundaries between politics and industrial relations' (Roche 1997:126).[1]

79

The policy choices

Why do governments seek to have an influence on the pay and working conditions of citizens? The answer self-evidently arises from government's role in the
management of national economies. In neutral terms, the overall government
aim might be defined as the achievement, maintenance and enhancement of
national prosperity; and that might perhaps involve the pursuit of objectives like
low inflation, a balance of payments surplus, favourable currency exchange
rates, full employment and so on. But there clearly are choices – political choices
– to be made about which of these will have priority. An important influence on
action will usually be the ideological disposition of the government in question:
whether, for example, its political approach is liberal-individualistic (as particularly evidenced in the 1980s in Ronald Reagan's United States and Margaret
Thatcher's Britain), social democratic (or traditional pan-European labour/
socialist) or even corporatist (on which see more below). The nature of a government's approach may also depend on whether it has sectional interests like
trade unions or employers to take care of. This is not to argue that governments
have no scope for independent, autonomous action: that they are always and
everywhere prisoners of ideology or of interest groups, or, indeed of the capitalist system itself (for further discussion, see Beaumont 1992: Ch. 1). It is simply
to note that we are dealing here with a matter of popular controversy and one
that lies at the very core of the social and economic policy-making process.

Crouch's taxonomy of industrial relations policy choices remains a useful
starting point. As he saw it in the early 1980s, the available options for governments in liberal democracies seeking to influence the conduct and outcomes
of industrial relations were as indicated in Table 5.1.

Table 5.1 *Industrial relations policy choices*

Prevailing ideology	Position of trade unions	
	Weak	Strong
Liberal	Neo-laissez-faire (or neo-liberalism)	Free collective bargaining
Corporatist	Corporatism	Bargained corporatism (or neo-corporatism)

Source: Based on C. Crouch (1982), *The Politics of Industrial Relations*, Glasgow: Fontana, p. 201.

Neo-laissez-faire/neo-liberalism

The word 'liberal' took on new and sometimes contradictory meanings during
the twentieth century. Crouch uses it in the British nineteenth-century sense,
suggesting a demand for the freeing of the individual from all forms of community, economic, moral and political restraints. In particular:

Freedom from interference by the state in the economy meant allowing market forces to work without interference. Similarly, individualism meant liberty for the individual to grasp opportunities available to him [*sic*]; but it also meant being forced to remain an individual and *not to combine with others*. (Crouch 1982: 142; emphasis added)

Revived in the 1980s as what is often called 'neo-liberalism', its three essential tenets are that:

- the pursuit by individuals of their own personal self-interest is the engine of national economic progress;
- the state must ensure that vested interests – trade unions in particular – are not permitted to interfere, by the exercise of essentially illegitimate collective power, with the totally free operation of markets; and
- there is no role for government in the setting of pay and conditions of employment, and no role for interest groups, such as employers and trade unions, in the formation of government policy.

To take the example of Britain in the late 1970s, when the trade unions were still strong, the neo-liberal approach essentially demanded that they be weakened; and this weakening was achieved in a variety of ways:

- new legal restrictions on trade union power in the workplace, intended to enable employers more easily to resist the unionisation of their workers, and to make it more difficult for unions to engage in strikes or other industrial action;
- 'deregulation' of the labour market by ending all forms of legal wage setting; banning 'trade union labour only' contracts; privatising state-owned industries; insisting on competitive tendering by private companies for the supply of services previously provided from within the public sector; eroding legally enforceable job security rights; accepting unemployment as a method of wage regulation; and
- the elimination of unions and employers from dialogue and influence on the formation of government social and economic policy.

Free collective bargaining

To operate in their purest forms, both neo-liberal and corporatist systems require a weak, or at least quiescent, trade union movement. It was thus the very growth of trade unionism – a way of dealing with the economic system not as an individual but as a member of an inevitably more powerful combination (or collective) of people – that forced governments away from laissez-faire individualism into an accommodation with collectivism.[2] The product of this late nineteenth-century accommodation with the new power of the unions was 'free collective bargaining', defined as the determination of the pay and conditions of employment of workers by means of voluntary negotiations between the independent trade unions that represented the workers and the management of the organisations that employed them. We should note in passing that collective bargaining was actually quite a costly business, since it meant real increases in pay and real improvements in the working conditions of ordinary people. However, for the UK and the US this was an adjustment that could be afforded – by the US because of its growing economic superpower status, and by the UK because of the vast resources and guaranteed markets of the Empire. And it is hardly to be wondered at that it was not until after those 'props' began to crumble that there was any serious move back to economic liberalism – to neo-laissez-faire.

The new collective bargaining dispensation was liberal in traditional terms, at least to the extent that the market economy remained intact. However, it was also liberal in a more modern sense, as meaning tolerant, progressive and defensive of diversity. Furthermore it retained the key liberal motif of non-interventionism: of the state as an 'auxiliary' – as a bystander almost – as regards industrial relations. This 'hands-off' approach derived from a conviction that the maintenance of order on the streets as well as social and economic justice were most likely to be served by totally unfettered free collective bargaining.[3] In the UK this 'auxiliary state' model was characterised by three main things:

- the continuing and well-nigh complete independence of the industrial relations system from government control;
- a general distrust of legislation and its effects on the system;[4] and
- the complete self-reliance and independence of trade unions, employers and employers' associations.

These 'freedoms' of the British collective bargaining system, which independent Ireland inherited, included the right of the parties to make whatever bargaining arrangements they wished, the non-legally binding nature of any agreements arrived at, and the (somewhat circumscribed) right of workers to withdraw their labour – in other words, to go on strike.

Moreover, so important were these rights considered to be that the only substantial interventions made by governments, in both Britain and Ireland, were designed either to offer further practical *support* for free collective bargaining, or to provide a *substitute* for it. Support took the form of state-funded conciliation and arbitration services, designed to assist in situations where 'normal' bargaining had been inconclusive or had ended in disagreement. The substitute mainly took the shape of what came to be known as Wages Councils (in Britain) or Joint Labour Committees (in Ireland). Made up civil servants and union and management representatives appointed by government, their task was to set minimum, legally enforceable wage rates for workers in industries in which union organisation was acknowledged to be inadequate or difficult to maintain. As to the levels of wages arrived at through the normal collective bargaining process, the very most a government operating a non-interventionist free collective bargaining policy was likely to do was to exhort the parties to moderation when the economic situation seemed to demand that.

Corporatism

Corporatism is, in a profound sense, the very antithesis of liberalism, and it is perhaps the strength of Europe's liberal legacy that explains why full-hearted corporatism has rarely, if ever, been encountered. It is worthy of some brief consideration in the present context, however, not because Ireland ever became corporatist, but because in spite of the ardent advocacy of corporatist ideas by some influential figures, it did not. Although there are arguably other sources, corporatism can be said to be rooted in the theory of 'vocationalism', a new component of nineteenth- and early twentieth-century Roman Catholic social thinking, which was vehemently opposed to the liberal objective of widening the choices available to individuals – to freeing them from the constraints of social and, above all, moral forces. Under corporatist arrangements:

> The economy remains capitalist in the sense of being privately owned, but the stability of the system is ensured through the close *integration* of political, economic and moral forces, rather than through their separation. And workers (and others) are subordinated not through individualism, but through the very fact that they belong to collectivities/organizations; the organizations which represent them also regulate them. (Crouch 1982: 145; emphasis in original)

Italy under fascism is often cited as the corporatist archetype; however, that claim hardly stands up to scrutiny because of the way organisations like trade unions, which were ostensibly to contribute to policy-making, were deliberately enfeebled. It might more convincingly be argued that Britain in the immediate post-World War II period was at least mildly corporatist, to the extent that trade unions were truly influential for the first time in policy-making – on the reconstruction of industry, the regeneration of the economy and the creation of the welfare state. This provided for a time a 'moral unity' between government and unions, making union leaders 'willing to use their organizational strength to restrain rather than press the demands of their members' (Crouch 1982: 146).

Bargained corporatism/neo-corporatism: 'classical' and 'competitive'

Bargained corporatism, or neo-corporatism as it is now more often called, is much more formally tripartite and institutionally based. It generally arises when unions are strong; and, more often than not, the central aim is to gain union and employer commitment to wage restraint in exchange for providing them with an influence in public policy determination.

> In a neo-corporatist system of pay determination ... collective bargaining over pay and conditions becomes directly tied to government decision-making, especially

in the areas of economic and social policy. Unions and employers admit the government as a negotiating partner ... [and] the government and the various agencies of the state gain direct influence over pay determination in the economy. In return, unions and employers gain direct influence over public policy in ... [matters such as] taxation, employment creation and social programmes. [The last part of the bargain is that] union and employer leaders are expected to co-operate with the state by 'delivering' their constituencies' support for jointly agreed policies, including the pay norms specified in pay agreements. (Roche 1997: 129)[5]

Britain in the 1970s provides several *ad hoc* examples of such agreements, but we must look to Scandinavia, Austria and the former West Germany for more deep-rooted, long-standing neo-corporatism. Based on the notion of a 'social partnership' of workers, employers and the state, in these countries it was also seen as part of the great post-World War II social settlement – a historic compromise between capital and labour intended to be of benefit to both.

Theoretical thinking has developed somewhat further since the early 1990s and two subtypes of *neo*-corporatist agreement are proposed. What have come to be described as 'classical' neo-corporatist agreements emerged in the 1960s and 1970s, usually under social democratic governments with a broadly Keynesian approach to economic policy. As well as the setting of pay norms and the introduction of taxation reforms favourable to both employees and employers, these agreements typically included commitments to the elimination of income inequality by means of social spending, which was often, in practice, financed by public borrowing. Also featured on occasion were legislative concessions to trade unions, which involved increased labour market regulation on matters such as the right to trade union recognition, and the protection of individual workers against unfair dismissal.

However, the widely perceived ideological shift to the neo-liberal right, together with international economic recession, globalisation of markets and the consequent decline in trade union power and influence – trade unionism, as it were, 'on the back foot' – is argued to have generated a new 'competitive' neo-corporatism. With Keynesian demand management apparently discredited, the classical neo-corporatist emphasis on an egalitarian or 'fairness' agenda was replaced by a focus on the enhancement of national competitiveness; on competitively sustainable levels of public expenditure, involving the reform of tax, pension and social security systems; and on promoting measures to increase the flexibility, skill and sometimes the quantity of the labour supply, including a range of measures falling, this time, under the broad heading of labour market *de*regulation. The political and economic context had clearly changed to a significant extent.

Ireland and free collective bargaining: 1922–45

We ought now to try to place industrial relations in independent Ireland in their own historical context.[6] The practices of free collective bargaining and the associated non-intervention by the state were already deeply embedded in the industrial relations system when the Irish Free State was established. Indeed, Cumann na Gaedheal, which formed the early Free State governments, as well as being devoted to liberal economic principles, was almost excessively wedded to non-interventionism, and refused to become involved in disputes even when this might well have proved helpful.

Most of the trade unions' efforts in Ireland in the 1920s were devoted to fighting pay cuts. Incomes declined and union membership declined with them; and there was little relief until the mid-1930s, when the new Fianna Fáil government's programme for industrial development began to take effect. The central component of this was tariff protection for Irish-made goods; and Fianna Fáil also adopted a generally more sympathetic, consultative approach to the trade union movement. This contributed further to a mood of union confidence, as well as to increases in incomes and in the extent of unionisation.

In what eventually transpired to be no more than a temporary diversion, the 1930s were also marked by increasing interest in vocationalism, sparked to some degree by the papal encyclical *Quadragesimo Anno*. Ireland also had its own small band of supporters (more or less) of fascism, called the 'Blueshirts' (see Manning 1970), who eventually merged with Cumann na Gaedheal to form Fine Gael. So the Blueshirts' devotion to vocationalism was inherited by the new party; but Fianna Fáil was also influenced. First evidence of this was the lodgement of the principle of vocationalism in the new 1937 Constitution of Ireland (Bunreacht na hEireann), essentially the creature of the taoiseach, Eamon de Valera of Fianna Fáil. In an effort to ensure parliamentary representation of major interest groups, the Constitution provided that the majority of members of the Seanad (or Senate), the second chamber of the Oireachtas (Parliament), be elected by five 'Vocational Panels': Agriculture, Culture and Education, Industry and Commerce, Labour, and Public Administration (see Collins and Cradden 2001: Ch. 5). A longer-term consequence of this cross-party interest in vocationalist/corporatist ideas was the setting up in the early 1940s of a Commission on Vocational Organisation, with the purpose of inquiring into its applicability to Irish circumstances.

In the event, Seanad elections quickly lost their ostensibly 'vocational' character and became almost exclusively party political; and the eventual Report of the Commission, which was mildly favourable to experimentation in vocationalism, had little influence in the face of the antipathy of three key groups. Leading trade unionists, including people who were to find themselves on different sides in an upcoming split in the trade union movement, were well aware of the roots of vocational ideas and were highly sceptical of the value of the corporatist thinking associated with them (see Cradden 1993: Ch. 3–VIII);

politicians, for their part, sensed a loss of power for themselves because of the possible devolution of elements of policy formation to unelected vocational groups; and senior civil servants, with some justice, regarded vocationalism as being incompatible with the principle of ministerial responsibility.

It has also been argued that there were structural factors constraining the growth of corporatism – in essence that the prospective 'social partners' were weak and divided (Roche 1997: 143). The weakness of the trade union movement had been all too evident in face of the Emergency Powers (No. 83) Order of 1941, better known as the Wages Standstill Order. This was only one of a series of measures considered necessary to control the economy during World War II (which was necessarily, if somewhat euphemistically, described in neutral Ireland as 'the Emergency'). Despite swearing themselves to a campaign to the bitter end against the implementation of the Order, the unions were unable to live up to that. Moreover, the astute Lemass, then at the helm at the Department of Industry and Commerce for a second time, made just enough concessions to take the edge off what remained of union anger.

The 'rounds' system: 1945–70

Remarkably it was Lemass, the least ideological of men, who in the post-war years proposed the transformation of the management of the economy of Ireland into truly corporatist mode. But both unions and employers remained strongly devoted to the existing system; furthermore the 1945 split in the trade union movement also made it impossible to produce the co-ordinated union approach which was vital to Lemass's purposes (see Cradden 1993: Ch. 4; McCarthy 1977: Ch. 6).[7] As a result, the Labour Court, the only component of his grand design which 'bedded in', emerged as a classical support mechanism of free collective bargaining. For instead of becoming, as intended, the cornerstone of a system for regulating wage levels 'in accordance with national economic imperatives', it developed into a typical European-style conciliation and arbitration service (Roche 1997: 145). The Lemass proposals finally expired with the advent of the first inter-party Coalition Government in 1948 – for the time being at any rate.

Though there were other influences, what came to be the principal identifying mark of Irish industrial relations in the 1950s and 1960s arose most immediately from the lifting of the Wages Standstill Order in 1945. This created a single 'starting line' for all groups, and effectively synchronised pay bargaining from then on. In a very short time intensive, concentrated, periodic negotiations between employers and unions became the norm – the phenomenon of pay 'rounds' had arrived. Covering the great majority of unionised workers, they were eventually given numbers, as in 'the fifth round', and the broad outcome of a round was often used as the basis for pay awards in the non-unionised sectors.

Inevitably there developed out of this the notion of 'the going rate', and a focus on the cost of living as an important determinant of this, with productivity, profitability and general national prosperity as additional influences. Inevitable also was that certain large groups of workers 'strongly influenced the general course of bargaining', creating by the 1960s clear 'wage leaders' and 'wage followers' (Roche 1997: 149–51). What is most remarkable about this 'patterned' free collective bargaining during the early rounds, however, is that apart from adopting the usual role of exhorting the parties to bear in mind the wider economic situation, the state played a negligible role in the process, thus differentiating Ireland quite clearly from the developing neo-corporatism of the other European countries already referred to.

It was difficult, none the less, to avoid the conclusion that the absence of a government input into wage bargaining was disabling in terms of macroeconomic management. Indeed, it was becoming clear that the rounds system was inherently inflationary, and threatened Ireland's already weak international competitive position. But while that particular nettle was not fully grasped until later, with Fianna Fáil back in power after the 1951 general election, Lemass's corporatist leanings led to the creation of several tripartite consultative institutions which enabled employers, unions and the state to build up some experience of working with each other on economic policy matters. Also most important for the future was the formation by the Federated Union of Employers (FUE) and the Irish Congress of Trade Unions (ICTU) of a bipartite forum, the Employer–Labour Conference (ELC).

Although it took most of the 1960s to woo a majority of Irish trade union leaders and activists away from their devotion to unrestricted free collective bargaining, what Roche has called a 'drift' to neo-corporatism was becoming plain nevertheless (1997: 156–60). The pressure for some kind of change was increased by what appeared to be a general deterioration in the industrial relations climate, marked in particular by a long and deeply damaging strike by key maintenance workers across Irish industry in 1969.

Centralisation, national agreements and neo-corporatism: the 1970s

The very first 'national agreement' was actually arrived at in 1948, when a government threat to impose a legally enforceable pay norm obliged unions and employers to arrive at a pact on pay. This threat remained in the government armoury and was used again to good effect, in 1964 and 1970, to produce two further such agreements. But 1970 was also the start of a decade of centralised bargaining, on a bipartite ELC basis to begin with, and later with the full participation of the government.[8] There were important changes in industrial relations terminology as well, with the expression 'social partnership' coming increasingly into use, and with the later agreements being labelled 'national understandings'.

The fundamental significance of the new tripartism which this pointed up was that the conclusion of national deals in the late 1970s began more and more to rely on the availability, in exchange for wage moderation, of tax and social security concessions from governments (of both Fine Gael/Labour and Fianna Fáil complexions). And as time went on agreements began to encompass matters typical of the 'classical' neo-corporatist tradition, such as reducing unemployment and improving state health and educational provision. However, the process did not always proceed smoothly, principally because of a serious division in the union camp.

On one side were the advocates of tripartism, who had a variety of motivations: there were a few who accepted the essentially anti-inflationary economic logic of tripartite agreements; still others found the notion of social partnership ideologically attractive; and then there were those representing generally low-paid workers whose members were more than likely to be direct beneficiaries. On the other side of the argument, among the opponents of tripartism, there were also a number of factions: the first consisted of those who had deep-rooted objections to any departure from free collective bargaining; the second came from the craft or skilled workers who stood to lose ground, in relative terms, to lower-paid workers, because the deals arrived at often tended to squeeze differentials; and the third was made up of members and officials of some British-based unions with substantial membership in the Republic of Ireland who were obliged to abide by their executive councils' policies against centralised bargaining, which had, of course, been influenced by UK rather than Irish economic and political conditions.

This opposition was often well organised and almost succeeded in killing off the 1979 national understanding; only a reversion by the government to the tactic of threatening a legal pay limit persuaded the delegates to an ICTU Special Conference to agree to the deal. Then, to the surprise of many, it was the turn of the employers to be awkward, and the FUE almost managed to bury the 1980 agreement. Refusing to budge on several points in spite of pressure from both the unions and the government, the FUE effectively brought about the collapse of the negotiations. But the Taoiseach, Charles Haughey, intervened and put what was later ruefully described as 'undue political pressure' on the FUE: the employers formally backed down on the strength of open pledges on matters of advantage to them to be included in the next budget by the Minister for Finance.

Evidence on whether this decade of centralised bargaining and embryonic bargained corporatism was a 'good thing' is generally on the negative side. Roche's judgement is as follows:

> Instead of a virtuous circle in which pay restraint contributed to positive economic outcomes, which in turn provided further support for tripartite bargaining, a vicious circle was set in train. Trends in disposable pay and trends in unemployment both worsened; employers in many sectors faced intensifying

competitive pressures and increasingly uncertain trading conditions; the state was forced simultaneously to raise tax levels on employees and to resort to borrowing to fund spending commitments. The cumulative effects of these trends undermined centralised bargaining in 1981. (Roche 1997: 171)

Back to free collective bargaining: 1981–87

In 1981 then, for all those reasons, the national agreement phase imploded – during the life, as it happens, of the short-lived Fine Gael–Labour coalition led by Garrett FitzGerald. The actual collapse of the process was due mainly to government and employer resistance to union demands, based on a general conviction that the unions had done better out of national agreements than either of the other two parties. But neither the coalition government nor its three successors took the serious strategic look at pay determination that was obviously required. And so the scene was set for six years of complete reversion to decentralised free collective bargaining and non-intervention by the state – except for the occasional urging of pay moderation in the private sector and *ad hoc* responses to particular crises arising in the public sector.

It seemed to begin with, moreover, that there would be a reversion to the rounds system; but there were soon such significant divergences in both levels of wage increases and settlement dates that the notion of the round as a focused period of bargaining activity became virtually meaningless. Indeed, by the time of the return to centralised bargaining in 1987, while much of the private sector considered itself to have completed the twenty-seventh round, the last pay increases in the public sector were considered to be in the twenty-fifth round! And what of the more obvious effects of all this? 'The "winners" and "losers" in the new [decentralised] pay regime were evident enough. Foreign-owned, export-oriented high technology firms tended to do relatively well, with manufacturing generally doing well relative to distribution and services. The public sector gradually fell well behind the rest of the field' (Roche 1997: 174).

Fianna Fáil and a new partnership: 1987

Whilst all this was going on, the tripartite bodies which had been so important in the neo-corporatist 1970s continued to function, though not especially productively. However, the National Economic and Social Council (NESC), which replaced an earlier body with roughly the same consultative and investigative functions, was to play a key role in the revival of neo-corporatism. In a report issued in 1986, it had detailed a comprehensive prescription for economic recovery including – most significantly, in view of the involvement of the unions in the NESC – the cutting of public expenditure. Implementation would, of course, only be possible with the agreement of the social partners:

government, unions and employers. But why should anyone want to go back
to social partnership?

For the unions there were several considerations. First, under tripartism
their weakest and lowest-paid members had been protected by agreed
minimum pay increases. Secondly, the wage dispersion of the early to mid-
1980s had widened the gap between the top and bottom levels of pay of
unionised workers, 'and threatened progressively to undermine the cohesion
and solidarity of the trade union movement'. Thirdly, falling membership levels
– and, linked to this, increasing unemployment – made union leaders 'fear that
what was happening to unions in Britain under the neo-liberal regime of
Margaret Thatcher might also occur in Ireland' (Roche 1997: 177–8). A return
to social partnership seemed to promise help on all these fronts.

For the employers, decentralised bargaining had actually been a mixed bless-
ing. The number of strikes had fallen significantly, and trends in wage levels had
begun to moderate. But until 1987, governments of all hues relied on borrowing rather than cutting public expenditure to meet social spending. And while
pay increases outstripped inflation and were thus a threat to competitiveness,
the 'social costs' of employment – taxation, pensions and social security contributions – had become increasingly burdensome as well.[9] Though the
employers were not exactly inspired by the idea, then, centralised tripartite bargaining, or social partnership, did seem to offer the possibility of linking economic and fiscal reform with pay determination, preferably with pay restraint.

Fianna Fáil's Shadow Cabinet surveyed the economic difficulties of the
1983–87 coalition government with more political concern than political
schadenfreude. The main reason was that it was becoming all too clear that they
were going to inherit those same difficulties – as in due course they did, in a
minority government led by Haughey. The Lemass 'social partnership' inheritance had been reasserting itself, and some astute wooing of leading ICTU
figures in advance ensured that the unions, at any rate, were already on side
when the new administration was formed. The FUE, for its part, was finally won
over by the possibility of pay moderation, and the result was a three-year tripartite agreement: the grandly titled Programme for National Recovery (PNR).
It set sharp limits on pay, with a 3 per cent increase per annum permitted on the
first £120 per week of earnings and 2 per cent thereafter, with an underpin-
ning minimum enhancement of £4. But its most significant economic features
were commitments to the control of public expenditure and a reduction in government borrowing.[10] And, like its national understanding predecessors in
1979 and 1980, the PNR included several other important if rather broadly
expressed non-pay commitments: to promote increased employment through
industrial development; to improve social welfare provision; and to reduce
direct taxation on lower-paid workers covered by the pay-as-you-earn (PAYE)
system (by which income tax is deducted from workers' pay by employers).

Most gratifying for its NESC architects was the widespread recognition by
employers and unions of the PNR's beneficial effects. This ensured that it was

followed by the Programme for Economic and Social Progress (PESP), covering the period up to 1993. This allowed of much the same kind of percentage increases (though these now varied year upon year) but also permitted an additional and 'exceptional' provision for an extra amount to be negotiated at enterprise or plant level, the expectation being that any such increases would be in exchange for improvements in productivity, flexibility and so on. The temptation to see this as a step back from centralisation to at least an element of free collective bargaining is hard to resist, especially since there was a more extensive use of the 'exceptional' clause than had been anticipated. Indeed, although the (renamed) Federation of Irish Employers (FIE) specifically enjoined its members to insist on concessions before agreeing to any such increase, the evidence suggests that genuinely exceptional reasons were the exception.

There were also some serious economic retreats during the period covered by the PESP, including a devaluation of the Irish pound which the government had tried hard to resist. As well as several pay-related crises, there were major rows over income tax increases and cuts in social welfare benefits, which were argued by the unions to be in clear breach of the terms of the PESP. Yet it still held together, and weathered a change of government when Haughey made a run for a majority in a snap election in 1989, failed, and was obliged to make a coalition pact with the Progressive Democrats (PDs). The PDs, with only a very small number of Teachtaí Dála (TDs, or Members of Parliament), had a 'new right' or neo-liberal economic agenda; yet this had no discernable effect on the government's approach to the PESP.

In 1992 that coalition government, by then headed by Albert Reynolds, was succeeded by a more left-leaning Fianna Fáil–Labour coalition. Against the background of a recovering economy a new agreement was inevitable, and the PESP was succeeded by the Programme for Competitiveness and Work (PCW), which ran until 1996. Its pay provisions followed much the same pattern as in the two previous pacts, but more attention was given to non-pay issues. In particular, PESP commitments to specific targets for cuts in public expenditure and a reduction in the national debt were renewed in the PCW after stringent revision. Roche's conclusion on the performance under these programmes is as follows:

> Overall, with the exception of the record on employment and the level of unemployment, developments [after] 1987 [were] in closer harmony with the objectives of tripartism than was the case in the previous period of sustained tripartism during the 1970s. Moreover, economic and industrial relations trends since 1987 show significant improvements over those recorded during the return to decentralised bargaining in the 1980s. (Roche 1997: 194)

Making partnership the theme

ICTU had a long record of interest in what has been variously described as industrial democracy, worker participation, employee involvement or (more recently) workplace partnership (see Kelly and Hourihan 1997); and some individual unions in Ireland began tentatively to co-operate in management-inspired employee involvement initiatives in the late 1980s. The human resource management (HRM) 'wave' was also important in this, all the more so as it began to be seen as a serious response to the excesses of the 'macho', 'smoking-gun' style of management associated with early neo-liberalism. HRM is distinguished from traditional personnel management in three important ways: by the centrality of strategic or long-term planning in which employees are the core consideration; by an emphasis on gaining employees' *commitment* to the work organisation and its objectives rather than their unthinking *compliance* with management orders; and by the need for the organisation to display a reciprocal commitment to the well-being of its employees as individuals.[11]

Included in a typical HRM 'package', therefore, might be: as much job security as possible, even 'a job for life'; a high level of investment in training, personal development and career planning; promotion 'from within'; individualised, performance-related and profit-related pay; employee share ownership; flexible working and multi-skilling; new channels of communication with employees so that they are fully informed on all aspects of the organisation's affairs; and, most important of all, opportunities for workers to influence organisational decision-making, through employee involvement and participation schemes of various kinds.

The reasons why these methods and techniques were generally viewed as a threat to traditional trade union rights and prerogatives are plain enough. They appear to undermine the collective bargaining bedrock; to breach lines of work demarcation and upset established pay relativities; to erode worker solidarity and commitment to their unions; and to bypass long-established methods of information transmission to workers via union shop stewards. Yet by the early 1990s it was beginning to be argued in some union quarters that the employee involvement which is at the heart of all this actually 'empowers' workers and democratises work in ways which traditional, adversarial, 'them-and-us' industrial relations could never, by their nature, achieve. It was further argued that it was perfectly possible for there to be a dual allegiance – for workers to be devoted both to their work organisation and to their trade union. What this required of the union was that it identify itself closely with the production, quality and competitive aims of the employer, and that it encourage the growth through participation of a greater sense of commitment on the part of its members to the organisation in which they work. Required of management was that it involve the union, as well as individuals and work groups, in all organisational decision-making and in its implementation (for more on this, see Cradden 1992).

Evidence from the US in particular suggested that this was more than mere pie in the sky (Kochan and McKersie 1990); and some of the experimentation in employee involvement in Ireland itself was seen to be successful, especially when there was the wholehearted dedication of all concerned to making it work (DoL 1989). Based on this experience, significant figures in the trade union movement, both at a central ICTU level and in individual unions, became even greater enthusiasts for a change of approach to the management of their members at work; and their influence began to spread.[12] But while the PNR and the PESP both contained references to the desirability of employee involvement, the most important consequence of the new mood was the setting up by ICTU of a working group to study new management methods. It eventually produced a mould-breaking report, approved by the 1993 ICTU Conference, which essentially argued for unions themselves to seize the initiative on employee involvement – in other words to echo the partnership at national level represented by the PNR and the PESP with partnership at the level of the enterprise, the plant and the office (ICTU 1993).

As its title suggests, one of the main non-pay issues addressed by the PCW was unemployment; but another important one was employee involvement, to which ICTU now wanted more than the lip service paid in the PNR and PESP. But although there was more verbiage about participation in the PCW, the Irish Business and Employers' Confederation (IBEC, the successor body to the FIE) fought hard against anything too prescriptive. There was further disappointment when post-agreement bipartite discussions produced little more of substance.

Partnership 2000 and the Programme for Prosperity and Fairness

The PCW ended on a sour note, with public service workers complaining that they had done poorly out of it in comparison with other groups. However, while this made the negotiation of a new agreement more difficult, the continuing economic success which attended the PCW ensured that a new deal would certainly be done in the end. Negotiating this time with a Fine Gael/Labour/Democratic Left government,[13] ICTU set itself very different targets than those which it had outlined for the PNR almost a decade before. As well as the obvious things – moderate pay increases combined with tax relief sufficient to secure real improvements in living standards – it also called for 'mechanisms to develop partnership at the workplace level; and a new focus on equality, long-term unemployment and social exclusion' (ICTU 2000).

The tone was set by the name of the new agreement. Called 'Partnership 2000' (or P2000), it included an important chapter devoted to what ICTU described as 'developing partnership in the workplace':

Congress sees *Partnership 2000* as a watershed in the evolution of social partnership in Ireland and believes that it will determine whether social partnership develops or dies. It is probably the last window of opportunity to widen and deepen the national partnership process into a genuine partnership at the level of the workplace. It is for this reason that the implementation of the chapter of the

programme [on partnership] is the most important challenge for *all* the parties ...
The extent to which partnership at the workplace becomes a reality during this
programme will be the trade union benchmark when we come to assess its success
or failure. (ICTU 2000: 3; emphasis added)

To support such development in the workplace, a National Centre for
Partnership was established, and private sector companies were also encouraged to reward employees for their contribution by means of profit-sharing.
However, P2000 also included commitments to 'promoting enterprise', and a
further institution, the National Competitiveness Council, was created for this
purpose. Each of these new bodies had a training remit, and in due time ran
courses for trade unionists and personnel managers on the implementation of
both partnership and competitiveness programmes.

The equality, employment and 'social inclusion' aspects of P2000 were a
particular response to the conundrum posed in the first paragraph of this
chapter: that many citizens of the Irish state had not, at least until 1997,
enjoyed any of the fruits of the Celtic Tiger. Targeted specifically were the long-
term unemployed, the educationally disadvantaged, those on low incomes, and
those living in the more deprived areas of the country. Of some significance in
regard to this 'fairness' agenda was the input for the first time in social partnership negotiations of the so-called 'social pillar', comprised of voluntary and
community bodies such as the National Youth Council, the National Women's
Council, the Irish National Organisation for the Unemployed (INOU) and the
Conference of Religious of Ireland (CORI).[14]

As measured by a range of indicators, the period covered by P2000 was a
highly successful one. In particular, the economy was booming on all fronts;
unemployment had dropped to its lowest level in living memory; the number of
days lost due to industrial disputes had fallen to an all-time low; there was widespread public approval for the continuation of social partnership; and to crown
the 'classical' achievements of neo-corporatist social partnership, it was
reported that expenditure in real terms on health, education and social welfare
had increased by 117 per cent, 71 per cent and 45 per cent respectively since
1987 (*IRN* 1999).

The successor to P2000 emerged on 26 January 2000, and this despite the
presence in coalition with Fianna Fáil (since 1997) of the PDs, with their undis-
guised neo-liberal leanings. Under the Programme for Prosperity and Fairness
(PPF), workers were to receive a 15 per cent increase in pay over a period of
thirty-three months, plus another 10 per cent as a consequence of tax cuts.
Those on the newly introduced national minimum wage and others on low
wages were to do even better; and a new Social Welfare Bill would provide
increases worth another Ir£5 a week to those earning under Ir£200 a week,
through Pay Related Social Insurance (PRSI) and health-levy exemptions. The
PPF also sought to extend and deepen the workplace partnership process begun
under P2000.

However, the agreement ran into trouble very quickly. The consumer price index for the twelve months to June 2000 had risen by 5.5 per cent, and the unions called for a 'review' of the PPF, which they insisted had been negotiated on the basis of an inflation expectation of just 3 per cent. IBEC at first resisted this, on the grounds that the agreement contained no provision for review. But, under fairly obvious pressure from government, by December the employers had reluctantly acquiesced to an additional 5 per cent pay increase over the life of the PPF.

Sticking with partnership?

This episode tested the Republic of Ireland's social partnership process most severely, and to some seasoned observers seemed to imply an early end to the adventure. By the beginning of 2002 the forces on both sides of the argument had begun to muster in earnest. Firstly, said commentators sympathetic to the neo-liberal view, the trade unions had clearly 'pushed their luck'. Moreover, ICTU could no longer claim to be the authentic, majority voice of the workers of Ireland; its affiliated unions now represented predominantly public sector employees, and they had failed to break the resolve of most green-field investors in Ireland – especially those US companies at the high-technology cutting edge – not to recognise trade unions. Secondly, the broad economic and social ambitions that had prompted the 'crisis' birth of social partnership in the late 1980s had been almost fully achieved, and what was needed now was a dose of truly free market, laissez-faire industrial relations to sharpen up the act of the unions, the management of Irish business, and their employees. Thirdly, the pay agreement at the core of the PPF was becoming a fiction, as increases in the booming parts of the private sector appeared to be exceeding the PPF's pay norms, and as pay militancy began to rise in the public sector. To be coldly realistic, could pay increases be held to between 2 and 3 per cent a year in a highly successful economy with real labour shortages? Fourthly, there was widespread 'partnership fatigue' on all sides arising from the more than twenty working groups set up under the PPF and its predecessors, and intended to address policy development and implementation in areas such as child care, family-friendly work, housing, gain-sharing, etc. The very least that this demanded was a return to the 'leaner' and less complicated agreements of the late 1980s and early 1990s.

As against all that, there were three main pressures for a continuation of social partnership agreements in the form in which they had developed by the turn of the twenty-first century. In the first place, there was the simple argument that the cumulative benefits of social partnership were so obvious that it would be foolish throw them all away. It would be even more regrettable to have to abandon the almost uniquely Irish neo-corporatist model – one that incorporated both 'classical' and 'competitive' characteristics, and represented, as it

were, neo-liberalism with a social conscience. Secondly, there was some appre-
hension that a return to unfettered free collective bargaining would be too
much of a shock for the industrial relations system; and after fifteen years of
national-level pay determination there was a worry too that many manage-
ments and trade union officials were ill equipped to deal with a return to the
face-to-face negotiating process at firm and plant level.

The third and perhaps most telling pressure for the retention of neo-
corporatism arose from economic downturn. With so much American industrial investment, Ireland was especially vulnerable to the effects of the US
recession of 2001, deepened as that was by the terrorist attacks of September
11. To make economic matters worse, soon after the 2002 general election,
which returned the Fianna Fáil–PD coalition for a second term, earlier suspi-
cions about looming problems in the public finances were proved to be justified.
Not only was government expenditure running well beyond expectations, but
tax receipts appeared to be in serious decline. This was plainly not the right
moment, so it was argued, to make any radical change of approach. Social partnership might indeed be essential to maintaining economic stability.

'Sustaining Progress'

In the event it was the influences for the continuation of partnership that finally
won the day. But there were several crisis points in the negotiations, and it was
only the last-minute intervention of the taoiseach that ensured that a new
agreement, entitled 'Sustaining Progress' (SP), was concluded in February
2003. In the foreword to the final document, he reflected the change of economic mood:

> When I formally launched the negotiations on a possible successor to the
> *Programme for Prosperity and Fairness* ... on 31st of October last, I said that in light
> of the present economic uncertainties, we would have to jointly take hard deci-
> sions ... We made similar hard choices in 1987 and they provided a solid platform
> for economic and social development from which all of the people subsequently
> benefited. While nobody wishes to go back to the bad old days, all of us have had
> to moderate our expectations so that we are in a good position to take advantage
> of the upturn in the world economy when eventually it comes. (DoT 2003: ii)

Like its predecessors, the SP is to last for three years. However, the uncertainty identified by the taoiseach was manifest in the pay provisions of the
agreement, which covered only an 'interim' period of eighteen months. In late
2002 there had also been a 'benchmarking' (income comparison) process covering public sector employees, the aim being to redress what was recognised to
have been a relative falling behind in the pay of the government's own employees during the course of the PPF. As a consequence, the SP agreement dealt separately with public sector pay, providing an implementation schedule for the

benchmarking outcomes, then a six-month pay pause, to be followed by a general increase of 7 per cent payable in three phases (3 per cent, 2 per cent and 2 per cent) ending in December 2004. As regards the private sector, the agreement provided for an earlier but similarly phased implementation of the same 7 per cent. And the national minimum wage was increased to €7 an hour with effect from February 2004.

Yet despite the focus on the possible effects of the agreement on competitiveness, there remained a clear traditional or 'classical' commitment to social improvement, including a strong recommitment to the development of workplace partnership. The comprehensive nature of Irish social partnership agreements, as well as the scope of SP in policy terms, is captured in Table 5.2.

Table 5.2 *Some key policy elements of the Sustaining Progress agreement*

Policy area	Themes
Macro-economic	Public expenditure
	Taxation
	Competitiveness and inflation
Building, maintaining and sharing	Infrastructure
Economic development and prosperity	The environment
	Adaptation to continuing change
Delivering a fair and inclusive society	Poverty and social inclusion
	Health and addressing health
	Inequalities
	Equality
	Access to quality public services
	Challenge of delivering a fair and inclusive society
Workplace relations and environment	Protecting employees' rights
	Ensuring greater equality
	Improving skills
	Promoting health and safety
	Achieving a better work–life balance
	Developing integrated policies for migrant workers
	Partnership in the workplace

Source: DoT (Department of the Taoiseach) (2003), *Sustaining Progress: Social Partnership Agreement 2003–2005*, Dublin: Department of the Taoiseach/Stationery Office.

The only substantial blemish on the new achievement was dissent from two of the social partners. Farmers had been suffering harsh economic times for a couple of years, and were loudly disappointed that the SP offered them negligible recompense. The Saint Vincent De Paul Society, the anti-poverty agency, and the housing charity the Simon Community, which were key components of

the 'social pillar' or community platform (now representing twenty-six separate organisations), were also unhappy. They said that insufficient attention
had been paid to the poor and the homeless, and dismissed the SP as little more
than a glorified national pay agreement. At the time of writing, the SP had not
been formally endorsed by the members of trade unions within the ICTU fold
and by IBEC's affiliates; but it seems unlikely to be rejected.

Conclusion

As well as those relating to Irish industrial relations, there are two main lessons
to be learned from the experience of social partnership. The first one is that neo-
corporatism is a real and substantial alternative to neo-liberalism. That a free
market US and a social partnership Ireland were both among the best perform-
ing economies in the world during the 1990s is adequate testimony to this. But
while it is consequently true that abject poverty is less evident in Ireland than
in the US, the third lesson is that the vessel holding those less-well-off citizens
that remained semi-submerged despite the Celtic Tiger's rising tide could well
be completely marooned by its ebb.

Notes

1 The author is indebted to Professor Bill Roche of University College Dublin for the
   benefit of his advice on, and insight into, the social partnership process.
2 Trade unionism presents a difficulty for liberal theory, to the extent that it seems at
   least as 'natural' an output or concomitant of capitalist development as, for
   example, the factory system. Henry Phelps Brown, the distinguished British labour
   economist, insists that the 'propensity to combination' and the growth of trade
   unions spring from drives 'that are basic to human nature' (1986: 20).
3 For a most elegant defence of the 'voluntarist', free collective bargaining tradition,
   and for a eulogy of one of its first intellectual analysts at the University of
   Wisconsin, see Barbash (1991).
4 Although industrial relations in the US were also essentially liberal collectivist until
   the Reagan era, in contrast to the position in Ireland and the UK the system relied
   on a mass of legislation.
5 On neo-corporatism generally, including the subtypes described below, see also
   Panitch (1980); Goldthorpe (1984); Traxler (2000).
6 The historical chronology provided here owes a great deal to Roche (1997), which
   remains the definitive historical and analytical account of the road to social partnership.
7 For more on Lemass's intended 'democratic partnership' with the unions, see Bew
   and Patterson (1982).
8 Roche points out that despite the formal position, the national agreements of the
   early 1970s were strongly influenced by government (1997: 158).
9 Roche notes that between 1980 and 1986, hourly earnings increased at a higher

rate in Ireland than in all other European Monetary System countries (EMS) (1997: 178–80).

10 The Fianna Fáil government enjoyed the open support of Fine Gael for its efforts under the PNR to bring public expenditure under control; but the new leader of Fine Gael, Alan Dukes, who had declared this as party policy (colloquially labelled the 'Tallagh Strategy'), was eventually dumped, in major part for seeming to be so supportive of the Fianna Fáil approach.

11 What is described here is perhaps better labelled 'soft' HRM, because some 'macho' management approaches also attracted the HRM title, and were often called 'hard' HRM.

12 See, for example, Geraghty (1991). Until his retirement in late 2003, Geraghty was General President of SIPTU, the largest union in Ireland.

13 Because of a failure of trust between the leaders of the two parties, Labour walked out of its coalition with Fianna Fáil in 1994. But there was no general election because this alternative, so-called 'rainbow' coalition was able to muster a Dáil majority.

14 The government was disappointed that CORI and INOU felt unable fully to endorse P2000, and the feeling was that the expectations of these bodies were pitched excessively highly for this first effort to involve them.

References

Barbash, J. (1991), 'John R. Commons and the Western Industrial Relations Tradition', in R. J. Adams (ed.), *Comparative Industrial Relations: Contemporary Research and Theory*, London: HarperCollins.

Beaumont, P. B. (1992), *Public Sector Industrial Relations*, London: Routledge.

Bew, P. and Patterson, H. (1982), *Sean Lemass and the Making of Modern Ireland*, Dublin: Gill and Macmillan.

Brown, H. P. (1986), *The Origins of Trade Union Power*, Oxford: Oxford University Press.

Collins, N. and Cradden, T. (2001), *Irish Politics Today*, third edition, Manchester: Manchester University Press.

Cradden, T. (1992), 'Trade Unionism and HRM: The Incompatibles?', *IBAR – Irish Business and Administrative Research*, Vol. 13, pp. 2–3.

Cradden, T. (1993), *Trade Unionism, Socialism and Partition*, Belfast: December Books.

Crouch, C. (1982), *The Politics of Industrial Relations*, Glasgow: Fontana.

DoL (Department of Labour) (1989), *Case Studies in Employee Participation*, Dublin: Department of Labour/Government Publications Office.

DoT (Department of the Taoiseach) (2003), *Sustaining Progress: Social Partnership Agreement 2003–2005*, Dublin: Department of the Taoiseach/Stationery Office.

Geraghty, D. (1991), *The Return of the Intelligent Worker*, Dublin: Scientific, Industrial, Professional, Technical Union.

Goldthorpe, J. H. (ed.) (1984), *Order and Conflict in Contemporary Capitalism: Studies in the Political Economy of West European Nations*, Oxford: Clarendon Press.

ICTU (Irish Congress of Trade Unions) (1993), *New Forms of Work Organisation: Options for Unions*, Dublin: Irish Congress of Trade Unions.

ICTU (Irish Congress of Trade Unions) (2000), Partnership 2000, www.iol.ie/ictu/
    p2000.htm.
IRN (Industrial Relations News) (1999), Vol. 42.
Kelly, A. and Hourihan, F. (1997), 'Employee Participation', in T. V. Murphy and W. K.
    Roche (eds), *Irish Industrial Relations in Practice*, second edition, Dublin: Oak Tree
    Press.
Kochan, T. and McKersie, R. (1990), *Human Resources, Organizational Governance and
    Public Policy: Lessons from a Decade of Experimentation*, Cambridge, MA: Sloan School
    of Management.
Manning, M. (1970), *The Blueshirts*, Dublin: Gill and Macmillan.
McCarthy, C. (1977), *Trade Unions in Ireland: 1894–1960*, Dublin: Institute of Public
    Administration.
Panitch, L. (1980), 'Recent Theorisations of Corporatism: Reflections on a Growth
    Industry', *British Journal of Sociology*, Vol. 31, pp. 159–85.
Roche, W. K. (1997), 'Pay Determination, the State and the Politics of Industrial
    Relations', in T. V. Murphy and W. K. Roche (eds), *Irish Industrial Relations in Practice*,
    second edition, Dublin: Oak Tree Press.
Traxler, F. (2000), 'National Pacts and Wage Regulation in Europe: A Comparative
    Analysis', in J. Fajertag and P. Pochet (eds), *Social Pacts in Europe: New Dynamics*,
    Brussels: European Trade Union Institute.

6

Health care: consumer purchase or social right?

Michelle Millar

Introduction

Access to adequate health care is now regarded as an important right of all citizens, regardless of ability to pay. This was not always the case; medical advances and the assertion of liberal-egalitarian values at the beginning of the twentieth century led to a gradual acceptance of considerable governmental responsibility for the health of the population. Health policy in Ireland traverses many areas: from hospitals to health promotion, from fostering services to food safety, and from crisis pregnancies to child protection. Indeed, health care is not just to do with the availability of good health services, but is dependent on a myriad of factors such as housing, sanitation, working conditions, environmental pollution, education, unemployment and the general economic conditions of the country.

In recent times the health services provided in Ireland have been subject to persistent criticism. Years of underfunding in the 1980s, staff shortages, waiting lists for operations, the contamination of blood products with hepatitis C, and an inequitable mix of public and private health care have combined to create a government department described by one former minister for health as 'Angola – a department full of unexploded landmines'! In this chapter we will begin by examining the roles of the state in relation to health care, which can take three forms: regulator, funder/purchaser and provider/planner. Any one health care system is likely to be constituted of a combination of all or most of these roles (Hill 1997: 99). We will then consider the role of the Irish state as regulator, funder and provider of health care, specifying what public policy is in these areas. A brief analysis of the current health care strategy as a blueprint for the future direction of health policy in Ireland is then considered. Finally, some of the salient problems in Irish health policy are discussed.

The state role in health care: regulator

There are two primary areas in the Irish health care system in which the state has a regulatory role: in respect of professions related to medicine; and with regard to voluntary health insurance schemes. The medical profession is at the core of health service provision, and the government is significantly dependent on doctors for the implementation of its health policies. However, the state's regulatory role in respect of health professionals and semi-professionals can be characterised as 'hands-off', it having delegated responsibility, under a self-regulation regime, to the professions themselves. The Medical Registration Act of 1858 established a common register for Great Britain and Ireland of persons qualified to practise medicine. In addition, the legislation established a General Medical Council to monitor the educational and professional standards of its members (Barrington 1987: 16). This was the beginning of what can be described as the 'professional autonomy' of the medical profession. The Medical Practitioners Act, 1978, established the Irish Medical Council, the role of which is to monitor professional education, to register doctors, to operate disciplinary procedures and to give ethical guidance to the profession.

As McKevitt notes, 'it is only in the last decade that there has been sustained government attention given to the curtailment or abridgement of these professional freedoms' (1998: 144). Much of this has come in the wake of the 'New Public Management' drive (see also Chapter 8), as governments seek to ensure efficiency and efficacy in service delivery, as well as keeping tighter control over public expenditure. A consequence has been efforts by government – as yet tentative – to curtail the freedoms of the medical profession. Under the Strategic Management Initiative, the Department of Health launched a four-year strategy, 'Shaping a Healthier Future' (DoH 1994), in which it signalled its intention to increase control over the health services by measuring the actual performance of the various components of the system. To date, however, no government has been willing to implement such regulatory control over the medical profession and, needless to say, strategy statements alone will not suffice. To change the state's regulation of the medical profession would require legislation, which is in turn dependent on political commitment and agreement with vested interests (Millar and McKevitt 2000).

By comparison with other countries, the Irish state plays a strong regulatory role in the area of private health insurance. This kind of insurance was first introduced in 1957 as a way of covering the hospital costs of the 15 per cent of the population who were not eligible for free public hospital services. Until 1994, the provision of private health insurance was subject to the 1957 Voluntary Health Insurance Act. Under this the semi-state Voluntary Health Insurance (VHI) body developed a virtual monopoly in the market, with other schemes being confined to vocational or occupational members and their dependents – including, for example, the Gardai (police officers), prison officers and employees of the state-owned Electricity Supply Board (ESB). In response to the European Commission Directive 92/49/EEC, member states were obliged to make arrangements to allow an internal European Union (EU) market in non-life insurance, including health insurance. This opened up the Irish market, and with the passage of the Health Insurance Regulations Act, 1996, the British United Provident Association (BUPA) commenced operating within the Irish state as BUPA-Ireland.

Under the 1994 and 2001 Health Insurance Acts, the three principles associated with private health insurance in Ireland are 'community rating', 'open enrolment' and 'lifetime cover'. As well as providing for competition, the legislation also required all new entrants to the private health insurance market to operate 'community rating', a unique feature of the Irish system. In practice it means that everyone in a given scheme pays the same premium for a specified level of cover, regardless of their age or state of health. In other words, the younger members pay the same premiums as older people; but since they place fewer demands on the health services they thus, in effect, subsidise the older members of the scheme. 'Open enrolment' is the practice whereby all applicants for private health insurance cover must be accepted by a health insurer, regardless of their risk status. Finally, 'lifetime cover' is a system that guarantees health insurance consumers the right to renew their policies, irrespective of factors such as age, risk status or claim history.

A government White Paper on private health insurance in Ireland (DHC 1999) contained, amongst other things, proposals to establish an independent regulator of the private health insurance business. This had been mooted since the 1994 Health Insurance Act, and the intention was to end the conflicting roles of the minister for health and children in being both shareholder in the VHI and regulator of the sector. The result was the creation in early 2001 of the Health Insurance Authority (HIA), the main responsibility of which was to safeguard the interests of private health insurance consumers in Ireland through regulation of the market.

One of the more recent additions to the government's regulatory remit in health policy is food safety. Following the onset of the bovine spongiform encephalopathy (BSE, or 'mad cow disease') crisis in 1996 there was a realignment of responsibility for food safety from the Department of Agriculture and Food to the Department of Health. This signified a major shift in the state's mindset, food being seen no longer merely in terms of its export potential but also as a matter of public health. The result was the establishment in 1998 of the Food Safety Authority of Ireland (FSAI), an independent body under the auspices of the Department (O'Sullivan 1998). In an editorial the *Irish Times* declared that the creation of the FSAI represented a watershed in Irish politics, marking the 'beginning of the end for the symbiotic relationship that has existed between the Department of Agriculture and the farm lobby, a situation in which consumers had been consigned to the role of bit players' (1998). To date the work of the FSAI has been impressive, with a commitment, first, to eliminating offending premises which fail to achieve acceptable standards of

food safety and, second, to greater transparency in the way regulation is formulated (see Taylor and Millar 2002).

The state role in health care: funder

As funder/purchaser the state's involvement takes many different forms. In
general, health systems tend to be funded or financed in one of three ways: by
the state from general taxation; by the state from compulsory social or health
insurance schemes; or by private finance (generally voluntary insurance). In
Ireland, there is a unique and complex system of funding, a hybrid involving a
combination of private finance based on voluntary health insurance, and
finance from state taxation revenue. Public funding currently accounts for 78
per cent of total expenditure on health care. Private funding through private
health insurance contributes another 8.5 per cent, and the remainder consists
of payments by individuals – such as payments to general practitioners (GPs)
by non-General Medical Services (GMS) patients (DHC 2001a).

Health expenditure in Ireland has increased considerably since the late
1990s, after a long period of decline. From the mid-1980s until the late 1990s
there was serious underfunding: between 1980 and 1996 Ireland reduced
health spending as a proportion of gross domestic product (GDP) by 20 per
cent, and by 1989, spending on health was, in volume terms, 6 per cent lower
than in 1980. However, in 2002 the allocation of gross current expenditure
from Exchequer funds to the health services was projected to exceed €8.027
billion which, as Wiley (2002) notes, is over twice the allocation of €3.648
billion estimated for 1997. Similarly, gross current health expenditure in 1997
accounted for 6.3 per cent of gross national product (GNP), while it was projected that health spending in 2002 would account for 7.7 per cent of GNP.
Indeed, the unprecedented increase in funding since the late 1990s 'has to a
great extent been made possible because of the exceptional growth of the
economy' (Wiley 2002).

Approximately two thirds of all health expenditure is taken up by employee
pay costs; and since 1997 numbers employed in the health sector have
increased by 28 per cent, to a total of 87,000. Table 6.1 highlights the allocation of current health care expenditure, and it will be noted that the hospital
programme receives almost half of this. Community health services include the
GMS and the subsidisation of drugs scheme. Care for the handicapped includes
residential and therapy services for individuals with physical and sensory disability. The community welfare programme is concerned with the provision of
certain social services. The psychiatric programme involves the deinstitution-
alisation of psychiatric treatment by developing mental health services in the
community. The general support programme funds a number of minor and
miscellaneous activities, and is particularly valuable in covering unanticipated
contingencies. And the community protection programme funds services such

Table 6.1 *Percentage breakdown of health care expenditure, 2001*

Allocation of health care funding	%
General hospital programme	47.5
Community health services	16.3
Programme for the handicapped	11.7
Community welfare	8.5
Psychiatric programme	7.2
General support programme	4.5
Community protection	4.3

Source: Adapted from M. Wiley (2002), 'Huge Cash Injections into Health Services Cannot Continue Indefinitely', *Irish Times*, 17 April.

as immunisation against infectious diseases and health promotion (Wiley 2002).

The state role in health care: provider

Hill has observed that 'a strong funder role tends to lead to the state wanting to be involved in the provision and planning of services' (1997: 100). The Health Act, 1970, remains the cornerstone of contemporary services, and was introduced by the then minister for health as the 'most rational solution to a number of problems' (Barrington 1987: 271). Many of these problems stemmed from the manner in which health services had been provided within the former 'Dispensary System'. The Poor Relief (Ireland) Act, 1851, placed a duty on the Irish Poor Law Commissioners to see that Boards of Guardians provided health care dispensaries and appointed medical officers to each of them. Each poor law 'union' was divided into a number of dispensary districts, each with a salaried medical officer whose priority was to treat the poor; however, the doctor concerned was also entitled to attend those outside this class of people as a private practitioner. The system was financed by a poor law 'rate', a local taxation levied on property owners (for more on the rating system see Chapter 4). The shortcomings of the system were manifold, in particular the variation by county in the criteria for eligibility for treatment, and the lack of choice of doctor for eligible persons; yet the basic system endured until the 1970 Health Act.

This legislation provided for the creation of eight regional health boards with a broad mandate as regards health policy, the scope of services to be provided, and how they should be organised. More recently the number of boards has increased, with the Eastern Health Board covering the greater Dublin area being done away with and three new health authorities established in its place. The Act also established the GMS; and it was innovative in one other important respect, in that eligible people no longer attended a dispensary but visited the doctor of their choice, in the same facilities as private patients (Hensey 1988). Section 45 of the Act effectively solidified the two-tier system of public and private health care – though there are actually two categories of eligibility for state-provided services, 'full' and 'limited'. Full eligibility is available, subject to an income limit, to 'adult persons unable without undue hardship to arrange general practitioner, medical and surgical services for themselves and their dependents'. Individuals in this category are entitled to the full range of health services without charge. Limited eligibility is available to people whose income is above the established threshold for full eligibility. They are entitled to free hospital care (there is a nominal nightly 'bed fee', effectively an accommodation charge), specialist services in out-patient clinics, and maternity and infant welfare services. Despite the two-tier system, public and private health care are provided, by and large, in the same hospitals and by the same consultants and nurses.

To add to the complexity, the minister for finance announced a range of social service measures for the over-70s, regardless of their means; as well as free electricity supply and free television licences (the licence payment being use to fund public service broadcasting), they also included free health services (O'Morain 2001b). The announcement was met with anger by the doctors; one GP described the scheme as having 'nothing to do with social compassion and equity. We are being asked to provide free drugs and nursing to retired judges and barristers, doctors and stockbrokers, while at the same time a young married couple with children and a high mortgage cannot access basic health care' (cited in Houston 2001b).

The Irish Medical Organisation (IMO, the doctors' professional body) described it as the government's plan to capture the 'silver haired voter'; the IMO also regarded the scheme as a perversion of the notion of social inclusion (or community interdependence), but agreed to 'participate in discussions' with the Department of Health (O'Morain and Houston 2001). In the event, the IMO was able to lever a valuable deal from the government – which could not of course go back on its promise to the over-seventies. At first the IMO sought a fee-per-service payment in respect of the patients concerned, but the government was not willing to concede this. Instead, despite the IMO's earlier protests about exclusion of the needy, the doctors voted to accept a government offer of Ir£365 (approximately €460) per over-70 patient per annum. In comparison with the rates paid to GPs for other patients this was a very significant sum. For example in 2001, GPs were paid the annual sum of Ir£39.50 (€49.50) for patients aged under 5, Ir£23 (€29) for 5–15-year-olds, increasing on a sliding scale to Ir£60 (€75) for those over 65 (Wren 2001a).

'Quality and Fairness'?

The government health strategy, called 'Quality and Fairness: A Health Strategy For You' (DHC 2001a), has been seen as unique for a number of reasons; not least of these is that the process of producing it involved widespread consultation and was based on a partnership of all key stakeholders in the health service. Lead responsibility for the production of the strategy lay with a steering group. In addition a National Health Strategy Consultative Forum, representative of stakeholders, was established to provide advice to the steering group. Within this forum subgroups were established to consider key themes in health provision.

As well as that, the government placed advertisements in the national press seeking submissions from members of the public and interested groups. The minister published the findings of this consultation, *Your Views about Health: Report on Consultation* (DHC 2001b), which were based on 1,512 submissions from members of the public and 300 from various interested organisations. In addition, Irish Marketing Surveys were commissioned by the Department of Health and Children to carry out market research on public views about health and health services. The key themes emerging from the consultation process included the need for more investment at all levels in health and health services; a demand for a holistic and seamless service; a refocusing of the health system on care in the community; 'respectful relationships' between health providers and patients; and a strong will to change what was seen as an inequitable system.

A key component of the new strategy arises from the proposal for a 'treatment purchase fund' from the Progressive Democrats (PDs, participants in government with a broadly neo-liberal agenda, but relative newcomers to the party political scene). The fund is intended to buy treatment, from either private Irish hospitals or abroad, for public patients on waiting lists. The aim is to have reduced waiting time by the end of 2004 to no more than three months after the patient has been referred from an outpatient clinic. This is, however, a target and not a guarantee; and it, like all other elements of this forward thinking, is contingent upon the availability of funding.

The strategy also aims to revise hospital consultant's contracts to achieve 'greater equity for public patients' (DHC 2001a). At present, the majority of hospital consultants who staff private hospitals are paid a salary to work in public hospitals. The strategy aims to change this arrangement by ensuring that newly appointed consultants treat only public patients during the early years of their contract, leaving them free to engage in private practice only at a later stage. In addition, the strategy aims to curb the inequitable use of public beds by private patients. Current rules require that patients must decide between fully private and fully public status in hospitals. However, particularly in the case of emergencies, it can happen that private patients are accommodated in public beds. The strategy aims to ensure that admissions are managed so that the designated ratio of 80:20 between public and private activity is adhered to. The Minister for Health and Children reported that there had been a slippage to a 70:30 ratio in 2001, and announced that to prevent this might require the suspension of some non-emergency hospital treatment of private patients (cited in Houston 2001c).

Another strategic objective is to establish a new National Hospitals Agency with the goal of depoliticising the hospital system – by taking decision-making regarding hospitals out of the political arena of the health boards, which are mainly comprised of local councillors and public representatives, and putting it into the less partisan hands of a state agency. This comes in the wake of criticism that in some health board areas hospital services were too 'thinly spread', with no centres of regional expertise. For example, one expert pointed out that the North Eastern Health Board had five hospitals for a population of 350,000, and the Midland Health Board just three hospitals for 222,000 people; moreover, none of these hospitals could be categorised as regional (cited in Healy 2002). The views of managers and professionals alike is that hospitals in an identifiable region, or geographic area, should collaborate to share (rather than duplicate) services.

However, moves in this direction in the past have led to protests, such as that against the Midland Health Board in 2000 when it attempted to establish a regional centre of excellence for cancer services in Tullamore, County Offaly. Residents of nearby Portlaoise, County Laois, just over 20 miles away, resorted to the streets and undertook a High Court action to challenge the choice of Tullamore (Wren 2000b). The National Hospitals Agency will in future advise on the configuration and location of acute hospital services and on the designation of national specialist services; it will also manage a new national waiting list database and co-ordinate actions to reduce waiting time (DHC 2001c). Thus a central independent agency will take some important decisions out of the hands of health boards, and provide advice directly to the Minister for Health and Children.

In addition to the launch of the overall health strategy, in the same week the government introduced a new programme, 'Primary Care: A New Direction' (DHC 2001c), the main objective of which is to create 'one-stop-shop' primary care teams (see also Houston 2001b). Each team will consist of doctors, dentists, nurses, therapists, pharmacists, social workers and community welfare officers, and will enable more treatment and rehabilitation to be dealt with in the community, rather than by clogging up an already overcrowded hospital system. The plan proposes that by 2011, 600 new primary care teams will be established; all members of a team will be accessible by use of just one telephone number; and the teams will offer 24-hour cover to the public. The full implementation of the project is, inevitably, reliant on the availability of funding; however, in October 2002 the Minister for Health and Children announced a pilot project to establish ten primary care teams in various locations around the country. Viewed by some as the 'first tangible development' since the announcement of the strategy, the teams will be operational as soon as additional staff have been recruited (Houston 2002b).

A sick system?

We must now consider some of the identifiable problems concerning health policy in Ireland. These include dilemmas posed by public and private health insurance (particularly the long-term viability of private health insurance schemes); what former Taoiseach Garret FitzGerald, labels our 'three-tier health care system' (2001); the question mark that looms over the funding of the health strategy; and the existence of serious health inequalities.

The future of private health insurance

An Economic and Social Research Institute (ESRI) study in 2001, funded by BUPA-Ireland, reported widespread dissatisfaction with the health services. The *Perceptions of the Quality of Health Care in the Public and Private Sectors in Ireland* study surveyed 3,000 households, and found that 95 per cent wanted the government to devote more money to health in order to reduce waiting lists and improve services. Waiting lists came in for particular criticism; the study found that one in fifteen people covered by the GMS were on a waiting list, compared to one in fifty of those with private health insurance. Indeed, the study confirmed that waiting times for people with private health insurance were substantially shorter than for those in the GMS or, needless to say, those with no cover (ESRI 2001).

More significantly, however, 62 per cent of those surveyed believed that if they needed hospital treatment, they would receive better care as private patients. Everyone in Ireland is entitled to free hospital care; why then is 45 per cent of the population in membership of private health insurance schemes? Since its establishment, membership of the VHI has steadily increased. By 1967, 300,000 individuals had private cover; by 1977 this had increased to 600,000. In recent years, growth has been exceptional and it is currently estimated that in excess of 1.5 million individuals have private health insurance (DHC 1999). This growth has been attributed to the increased number of people in employment and to the provision of health cover as an employee benefit by many companies – something estimated to account for 20 per cent of all premiums to private health insurers. However, the ESRI report referred to above suggests that considerations of a sense of security and easier access to health services were cited as the main reasons why people have private health insurance (ESRI 2001).

Health care funding derived from private health insurance only contributes 9 per cent to the total expended, yet this small contribution guarantees its members a major and tangible benefit: speedier access to hospitals. Moreover, health insurance does not pay the full economic cost of the use of hospital beds, meaning that private hospital treatment is heavily subsidised by all taxpayers. Public hospitals get back only half the cost of caring for private patients from the insurance companies. If the full economic cost were to be met, a 25 per cent rise in premiums would be needed. Moreover, there is a further loss to the Exchequer in that health insurance subscribers receive tax relief on their premiums as an incentive to remain in membership.

As the increase in numbers subscribing to health insurance in Ireland seems set to continue, private health care as it exists in its present form may not be sustainable in the longer term. The Society of Actuaries, in a submission on the government's White Paper on private health insurance, argued that the 'symbiotic relationship that has developed is beginning to eat away at the system'(cited in Kerby 1998) – that is, that the availability of private health insurance has eased the pressure on the public services. Yet ironically its success in enabling 'queue jumping' over public patients could also be its ruination, since the more members join, the more pressure there is on hospital beds and services. This, the Society argues, could eventually lead to waiting lists for private patients and remove the very rationale for people subscribing to such insurance.

To add to all this, the HIA is currently advising the government on the introduction of risk equalisation to the Irish health insurance market. The White Paper on private health insurance defined risk equalisation as 'a process which aims to equitably neutralise differences in health insurers' costs that arise due to variations in risk profiles. This results in cash transfers from health insurers with healthier than average risk profiles to those with less favourable risk profiles' (DHC 1999: 72). The issue is a complex one and the HIA is engaged in yet another consultation process (HIA 2002a) to ascertain how it can best serve the overall interests of consumers in relation to risk equalisation. In its eventual policy paper on risk equalisation the HIA takes the view that this could be justified in appropriate circumstances. 'However ... intervention may not always be appropriate to address difficulties in the private health insurance market and where intervention is necessary risk equalisation may not be the most appropriate or even an appropriate from to take' (HIA 2002b: 4).

Additionally, the HIA has begun a consultation process concerning 'lifetime cover' (HIA 2002c). In the 1999 White Paper the government indicated its intention to allow insurers the discretion to move from the current 'single' community rating system to a system of 'lifetime' community rating. It said such a move would 'underpin the future viability of community rating' and be 'inherently fairer than the present system' (DHC 1999: 33–4). As the HIA explains, under the current system people's age of entry does not determine the level of premium that they pay. So a person aged 60 taking out private health insurance for the first time will pay the same amount as another sixty-year old who has been insured since the age of thirty, or indeed the same as a person aged thirty taking out insurance for the first time (assuming they all have the same level of insurance, with the same insurer) (HIA 2002c: 2).

The difficulty here is that what we might call 'intergenerational solidarity' may break down if young people do not continue to subscribe in the numbers they have until now. The alternative, lifetime community rating, would in practice mean that the premium people pay would rise with the age at which they enter the private health insurance market. Already, late-entry premium loadings are provided for in the Health Insurance Act, 2001, and the preparation of the appropriate regulations is under way. All this would indicate that private health insurance is about to change to meet the demands placed on it.

The 'three-tier' system

Maev-Ann Wren, a media watchdog on Irish health policy, has written that if private insurance cover continues to grow, the fate of public patients will cease to be an issue 'which exercises most politicians ... As in America, Ireland's system will be essentially dominated by private insurance companies' (2000a). As employment levels have increased, fewer families and individuals are eligible for GMS medical cards – which, as we have noted, entitle them to a full range of health services without charge. However, with 30 per cent of the population still covered by the GMS, and 45 per cent or so with private health insurance, there remains 25 per cent of people who have neither medical cards nor any kind of insurance. The individuals who constitute this group must of course pay for every GP visit, but will receive free hospital care for a nightly 'bed fee'.

The IMO estimates that 250,000 people are unable to afford health treatment, yet the government does not intend extending the eligibility threshold for the GMS before the end of 2003, due to budgetary considerations. At its 2001 annual meeting the IMO called for a change in the way the GMS is operated; one delegate put it very simply: 'we have had thirty years of the GMS scheme. It must now be replaced' (cited in the *Irish Times*, 23 April 2001). In particular, the IMO has called for free GP care to be extended to all citizens on low incomes, by a lowering of the qualification threshold, for there is continuing concern about those families with young children.

Health care spending

Is it simply the case that health spending in Ireland has remained low since the severe cuts of the 1980s, and that there is now a need to catch up? Or does the problem lie in the health services themselves – is the problem more to do with the *way* money is spent than the *amount* that is spent? Certainly in other countries many of what in Ireland are regarded as health services are rather viewed as social services. Irish health boards are responsible not only for hospitals, clinics and primary health care, but also for things like the welfare of asylum seekers and refugees, for children at risk, and for local food safety. So whilst expenditure on health has evidently increased, so too has the range of services that have to be paid for out of 'health' funding.

Analysts have predicted that if the government's new health strategy were to be implemented by 2011, spending would have to increase from approximately 9 per cent of GNP to over 12 per cent. It is of some interest that the EU average – adjusted for variations in the responsibilities of health authorities in different member states – is currently 8 per cent (Houston 2002a). The eventual total cost of implementing the strategy will be €12.7 billion. At the time of writing many deadlines have been passed without being met; so a question mark looms over the future of the strategy: how committed is the government to funding this ambitious programme?

The Minister for Finance, writing in the *Irish Medical Times* in early 2002, said he had been concerned for some time

> that the output of the health service has not kept pace with the massive increase in funding delivered to the sector in recent years. Furthermore, he added, in the absence of systems to identify such outputs and outcomes being delivered by the present level of funding 'no prudent Minister for Finance can justify committing more money to health'. (cited in the *Irish Times*, 1 April 2002)

A couple of months later the government announced increased charges to patients for hospital services and drugs, something viewed as yet another 'sign of a health system struggling to keep its head above water' (*Irish Times* 2002).

On the other hand, there are those who insist that throwing more money at health care is not the solution. O'Connor writes that the relationship between the health services and funding is similar to that of 'a barrel of sawdust and water: you can keep on pouring and it will keep soaking it up' (1998). There have been many calls to restructure and reform the manner in which the health services are organised, yet the 2001 strategy document avoids addressing the possibility of any dismantling of the current structure. Instead, the minister explained that 'what we're about is transforming people ... we stood back from the abolition or amalgamation of health boards and concentrated on the human resource issue' (Houston 2001c).

Fundamentally, however, says Bowers, 'the strategy will live or die on the basis of adequate funding and the ability of the health system to reform. History tells us that we should be sceptical about reports on health as so many have failed to be implemented in the past' (2001a; see also Bowers 2001b). Indeed, a recent review by the ESRI of the progress of *Shaping a Healthier Future* concluded that the Department of Health and Children was unable to provide information on whether and when the targets set out in the strategy – such as improving nutrition and diet and preventing causes of accidents – were being met. The ESRI report concludes that the strategy was more aspirational and philosophical than operational in nature, paid little attention to health inequal-ities, and lacked explicit monitoring and implementation systems, and stated that some viewed it as being 'more about style than substance' (cited in *irishhealth.com* 2002).

Taking a slightly different tack, some analysts claim that reform of the way health care is administered or managed is what is needed most. In response to this and similar assertions, the government commissioned a 'value-for-money' report on the operation of the health boards, the Department of Health and Children, and the delivery of the health services overall. Published in late 2001, it made particular criticism of the health board system, saying that there are too many boards for such a small population, and pointing to their political nature and their apparent inability adequately to deliver health care (Deloitte and Touche 2001). Yet the health strategy document itself states that the government is 'satisfied that changing the number of boards would not of itself lead to improvements in services' (DHC 2001a).

Health inequalities

In contrast to the interest shown in health inequalities and their consequences in other countries, O'Shea and Kelleher argue that 'the volume of research output on socio-economic differences in mortality has been low in Ireland' (2001: 269). Health inequalities can be defined as 'differences in health status which are unnecessary and avoidable and judged to be unjust and unfair' (Whitehead 1990: 6). Information about the extent of inequalities, as well as their underlying determinants, has been growing steadily in most developed countries. This shows that health inequalities take the form of gradients across the socio-economic scale, to the extent that at any given level on the gradient, one has a lesser chance of good health than at the next level up, and a better chance of good health than at the next level down (Whitehead 1990). Quite simply, health inequalities are a consequence of the differences in the incidence of health problems between individuals of higher and lower socio-economic status.

In 2001, filling the information gap identified above for the period 1989–98, the first report on all-Ireland mortality (in both the Republic and Northern Ireland) since the early 1920s was produced. In it the Institute of Public Health (IPH) lays bare real evidence for the first time of long-suspected health inequalities. The study looked at death rates related to specific causes of mortality by social class, and in both jurisdictions members of the lowest socio-economic group were 100 per cent more likely to die of cancer than the highest socio-economic groups, 120 per cent more likely to suffer heart attacks and strokes, and 200 per cent more susceptible to diseases of the lung and other respiratory problems (IPH 2001). To add to that, Irish health and lifestyle surveys show that GMS medical card holders generally report lower levels of health and quality of life than non-medical card holders. The Survey of Lifestyles, Attitudes and Nutrition (SLAN), conducted at the National University of Ireland, Galway (Kelleher et al. 1999), found that those who hold medical cards consistently do worse than non-GMS patients on every measure, from health care need and utilisation through to smoking and drinking patterns. Moreover, self-rated health is a powerful proxy for morbidity and mortality – in other words, there is a clear and direct relationship between what people themselves discern as being their state of health and the likelihood that they will experience sickness and even death.

The Chief Medical Officer (CMO) of Ireland also highlighted the existence of health inequalities in his annual report for 1999, especially the poorer health and earlier death rates associated with low socio-economic status. The report emphasised that the identification and understanding of the determining factors in health inequality, together with the development of strategies to deal with, it are 'arguably the most pressing priorities facing us in the health field'. The CMO concluded that 'inadequate medical care' was a contributory factor to such inequalities: put bluntly, 'there is evidence that the less well off in society have poorer access to health services' (CMO 1999: 30).

While broad structural factors such as unemployment, poverty and education are implicated in contributing to health inequalities, these are also related to the levels of health service provision and, crucially, to access to such services. Whilst there is a distinction to be made between health inequalities and inequalities in health care provision, the two are obviously related. That there are, as we have noted, two separate waiting lists for hospital treatment – public and private – plainly leads to inequity of service; access ought surely to be on the basis of medical need, or capacity to benefit from care, and should not be determined by factors such as ability to pay or geographical location. The National Economic and Social Forum recently produced a report on *Equity of Access to Hospital Care* (NESF 2002). With a particular focus on the promotion of equity in access to hospital care, specifically as regards reducing waiting lists and waiting times for public patients, it also addressed the question of giving greater priority to tackling inequalities in health status. The report concludes that structural change may be necessary in the current public–private mix to ensure that hospital patients are dealt with equitably. The government's health strategy does not, however, envisage any such structural change to the public–private mix in Irish health care.

Conclusion

'The healthcare a society develops reflects its values. In the US the provision of healthcare is not seen as society's obligation but as a voluntary consumer purchase', writes Wren (2001b). She further notes that 'Ireland's two-tier healthcare system reveals values than are closer to Boston than Berlin' – in other words that they more closely reflect US health care values than those of welfarist Germany. For Ireland's health care system to change, Irish people must decide that they want such a change – or be persuaded by political leadership that change is necessary. The secretary general (the most senior civil servant) at the Department of Health and Children recently told an audience at the Royal Academy of Medicine that 'We live in a low taxation, low public spending economy by European standards. That's a fact; that's by choice of the Irish community. We live in a democracy' (cited in O'Morain 2001a). Serious change in the Irish health care system would involve more spending, which would in turn require higher taxes. Thus, whatever improvement changes in institutional structures and better management and administration can make, the real key to the future of health policy, and to the success of the government's far-reaching health strategy, remains finance. Everything being contingent on 'budgetary considerations', Irish society must answer the question posed by Wren: 'Do we perceive healthcare as a consumer purchase or do we believe in social solidarity?' (2001b).

References

Barrington, R. (1987), *Health, Medicine and Politics in Ireland 1900–1970*, Dublin: Institute of Public Administration.

Bowers, F. (2001a), 'Strategy: Reviving an Ailing Service', *irishhealth.com*, 26 November 2001, www.irishhealth.com/index.html, accessed 24 July 2002.

Bowers, F. (2001b), 'Government Will Not Expand Medical Card Scheme Next Year', *irishhealth.com*, 28 November 2001, www.irishhealth.com/index.html, accessed 24 July 2002.

CMO (Chief Medical Officer) (1999), *Annual Report*, Dublin: Chief Medical Officer/ Stationery Office.

Deloitte and Touche (2001), *Audit of the Irish Health Service for Value for Money*, Dublin: Department of Health and Children.

DHC (Department of Health and Children) (1999), *White Paper on Private Health Insurance in Ireland*, Dublin: Department of Health and Children/Stationery Office.

DHC (Department of Health and Children) (2001a), *Quality and Fairness: A Health System for You*, Dublin: Department of Health and Children/Stationery Office.

DHC (Department of Health and Children) (2001b), *Your Views about Health: Report on Consultation*, Dublin: Department of Health and Children/Stationery Office.

DHC (Department of Health and Children) (2001c), *Primary Care: A New Direction*, Dublin: Department of Health and Children/Stationery Office.

DoH (Department of Health) (1994), *Shaping a Healthier Future*, Dublin: Department of Health/Stationery Office.

ESRI (Economic and Social Research Institute) (2001), *Perceptions of the Quality of Health Care in the Public and Private Sectors in Ireland*, report to the Centre for Insurance Studies, Graduate Business School, University College Dublin, Dublin: Economic and Social Research Institute.

FitzGerald, G. (2001), 'Proposed BUPA Scheme is Fatal for Our Health Service', *Irish Times*, 28 December.

Healy, A. (2002), 'Healthcare Suffers from Politicisation', *Irish Times*, 11 May.

Hensey, B. (1988), *The Health Services of Ireland*, fourth edition, Dublin: Institute of Public Administration.

HIA (Health Insurance Authority) (2002a), *Consultation Paper: Risk Equalisation in the Private Health Insurance Market in Ireland*, Dublin: Health Insurance Authority.

HIA (Health Insurance Authority) (2002b), *Policy Paper: Risk Equalisation in the Private Health Insurance Market in Ireland*, Dublin: Health Insurance Authority.

HIA (Health Insurance Authority) (2002c), *Consultation Paper: Lifetime Community Rating*, Dublin: Health Insurance Authority.

Hill, M. (1997), *Social Policy: A Comparative Analysis*, Harlow: Prentice Hall.

Houston, M. (2001a), 'Shake-Up Would Benefit Both GPs and Patients', *Irish Times*, 23 April.

Houston, M. (2001b), 'Primary-Care Plan Augurs Major Change', *Irish Times*, 28 July.
Houston, M. (2001c), 'Martin's Mission: To Get Health Back On its Feet', *Irish Times*, 1 December.
Houston, M. (2002a), 'Few Signs of Life in National Health Strategy', *Irish Times*, 1 April.
Houston, M. (2002b), 'Minister Approves Plan for 10 Primary Care Teams', *Irish Times*, 9 October.
IPH (Institute of Public Health) (2001), *Inequalities in Mortality 1989–98*, Dublin: Institute of Public Health.
irishhealth.com (2002), 'Health Strategy Failure Revealed', www.irishhealth.com/index.html.
Irish Times (1998), Editorial, 31 August.
Irish Times (2002), 'Health Charges Rise Again', 16 July.
Kelleher, C. et al. (1999) *Results of the National Health and Lifestyle Surveys (SLAN)*, Dublin: Health Promotion Unit, Department of Health and Children, and Centre for Health Promotion Studies.
Kerby, J. (1998), 'Private Health Cover Creates as Many Problems as it Solves', *Irish Times*, 28 August.
McKevitt, D. (1998), *Managing Core Public Services*, Oxford: Blackwell.
Millar, M. and McKevitt, D. (2000), 'Accountability and Performance in Irish Health Care', *International Review of Administrative Science*, Vol. 66, No. 2, pp. 285–96.
NESF (National Economic and Social Forum) (2002), *Equity of Access to Hospital Care*, Dublin: National Economic and Social Forum.
O'Connor, A. (1998), 'Extra Health Spending Must Be Accompanied by Reforms', *Irish Times*, 16 November.
O'Morain, P. (2001a), 'Public and Private Health Mix Under Government Scrutiny', *Irish Times*, 19 February.
O'Morain, P. (2001b), 'All Over-70s to Get Free GP Treatment Under New Deal', *Irish Times*, 29 June.
O'Morain, P. and Houston, M. (2001), 'Medical Cards for Over-70s an "Election Ploy" – Doctors', *Irish Times*, 23 April.
O'Shea, E. and Kelleher, C. (2001), 'Health Inequalities in Ireland', in S. Cantillon et al. (eds), *Rich and Poor: Perspectives on Tacking Inequality in Ireland*, Dublin: Oak Tree Press.
O'Sullivan, K. (1998) 'Salmonella Cases Highlight Importance of Food Safety', *Irish Times*, 31 August.
Taylor, G. and Millar, M. (2002), 'The Appliance of Science: The Politics of European Food Regulation and Reform', *Public Policy and Administration*, Vol. 17, No. 4, pp. 125–46.
Whitehead, M. (1990), *The Concepts and Principles of Equity and Health*, Copenhagen: World Health Organisation.
Wiley, M. (2002), 'Huge Cash Injections into Health Services Cannot Continue Indefinitely', *Irish Times*, 17 April.
Wren, M-A. (2000a), 'Health System Needs Urgent Funding', *Irish Times*, 3 October.
Wren, M-A. (2000b), 'Arguments on Rural Hospitals Continue to be Political Dynamite', *Irish Times*, 5 October.
Wren, M-A. (2001a), 'GPs are Ready for a State-Run Health Service', *Irish Times*, 6 February.
Wren, M-A. (2001b), 'In Sickness and in Health, It's All About Values', *Irish Times*, 27 October.

7

Environmental policy:
managing the waste problem

Gerard Mullally and Aodh Quinlivan

Introduction

Hardly a day goes by without animated debate or commentary in the Irish media on the causes of and solutions to waste problems: news of illegal dumps; public opposition to proposed new disposal facilities; official rebukes by the European Commission; or growing exhortations to reuse and recycle, in a plethora of public awareness initiatives. While the debate is wide-ranging and often acknowledges the multifaceted nature of the problem, there has been a tendency of late to focus on the issue of household or post-consumer waste and on the responsibility of individual households to 'domesticate' the waste crisis. Waste has become one of the most contentious environmental issues in contemporary Irish politics (Boyle 2002), and a number of official publications have begun to take stock of Ireland's environmental performance to date and to look to the challenges ahead (OECD 2000: 1–2). The OECD *Environmental Performance Review* has highlighted both Ireland's 'remarkable economic performance' and the emergence of 'a modern and coherent body of environmental law'. Yet waste management is singled out for particular attention by the Irish government as the environmental area that has, until recently, received the least attention (DoELG 2002b).

The Minister for the Environment and Local Government has identified waste as intrinsic to modern social life: 'Waste has become a defining characteristic of our modern consumer society; the generation of waste in Ireland continues to increase, reflecting economic growth, improved manufacturing and industrial performance, increased population and changing consumption patterns' (quoted in *Irish Times*, 14 August 2002).

The minister's statement goes on to reflect upon the 'reality' that the waste crisis cannot be totally resolved; but what are the consequences of the waste debate for Irish politics? Beck's influential thesis on the politics of late modern society cryptically refers to the 'unintended consequences of unintended consequences in institutions' (Beck 1999). Beck is alluding here to the fact that

117

environmental risks, often understood as the unintended result of contemporary modern life in the form of pollution and waste, have manifested themselves
as risks to the stability of the economy and the decision-making structures of
the political system. The management of environmental risks is therefore
increasingly being recognised not simply as a technical problem, but as a
problem that demands the skills of 'governance' (De Marchi and Ravetz 1999)
– 'governance' referring to new styles of governing in which the boundaries
between the public and private sectors, and the national and international
levels, have become blurred.

The politics of waste management in Ireland are being conducted at multiple levels of government, from the European Union (EU) to national, regional
and local levels. What was formerly regarded as simply a reserve function of
Irish local authorities (see Chapter 4) has become involved in a political drama
involving a whole range of actors: politicians, government departments, institutions of the EU, environmental groups, community organisations, business
representative organisations, and a cast of supporting characters drawn from
engineering and economic consultancies. In this chapter, we critically examine
the notion that environmental policy has become implicated in a broader shift
from government to governance in Irish politics, using the issue of waste management as an illustrative case. The chapter first explores the evolution and
modernisation of Irish environmental policy, and places recent Irish environmental policy in the context of the growing importance of sustainable development on a global and EU level. The chapter then examines the growing
significance of waste management in environmental and sustainable development policy and highlights some of the recent controversies and contradictions
that have arisen at the local level in Ireland. The chapter concludes with a discussion of the future priorities and prospects for Irish environmental policy.

Governance and environmental policy

The concept of governance has become an umbrella term for a variety of
changes that are taking place in the way that contemporary society is governed.
John (2001) makes a distinction between *government* as the formal procedures
and institutions that societies have created to express their interests, to resolve
disputes and to implement public choices; and *governance* as a flexible pattern
of public decision-making based on loose networks of individuals (2001: 6–9).
Although governance is characterised by more reliance by the state on net-
working and negotiated agreements than on binding regulation, there is still an
emphasis on the ability of governing systems to co-ordinate public policy and
solve public problems.

In the Irish context, the shift from government to governance has been
explored most frequently in relation to the use of social partnership as a co-
ordinating instrument for development policy on a national, regional and local

level (Adshead and Quin 1998; Ó'Broin 2002; see also Chapter 5). Recently, a number of innovations in Irish environmental policy have also focused the attention of analysts on the role of policy networks (Taylor 2001), new environmental policy instruments (Scott 2001; Curtis 2002; Flynn 2003), and mechanisms to increase public participation in addressing environmental problems (Skillington 1997; Taylor 1998; Keohane 1998; Motherway 2002). In general, analyses of the Irish situation tend to focus on whether or not we are witnessing the modernisation of environmental policy in line with recent European trends, such as eco-taxation (including charges and levies), market-based instruments (subsidies, deposit and return schemes), voluntary agreements (codes of conduct, negotiated agreements), and eco-labels that provide consumers with information about the environmental impact of goods and services (Hanf and Jansen 1998; Jordan et al. 2003). In particular, these analyses examine the idea, current in much of the political science literature on environmental issues, that there is a positive link between enhanced democratic participation in decision-making on environmental issues and better environmental policies (Hajer and Kesselring 1999).

The emergence of Irish environmental policy

In the 1970s, throughout most of the Western world, government departments with responsibility for the environment and environment-related issues were added to the apparatus of central government. In Ireland, the Department of Local Government was transformed into the Department of the Environment in 1978. The 'new' department was assigned a leading policy role in promoting the protection and improvement of the physical environment. However, the protection of the environment was only one among the many concerns of a large and diverse government department (Taylor and Horan 2001; Flynn 2003).

Adapting to European policy

The primary basis of environmental policy in the 1970s and 1980s was a combination of central government legislation and European directives that were incorporated into the Irish environmental regime by making regulations under the EEC Act, 1972 (Taylor 2001). The responsibility for the implementation of environmental legislation, however, was placed not with central government but upon the local authorities. A series of legislative innovations, including the Local Government (Planning and Development) Acts, 1963 and 1976, the Local Government (Planning and Development) Regulations, 1977, and the Local Government (Water Pollution) Act, 1977, made local authorities responsible for air- and water-pollution control, sanitation and waste management (Taylor 2001: 9). Current environmental legislation in Ireland has been much

more heavily influenced by the EU, a process that began in earnest with the Air
Pollution Act, 1987 (McGowan 1999).

The dynamic of environmental policy-making in Europe has been described
as a process involving 'leaders and laggards' (Haas 1993). A feature of this
process has been that the domestic environmental politics of 'leader' countries
such as Germany, the Netherlands and Denmark has tended to drive the development of EU environmental policy (Sbragia 1999). European environmental
policy is, however, characterised by tension between the proponents of stringent standards and the more reluctant, or 'laggard', member states. The process
of national adaptation by member states to more stringent European requirements depends on the degree to which systems and structures for the protection of the environment are already established and embedded in the national
policy context (Knill 1998). The incorporation of EU laws and directives at
member state level also depends on the 'interplay between legislation and
implementation' (Andersen and Eliassen 2001: 17). The adaptation of the Irish
environmental regulatory regime to the demands of European directives 'followed a well-worn path where governments simply added on new elements to
the remit of local authorities' (Taylor 2001: 9). Yet, despite an abortive attempt
in the late 1970s and early 1980s to develop a national 'policy for the environment', Irish local government was operating in the absence of a coherent
national environmental policy programme.[1] The combination of a relatively
weak domestic legislative framework, a lack of both financial and human
resources, and a culture of regulation that relied heavily upon negotiated compliance were all significant impediments to the capacity of local authorities to
monitor and police a growing body of environmental regulations (Coyle 1994;
Leonard 1988). All of these elements combined to create a policy style that was
both 'adversarial and litigious at the implementation stage' (Flynn 2003: 138),
and contributed to a number of high-profile environmental controversies
(Baker 1990).

Environmental politics in the 1980s

In the course of the 1980s a fragmented though highly politicised environmental movement challenged the legitimacy and performance of Irish local
authorities in environmental protection. The received wisdom regarding environmental protest during the decade is that it was largely directed at industrial
pollution and associated mining and dumping (MacSeoin 1999; Allen and
Jones 1990). The debate tended to be conducted in stark terms as a choice
between economic development and environmental protection (Baker 1990).
Critics thus perceived a conflict of interests in respect of the regulatory function
of local authorities; for they were charged with regulating, monitoring and
policing the environment while at the same attempting to encourage inward
investment to their areas (Coyle 1994). As a result, environmental regulation
in the 1980s has been characterised as consisting of 'negotiated compliance'

rather strict enforcement (Leonard 1988). At a national level, in an economic climate characterised by recession, unemployment and emigration, the fear that stringent regulation would result in the withdrawal of multinational capital acted as a disincentive to central government to introduce stricter environmental regulation (Baker 1990). Yet, by the end of the 1980s, industrial interests were actually calling for the rationalisation of the existing regulatory regime, such as it was (Allen and Jones 1990). Opposition to a number of large-scale investments by the multinational pharmaceutical industry, involving protracted planning and legal battles, had resulted in serious delays to high-profile projects and were threatening the state's industrial policy of attracting foreign direct investment (FDI). In east Cork, the controversy surrounding the proposal by chemical giant Merrel Dow to locate a plant in an agricultural area became a national political issue, and the demand for a national environmental policy crystallised in the 1989 general election.

The election manifestos of all of the major political parties featured an emphasis on the protection of the environment and called for the creation of a new environmental agency (Taylor 2001). The election in 1989 of the first Green Party Teachta Dála (TD, or Member of Parliament), Roger Garland, was symbolic of the growing political significance of environmental issues. More concretely, however, the Fianna Fáil/Progressive Democrat coalition programme for government proposed the creation of an Office for the Protection of the Environment within the Department of the Environment, and signalled the intention to establish the Irish Environmental Protection Agency (Mullally 2001a). The announcement by the taoiseach, Charles Haughey' that the Irish presidency of the EU beginning in January 1990 was to be a 'Green presidency' could be interpreted as indicating the shift 'from laggard to proactive participant' in environmental policy (McGowan 1999: 165). Alternatively, it could also be seen as part of a bid to secure for the Irish government the cachet of being the location of the EU's new Environmental Protection Agency (O'Neill 1997). In any event, the publication of the *Environmental Action Programme* in 1991 was the first comprehensive environmental policy document ever adopted by an Irish government. It was primarily concerned with the regulation of the natural media as regards pollution (air, inland waters and the marine environment) as well as tracking the effects of the various economic sectors (agriculture, industry, forestry) on the environment (DoELG 1990). The programme also tentatively embraced the integration of environmental protection and economic growth by highlighting the benefits of clean technology, environmentally friendly industry and the positive growth potential of the environmental technology sector (Mullally 2001b). A critical feature of the policy programme was the commitment to establish the Irish Environmental Protection Agency (IEPA).

The Environmental Protection Agency Act, 1992, provided the legal basis for the establishment of an independent statutory authority for the protection of the environment. The IEPA commenced operations in 1993 and was endowed with a range of statutory regulatory, monitoring and enforcement functions. In 1994, it became responsible for the licensing and regulation of large and/or complex industrial and other processes with significant pollution potential through the introduction of Integrated Pollution Control Licensing (IPC). This merged a range of previous licensing arrangements into a single procedure under the remit of the IEPA. By the end of 2001, over 500 of these new licences had been issued. An important feature of this regime is that it encourages the improvement of environmental performance through an environmental management system, and promotes the uptake of cleaner production processes. In order to support improvements in environmental performance, the IEPA also co-ordinates research: for example, the Cleaner Greener Programme is designed to encourage research on environmental products and services under the government's Productive Sector Operational Programme 2000–2006 (DoELG 2002a).

The modernisation of Irish environmental policy in the 1990s can be interpreted as a consequence of dynamic interaction between local, national and international political developments: the government recognised the need to accommodate the environmentalist critique of the 1980s, but without threatening the free market ethos that came to underpin the politics of the 'Celtic Tiger' economy through the 1990s (Taylor 1998; see also Chapter 1). The ascendance of the concept of sustainable development in policy discourse at the global and European levels has proved to be a particularly important stimulus in the dynamics of Irish environmental policy.

Environmental policy and sustainable development

The First Environmental Action Programme committed the Irish government to the integration of environmental considerations into all policy areas; to the 'precautionary principle' (i.e. in conditions of scientific uncertainty, 'decision-makers should prevent potentially serious or irreversible environmental harm' – see also Chapter 9); and to the principle of sustainable development (Connelly and Smith 2003: 144).

Sustainable development and Agenda 21

The current emphasis on sustainable development in Irish and European policy stems from *Our Common Future*, a report issued by the World Commission on Environment and Development (WCED) in 1987. *Our Common Future* defined sustainable development as 'development that meets the needs of the present without compromising the ability of future generations to meet their own needs' (WCED 1987: 8). This interpretation of sustainable development emphasises the mutual reinforcing of economic growth, social development and environmental protection.

In 1992, the United Nations Conference on Environment and Development (UNCED) or 'Earth Summit' was held in Rio de Janeiro, where a number of agreements, including Agenda 21, were signed up to by governments from all over the world. Agenda 21 is an international programme of action for achieving sustainable development into the twenty-first century (Koch et al. 1993); it consists of some forty chapters divided into four major sections covering different aspects of sustainable development. The first section links environmental problems to social and economic issues like poverty, health, trade, debt, consumption and population. The second section deals with the need to conserve and manage physical resources such as land, seas, energy and wastes to further sustainable development. The third section emphasises the need to strengthen the role of major groups in the movement towards sustainable development – through partnership with women, indigenous populations, non-governmental organisations (NGOs), scientists, farmers, workers and trade unions, business and industry, and local authorities (Connelly and Smith 2003: 240). This section stresses that 'one of the fundamental prerequisites for the achievement of sustainable development is broad public participation in decision-making' (UNCED 1992: Ch. 23). It also stresses that 'as the level of governance closest to the people, local authorities play a vital role in educating, mobilising and responding to the public to promote sustainable development'. As a result of this type of reasoning, UNCED proposed that 'by 1996, most local authorities in each country should have undertaken a consultative process with their populations and achieved a consensus on "a Local Agenda 21" for the community' (UNCED 1992: Ch. 28). The final section deals with the role of governments, and Ireland, both independently and as a member of the EU, has made a firm commitment to implement Agenda 21.

Sustainable development and environmental policy in the EU and Ireland

The European Commission has used the instrument of environmental action programmes (EAPs) to set out its policy intentions since 1973. However, the legal competence of the EU in environmental matters was established with the Single European Act in 1987, and extended by the Treaty on European Union in 1993 (Baker et al. 1994). The function of EAPs is to suggest specific proposals for legislation, to discuss broad ideas on environmental policy, and to propose new directions for the future (Haigh 1992). Not surprisingly, EU environmental policy has undergone significant changes since 1973; the first two EAPs (1973–77 and 1977–81) focused on pollution control and remedial measures, and also stated the basic principles of emerging European Community (now EU) environmental policy. The third and fourth EAPs (1983–86 and 1987–92) emphasised preventative measures and the integration of environmental protection into other policies (Connelly and Smith 1999: 227). The fifth and sixth programmes (1993–2000 and 2001–10), however, placed a central emphasis on sustainable development as the main objective of environmental policy.

In 1997 the Treaty of Amsterdam confirmed the legal status of sustainable development as a horizontal principle of EU programmes and policies. In the same year, Irish environmental policy was placed more forcefully within the frame when it was subsumed into the larger framework of *Sustainable Development: A Strategy for Ireland* (DoELG 1997). The main focus of this strategy is on the measures required to place the major economic sectors of Irish society on a path towards sustainable development. The strategy also laid the basis for a new institutional framework linking national, regional and local government in the implementation of Agenda 21. At a national level this involved the creation of Comhar – the National Sustainable Development Partnership – as 'a forum for national consultation and dialogue on all issues surrounding the pursuit of sustainable development' (DoELG 2002a: 113). Regional authorities were given the responsibility of co-ordinating the activities of their constituent local authorities in pursuit of the sustainability goal. Meanwhile local authorities were ascribed a pivotal role in its implementation through Local Agenda 21, and the Environmental Partnership Fund was created as a mechanism for joint projects with local communities (Mullally 2001b). Since the publication of the Irish strategy the EU has reaffirmed its own commitment in 'A Sustainable Europe for a Better World', adopted by the Gothenburg European Council in 2001. More recently the Council of Environment Ministers and the European Parliament agreed the sixth EU EAP, which identifies four priority areas for action. These are: climate change; nature and biodiversity; environment and health; and resource efficiency and waste management. In the Irish national report to the World Summit on Sustainable Development in Johannesburg 2002, the government indicated that its own policy priorities fell within these broad areas, including, in particular, waste management (DoELG 2002a).

Waste management policy and the politics of waste

McCormick (2001: 168) notes that the EU has adopted eighty-five laws, a myriad of strategies and a variety of policy initiatives since the 1980s in the area of waste management alone. In 1999, the basic elements of the European Commission's policy were established in the *Community Strategy for Waste Management*, which enshrined sustainable development and a high level of environmental protection as its key commitments. Boyle (2002) argues that, of all the legislation stemming from the strategy, the Waste Framework Directive is of the greatest interest because it introduced 'the waste management hierarchy' as the basis of waste management in Europe. The hierarchy establishes the priorities for waste management on a continuum from the most to the least favoured options for dealing with waste, that is: prevention, minimisation, reuse, recycling, energy recovery and, finally, disposal. Boyle usefully characterises the logic behind the waste hierarchy as follows:

> Priority must be given to waste prevention and minimisation through the application of technologies that produce cleaner production processes and that reduce packaging wastes used at the point of consumption ... the next preferred options are the re-use and recycling of waste. Only in circumstances where it is impossible to reintegrate waste into economic systems should the issue of waste disposal be considered. In the event that the disposal of waste is required, waste to energy or thermal treatment facilities should be prioritised as causing less environmental damage than the landfill solution,[2] which is identified ... as the strategy of last resort. (Boyle 2002: 182)

The main effect on member states is the requirement to develop plans indicating how the waste management hierarchy is to be implemented. In spite of many of the developments in environmental policy described here, the European Environment Agency argues that there is still 'an urgent need for the integration of waste management strategy into a strategy for sustainable development, where waste prevention, reduction of resource depletion and minimisation of emissions at source is given high priority' (cited in Fagan et al. 2001: 2).

Waste management in Ireland

In Ireland, the strategy of last resort has traditionally been the first port of call, with some 90 per cent of waste being diverted to landfill. Frank McDonald, environment correspondent of the *Irish Times*, points out that the rapidly increasing volumes of waste now being generated in Ireland represent 'a crisis of mega-proportions' (12 August 2002). A report in July 2002 by Peter Bacon and Associates (Bacon 2002) predicted that by mid-2003 the available landfill capacity would not even be enough to cater for post-recycling household waste. The Bacon report also predicted a deficit in landfill capacity of 400,000 to 500,000 tonnes per annum in the Greater Dublin Area alone in the period from 2002 to 2009. While the overwhelming emphasis in that report is on the effects of the waste crisis on Irish economic competitiveness, in the last few years waste management has provoked a political crisis. This is being experienced most acutely at local authority level, where councils are faced with a diminishing number of operational landfill sites and growing public opposition to the location of new sites and waste incinerators.

At a national level, attempts to overhaul the waste management system can be traced back to the Waste Management Act, 1996, and the Waste Management (Planning) Regulations, 1997. A central feature of the redirection of policy was to shift the emphasis away from landfill towards the implementation of the EU waste hierarchy. The Waste Management Act, 1996, gave the IEPA the authority to license landfill sites operated by local authorities and private interests. The main thrust of the new direction, however, was contained within the policy statements *Changing Our Ways* (DoELG 1998) and *Preventing and Recycling Waste: Delivering Change* (DoELG 2002b). In these documents the minister for the environment and local government established targets for the next fifteen years for: the diversion of 50 per cent of household waste from landfill; the recovery of 50 per cent of all packaging waste by 2005; and the recycling of 35 per cent of municipal waste and 50 per cent of construction and demolition waste by 2003, with the figure for both rising to 85 per cent by 2013 (DoELG 2002b). The execution of the new policy has, however, been beset by controversy, and its implementation delayed by the politicisation of waste management at a subnational level, as many local councils have refused to adopt a waste management plan.

Waste management plans are a central feature of the new approach, in line with the requirements of EU policy. However, the government decided that these plans should involve dealing with the issue at a level above that of individual local authorities – to 'scale the problem of waste management primarily at the regional level' (Boyle 2002: 183). The reasoning was that the economies of scale that could be achieved by creating regional groupings of local authorities would facilitate the development of a recycling infrastructure, create a sufficient market to support a small number of incinerators and allow the development of fewer but larger and better-run landfill sites (Boyle 2002). For the purpose of waste management, local authorities were not required to remain within the confines of the eight regions established for the purpose of drawing down EU structural funds (see Chapter 4), but were left to choose which other local authorities they would link up with to develop regional plans. A total of seven regional groupings were eventually formed; however, many individual local authorities refused to endorse the plans, largely in the face of public opposition to the incineration of waste.

In many ways, incineration has emerged as one of the most problematic areas of waste management, with strong campaign groups coming to the fore, such as the Cork-based CHASE (Cork Harbour for a Safe Environment), the No Incineration Alliance in Meath and the South Tipperary Anti-Incineration Campaign. The 2002 general election also saw an anti-incineration candidate running (unsuccessfully) in the Cavan-Monaghan constituency. Meanwhile, the consequent delays drew down the ire of the European Commission, which initiated proceedings against the Irish government in the European Court of Justice in 1999 for its failure to ensure that waste management plans were in place (Boyle 2002). The Irish government responded with the introduction of the Waste Management (Amendment) Act, 2001, which effectively removed the power from elected local councillors to decide on waste management plans and transferred it to the city and county managers (on the duties and powers of elected councillors as against those of managers, see Chapter 4).

From local government to local governance?

As noted above (and as discussed also in Chapter 4) recent reforms in Irish local government have been designed to give effect to a shift from local *government* to local *governance*. Clarke (1996: 37) explains the shift as involving 'the mixed economy of provision, the greater differentiation of organisational provisions within the local public sector', and the increased importance of partnerships. This has effectively resulted in a localisation of the national social partnership model (see Chapter 5); local authority policy is now formulated in strategic policy committees (SPCs), on which at least one third of the membership is drawn from sectoral representatives who are not elected by the public. County/city development boards (CDBs) were also established in 2000 to oversee the development and implementation of a strategy for the economic, social and cultural development of cities and counties. The CDBs are led by local government and are also representative of local development bodies together with state agencies and social partners operating locally. *Towards Sustainable Local Communities* (DoELG 2001: 98) identifies these new structural arrangements as a crucial mechanism promoting 'greater participation in, and ownership of, sustainable development at local and regional levels'. A complex policy issue such as waste management and the local controversies that it creates highlight the importance of including stakeholders in the decision-making process – stakeholders being the 'decision-makers within the organisation and its environment who have an interest in organisational performance and can help or hinder the choice and implementation of strategies, (McCaffery 1989: 195). The message from McCaffery is that external stakeholders (e.g. the sectoral interests represented on the SPCs and CDBs) need to be managed in a way that will permit them to assume ownership of strategic policies such as local waste management plans. The partnership model involves a recognition that managing in the public sector now has far more to do with managing interests and stakeholders than it did in the past. At the same time, as local communities are being encouraged to take ownership of local sustainable development, the power of local elected representatives to decide on issues relating to the implementation of national waste management has shifted to the manager.

Waste management: implementation deficit or democratic deficit?

Nutt and Backoff (1992) point out that policy implementation can be particularly difficult at the local level of the public sector as 'publicness brings with it constraints, political influence, authority limits, scrutiny and ubiquitous ownership' (1992: 201). An editorial in the *Irish Times* argued that 'it has been evident for years that the elected representatives of some local authorities are reluctant to take difficult and unpopular decisions concerning the increasing amount of waste generated by our consumer society' (24 March 2001). This reluctance is put in context by a former local councillor as follows:

some councillors would gladly take on more powers, but for many others, the existing system suits them well enough. They can come to a meeting, argue a particular point or case in a matter before the council, knowing that the manager will make the final decision. The County Manager has, knowingly or unknowingly, often provided welcome cover for many a councillor at stormy public meetings. (Gallagher 2001: 94)

In the case of waste management plans, the formal transfer of power to the manager was made to address the problem of 'a local implementation deficit' with respect to waste management (Quinlivan 2002). But in doing so, has it contributed to a 'democratic deficit'?

The removal of decision-making from elected councillors illustrates an interesting tension between democratic legitimacy and effectiveness in Irish environmental policy. The new policy direction indicated in *Changing Our Ways* had emphasised that waste management planning should include effective public consultation and participation (Fagan et al. 2001). However, the Minister for the Environment and Local Government has described the planning process on waste management as 'over-democratised' (*Irish Times*, 13 August 2002). He has raised the idea of fast-tracking plans for incinerators, landfill sites and other waste management facilities by sending them directly to An Bord Pleanala (the state planning approvals agency), eliminating local authority involvement entirely. In addition to the problems surrounding the case of waste management plans, the local implementation deficit is particularly apparent on at least two other issues, namely waste charges and the problem of illegal dumping.

Attempts by local authorities to levy waste service charges have frequently met with strong opposition on the grounds that the charges represent double taxation. Increasingly, central government has not been in a position to finance waste management adequately, as the general tax take has failed to keep pace with rising waste management costs (Curtis 2002: 85). The question of charges has led to tensions within local authorities as well, most notably in Cork, where a local councillor took Supreme Court action against the city council. He successfully argued that his council's policy of not collecting refuse from houses where charges were not paid represented an unjust social levy. However, the Protection of the Environment Bill, 2003, includes provisions that effectively negate the Supreme Court decision in this case, by giving local authorities the explicit power to stop collecting domestic waste from householders who have not paid charges. The Bill also copper-fastens the previously informal decision-making power of the manager (see Chapter 4) on waste management issues, in particular with regard to the power to decide on waste charges. This creates a difficult situation for councillors, since 'elected councils which oppose waste charges would only have the option of voting down the [full] annual estimates, thereby risking [their] abolition' (*Irish Times*, 31 January 2003). The Minister for the Environment and Local Government has indicated his intention to introduce weight/volume-based charging for waste services by 2005 (DoELG 2002b: 97). In a recent address to the General Council of County Councils he warned householders that they would have to pay annual waste charges of €700 unless they recycled their rubbish (*Irish Examiner*, 31 May 2003). The chairman of the General Council of County Councils, however, has expressed concern about the 'diminution of the power' of elected representatives contained in provisions of the Bill (*Irish Examiner*, 21 May 2003).

In highlighting waste management as a key priority for the future, the Irish national report to the World Summit on Sustainable Development identifies an important implementation failure in the enforcement of existing policy. It states that 'while greater prevention/minimisation and recycling are needed, provision must also be made for the disposal of the waste that does arise. Action will also be taken to deal with the legacy of poor management and inadequate control systems evidenced by the alarming extent of illegal dumping' (DoELG 2002b: 97). Cases of this kind have attracted a large degree of media attention over the last few years. For example, illegal dumping of builders' waste took place for three years in close proximity to a special area of conservation and natural heritage in Newrath, just 250 metres from an area office of Kilkenny County Council (*Irish Times*, 17 January 2002). A massive illegal dumpsite was also discovered in Rockchapel, County Cork, in March 2002, in which the rubbish was piled to a depth of 3 metres in a forested area of over 1 acre (*Irish Examiner*, 5 March 2002). However, perhaps the most startling case of illegal dumping was discovered in Wicklow, near the famous Glen of Imaal. Wicklow County Council was itself heavily involved, to the extent that it had been depositing up to twenty-five truckloads of waste a week into a largely disused quarry (*Irish Times*, 11 March 2001). The council had neither planning permission nor a waste licence for this from the Environmental Protection Agency. Perhaps in response to all this, the 2002 Fianna Fáil/Progressive Democrat Agreed Programme for Government provides for the establishment of an Office for Environmental Enforcement: to audit the performance of local government in discharging its enforcement function; to monitor compliance by public authorities with their environmental obligations; and to prosecute cases where significant breaches of environmental legislation occur, and assist local authorities in doing so.

Priorities and prospects for the future

Fagan et al. (2001) suggest that in terms of waste management strategy, 'government by central decree would need to be replaced by a more consensual model based on multi-agency partnerships, the blurring of responsibilities between public and non-public sectors, and the emergence of self-regulating networks concerned with waste management as a central issue in sustainable development' (2001:4). However, regulation, or 'command and control', remains one of the main ways to achieve environmental and sustainable development policy goals (DoELG 2002a). Recent indications suggest the use of an expanded range of policy instruments in the future, including greater use of market-based instruments, and by making producers responsible for packaging waste and a range of other end-of-life products. Flynn (2003) argues that there is a general opposition to eco-taxation among business interests and in the Department of Finance, as well as 'a widespread cultural antipathy towards taxation in Irish society'. He also points out that the type of fiscal innovations experimented with in the 1990s have 'taken a marked neo-liberal direction in the form of significant reductions in capital and income taxes' (2003: 152). The 15 cents levy on plastic shopping bags and the landfill levy of €15 per tonne of waste, introduced by central government in 2002, have in fact met with less opprobrium than might have been expected. Curtis (2002: 84) points out that the plastic bag levy gained widespread acceptance 'because it addressed the problem of the ubiquitous plastic bag; and equally important, the revenue from the tax was earmarked for environmental problems instead of general government expenditure'. The policy has resulted in an estimated reduction of 90 per cent in plastic bag usage (*Irish Times*, 14 August 2002). The proceeds from the landfill levy are also earmarked for the Environment Fund, which will help to fund waste management initiatives.

Flynn (2003) points out that the limited range of 'new environmental policy instruments' used in Ireland, such as eco-taxation, voluntary agreements and eco-labels, 'were a welcome departure from the traditional emphasis on legal instruments of the preceding decades' (2003: 153). However, he also points out that the relationship between conventional regulation and these new instruments has been particularly poor. We find a similar lack of fit between initiatives designed to enhance public participation in environmental issues and local sustainable development, and the government's approach to developing a waste management strategy. Local Agenda 21 has not been as actively pursued by Irish local authorities as it has by their counterparts in the rest of Europe (Mullally 2001a; Neill and Ellis 2002). A study in the United Kingdom of waste management initiatives, conducted in the context of Local Agenda 21, has shown that while community engagement is certainly no panacea for the waste crisis, it has allowed local authorities to build bridges with their communities (Robbins and Rowe 2002). In Ireland, the government's Environmental Partnership Fund and EU funding have allowed local authorities to engage in a variety of partnership projects on recycling and composting. By and large, however, these projects tend not to be linked directly into the implementation of national waste management policy. The potential for the integration of local participation into decision-making at higher levels of governance certainly exists, as the proliferation of new institutional structures for sustainable development amply demonstrates (Mullally and Henry 2003). The key question, however, is whether the political will exists to find a more democratic solution to resolving the waste crisis.

Notes

This chapter draws on a PRTLI Cycle 2 research project on Environmental Management.
1 In 1978, following the transformation of the Department of Local Government into the Department of the Environment, an Environment Council was established by the minister to examine proposals for a national policy for the environment. It was a further ten years, however, before a national environmental policy programme was introduced.
2 Landfill involves the dumping of waste on an open site, where it is sometimes compressed and allowed to degrade naturally, or be covered with non-degradable material. The main problem is that much waste is non-degradable, or will degrade only very slowly.

References

Adshead, M. and Quin, B. (1998), 'The Move from Government to Governance: Irish Development Policy's Paradigm Shift', *Policy and Politics*, Vol. 26, No. 2, pp. 209–25.

Allen, R. and Jones, T. (1990), *Guests of the Nation: People of Ireland versus the Multi-Nationals*, London: Earthscan.

Andersen, S. S. and Eliassen, K. A. (eds) (2001), *Making Policy in Europe*, second edition, London: Sage.

Bacon, P. (2002), *Strategic Review and Outlook for Waste Management Capacity and the Impact on the Irish Economy*, report by Peter Bacon and Associates, Vol. 1, Issue 1.

Baker, S. (1990), 'The Evolution of the Irish Ecology Movement', in W. Rüdig (ed.), *Green Politics One*, Edinburgh: Edinburgh University Press.

Baker, S., Milton K. and Yearly, S. (eds) (1994), *Protecting the Periphery: Environmental Policy in the Peripheral Regions of the European Union*, London: Frank Cass.

Beck, U. (1999), *World Risk Society*, Cambridge: Polity.

Boyle, M. (2002), 'Cleaning Up after the Celtic Tiger: Scalar Fixes in the Political Ecology of Tiger Economies', *Transactions of the Institute of British Geographers*, Vol. 27, pp. 172–94.

Clarke, M. (1996), *Renewing Public Management: An Agenda for Local Governance*, London: Pitman.

Connelly, J. and Smith, G. (1999), *Politics and the Environment: From Theory to Practice*, London: Routledge.

Connelly, J. and Smith, G. (2003), *Politics and the Environment: From Theory to Practice*, second edition, London: Routledge.

Coyle, C. (1994), 'Administrative Capacity and the Implementation of EU Environmental Policy in Ireland', in S. Baker, K. Milton and S. Yearly (eds), *Protecting the Periphery: Environmental Policy in the Peripheral Regions of the European Union*, London: Frank Cass.

Curtis, J. A. (2002), 'Advancing Waste Management Beyond Crisis', *Administration*, Vol. 50, No. 3, pp. 83–93.

De Marchi, B. and Ravetz, J. (1999), 'Risk Management and Governance: A Post-Normal Science Approach', *Futures*, Vol. 31, pp. 743–57.

DoELG (Department of the Environment and Local Government) (1990), *An Environmental Action Programme*, Dublin: Department of the Environment and Local Government/Stationery Office.

DoELG (Department of the Environment and Local Government) (1997), *Sustainable Development: A Strategy for Ireland*, Dublin: Department of the Environment and Local Government/Stationery Office.

DoELG (Department of the Environment and Local Government) (1998), *Changing Our Ways*, Dublin: Department of the Environment and Local Government/Stationery Office.

DoELG (Department of the Environment and Local Government) (2001), *Towards Sustainable Local Communities*, Dublin: Department of the Environment and Local Government/Stationery Office.

DoELG (Department of the Environment and Local Government) (2002a), *Making Ireland's Development Sustainable: Review, Assessment and Future Action*, Dublin: Department of the Environment and Local Government/Stationery Office.

DoELG (Department of the Environment and Local Government) (2002b), *Preventing and Recycling Waste: Delivering Changes*, Dublin: Department of the Environment and Local Government/Stationery Office.

Fagan, H., O' Hearn, D., McCann, G. and Murray, M. (2001) *Waste Management: A Cross Border Perspective*, Working Paper, National University of Ireland, Maynooth: National Institute for Regional and Spatial Analysis.

Flynn, B. (2003), 'Much Talk but Little Action? "New" Environmental Policy Instruments in Ireland', in A. Jordan, R. K. W. Wurzel and A. R. Zito (eds), *'New' Instruments of Environmental Governance? National Experiences and Prospects*, London: Frank Cass.

Gallagher, P. (2001), 'The Experience of Being a Councillor', in M. Daly (ed.) *County and Town: One Hundred Years of Local Government in Ireland*, Dublin: Institute of Public Administration.

Haas, P. (1993), 'Protecting the Baltic and North Seas', in P. Haas, R. Keohane and A. Levy (eds), *Institutions for the Earth: Sources of Effective International Environmental Protection*, Cambridge, MA: MIT Press.

Haigh, N. (1992), 'The European Community and International Environmental Policy', in A. Hurrell and B. Kingsbury (eds), *The International Politics of the Environment: Actors, Interests and Institutions*, Oxford: Oxford University Press.

Hajer, M. A. and Kesselring, S. (1999), 'Democracy in the Risk Society: Learning from the New Politics of Mobility in Munich', *Environmental Politics*, Vol. 8, No. 3, pp. 1–23.

Hanf, K. and Jansen, A. I. (eds) (1998), *Governance and Environment in Western Europe: Politics, Policy and Administration*, Harlow: Addison, Wesley Longman.

John, P. (2001), *Local Governance in Western Europe*, London/Thousand Oaks/New Delhi: Sage.

Jordan, A., Wurzel, R. K. W and Zito, A. R (eds) (2003), *'New' Instruments of Environmental Governance? National Experiences and Prospects*, London: Frank Cass.

Keohane, K. (1998), 'Reflexive Modernization and Systematically Distorted Communications: An Analysis of an Environmental Protection Agency Hearing', *Irish Journal of Sociology*, Vol. 8, pp. 71–92.

Knill, C. (1998), 'European Policies: The Impact of National Administrative Traditions', *Journal of Public Policy*, Vol. 18, pp. 1–18.

Koch, M., Grubb, M., Thomson, K., Munson, A. and Sullivan, F. (1993), *The 'Earth Summit' Agreements: A Guide and Assessment*, London: Royal Institute of International Affairs.

Leonard, J. H (1988), *Pollution and the Struggle for the World Product: Multi-National Corporations, Environment and International Competitive Advantage*, Cambridge: Cambridge University Press.

MacSeoin, T. (1999), 'Rural Siting Conflicts in Ireland, 1999–2000', *Irish Journal of Sociology*, Vol. 9, pp. 115–20.

McCaffery, J. L. (1989), 'Making the Most of Strategic Planning and Management', in Cleary, Henry and Associates, *Managing Public Programmes: Balancing Politics, Administration and Public Needs*, San Francisco: Jossey-Bass.

McCormick, J. (2001), *Environmental Policy in the European Union*, Basingstoke: Palgrave.

McGowan, L. (1999), 'Environmental Policy', in N. Collins (ed.), *Political Issues in Ireland Today*, second edition, Manchester: Manchester University Press.

Motherway, B. (2002), *Public Involvement in Environmental Decision-Making in Ireland*, Policy Institute, Trinity College Dublin, Working Paper No. 3, Dublin: Policy Institute.

Mullally, G. (2001a), 'Environment, Democracy and Local Agenda 21: Towards a Sociology of Sustainable Development in Ireland', unpublished PhD dissertation, National University of Ireland, Cork.

Mullally, G. (2001b), 'Starting Late: Building Institutional Capacity on the Reform of Sub-national Governance', in W. M. Lafferty (ed.), *Sustainable Communities in Europe*, London/Sterling, VA: Earthscan.

Mullally, G. and Henry, A. (2003), 'Contra-Indications? Evaluating the Role of Deliberative Democracy in Regional Sustainable Development', paper presented to Workshop III of the EU Thematic Network project REGIONET – Evaluation for Regional Sustainable Development, Manchester, 11–13 June.

Neill, W. J. V. and Ellis, G. (2002), 'Local Agenda 21 and Civic Identity: Reflections on Belfast and Dublin', in F. Convery and J. Feehan (eds), *Achievement and Challenge: Rio + 10 and Ireland*, Dublin: Environmental Institute.

Nutt, P. C. and Backoff, R. W. (1992), *Strategic Management of Public and Third Sector Organisations: A Handbook for Leaders*, San Francisco: Jossey-Bass.

O'Broin, D. (2002), 'Participation on the Periphery: Community Participation in Reformed Local Government Structures', *Journal of Irish Urban Studies*, Vol. 1, No. 1, pp. 47–60.

OECD (Organisation for Economic Co-operation and Development) (2000), *Environmental Performance Reviews: Ireland*, Paris: Organisation for Economic Co-operation and Development.

O'Neill, M. (1997), *Green Parties and Political Change in Contemporary Europe: New Politics, Old Predicaments*, Aldershot: Ashgate.

Pierre, J. and Peters, B. G. (2000), *Governance, Politics and the State*, Basingstoke: Macmillan.

Quinlivan, A. (2002), 'European Standards and Waste Management in Ireland: Examining the Local Implementation Deficit', *Administration*, Vol. 50, No. 2, pp. 67–79.

Robbins, C. and Rowe, J. (2002), 'Unresolved Responsibilities: Exploring Local Democratisation and Sustainable Development through a Community Based Waste Reduction Initiative', *Local Government Studies*, Vol. 28, No. 1, pp. 37–58.

Sbragia, A. (1999), 'Environmental Policy', in W. Wallace and H. Wallace (eds), *Policy-Making in the European Union*, Oxford; Oxford University Press.

Scott, S. (2001), 'Environmental Hazards of Prosperity', *Studies*, Vol. 90, No. 347, pp. 17–28.

Skillington, T. (1997), 'Politics and the Struggle to Define: A Discourse Analysis of the Framing Strategies of Competing Actors in a "New" Participatory Forum', *British Journal of Sociology*, Vol. 48, No. 3, pp. 493–513.

Taylor, G. (1998), 'Public Registers, Oral Hearings and Environmental Democracy in Ireland: "Me Thinks Thou Dos't Protest too Much"', *Irish Planning and Environmental Law Journal*, Vol. 5, No. 4, pp. 143–52.

Taylor, G. (2001), *Conserving the Emerald Tiger: The Politics of Environmental Regulation in Ireland*, Galway: Arlen Press.

Taylor, G. and Horan, A. (2001), 'From Cats, Dogs, Parks and Playgrounds to IPC Licensing: Policy Learning and the Evolution of Environmental Policy in Ireland', *British Journal of Politics and International Relations*, Vol. 3, No. 3, pp. 369–92.

UNCED (United Nations Conference on Environment and Development) (1992), *Agenda 21: A Programme for Action for Sustainable Development*, New York: United Nations Conference on Environment and Development.

WCED (World Commision on Environment and Development) (1987), *Our Common Future*, Oxford: Oxford University Press/World Commission on Environment and Development.

8

Citizens as consumers: process, practice, problems and prospects

Patrick Butler and Neil Collins

Introduction

The conceptualisation of citizens as consumers of public services presents both opportunities for improved service delivery and potential threats to democracy. By borrowing from private sector experiences in streamlining the design, development and delivery of public services, government, the public sector and citizens can benefit from efficiencies and improvements in the provision of goods and services. However, pressing the business analogy in this area can exacerbate political inequalities.

In this chapter, the process of recasting citizens as consumers is shown to be underpinned by the influential New Public Management developments in Western democracies, involving a reorientation of approach to the delivery of services to citizens. The role of marketing in this broad managerialist thrust is particularly important in examining consumer and customer ideals, given its focus on market operations and the management of customer service. In the Republic of Ireland, the consideration of citizens as consumers of public sector services may be examined in the light of the Strategic Management Initiative and the Customer Action Plans recently produced by government departments and agencies. A review of the plans and their intent provides some insights into the practice of considering citizens as consumers.

Problems with the central analogy arise, however, when the distinctive characteristics of the public 'marketplace' reveal important differences from private sector contexts. The lack of clarity in applying the concepts and language of marketplace management to the public sector are among the possible criticisms here. The ultimate paradox is that better utilisation of management technologies may damage political processes and institutions, because treating citizens as consumers involves both positive and negative outcomes. For all its contributions to more efficient service delivery, the managerialist approach of perceiving and treating citizens as consumers is challenged by new models of governance in which market-based solutions are questioned. Problems associated with the separation of politics and administration are raised in this context. Initiatives relating to the provision of government services by electronic means (often called 'eGovernment') that primarily emphasise customer service delivery will also be vulnerable to such difficulties.

The process of considering citizens as consumers

The political system in Ireland reflects in large part those of other liberal democracies. It facilitates, however imperfectly, the translation of citizens' needs into political action. These needs may include material, ideological, social and even spiritual dimensions. Politics may be represented as a neat sequential processing model, though the reality is usually more chaotic or confusing. For the purpose of this chapter, the political system can be seen as one which recognises people's needs, provides alternative ways of meeting them, chooses between the options and sets up mechanisms to implement the solution. In this simplified model, politicians' functions begin with the recognition of the problem – for example, a shortage of affordable housing for families of modest income, or feelings of insecurity among elderly people. Sometimes, the electorate may not have recognised the nature of the difficulties they are experiencing. In these cases, politicians may act to give expression to a general discontent among the population. In either case, the identification of the problem may lead to a demand that 'something' be done to address the issue, as articulated by individual politicians or political parties. Alternative understandings of the problem and formulations of a solution will be placed in the political arena for the approval of the public, either as voters or party activists, or as part of collectives such as trade unions, pressure groups or local communities.

Viewing politics as a system rather like a production process does not do justice to the complexity of rhetoric and political debate by which citizens' views are articulated and aggregated by the media, politicians, pressure groups and the like. It does, however, point to the traditional solution to political problems which is that 'the government should do something'. This, in turn, has generally meant that the state has created a programme, a budget or even a department to provide a new or enhanced service. There is an outstanding record of achievement in the direct state provision of public services in Ireland – in schools, hospitals, airports, security forces and the like. Typically, state agencies are monopolies with a bureaucratic structure designed to facilitate equity and accountability as well as provide a service to the public. Operating through its various departments and agencies, the state in Ireland now represents 16 per cent of gross national product (GNP). It also controls a wide range of commercial and utility services through state-sponsored bodies such as Aer Rianta (the state airports authority) and Bord Gais (the semi-state company responsible for the provision of natural gas to homes and commercial customers). These forms of public provision have, however, been the subject of crit-icism. It is asserted that the state is now so 'big', and its scope so wide, that it is inhibiting private enterprise and, more significantly for the purposes of this chapter, failing to satisfy the criteria of effectiveness, efficiency and responsive-ness to public needs. These criticisms are crystallised in the concept of New Public Management (NPM), a school of thought that has influenced politics not only in Ireland but also in other liberal democracies. A crucial element of NPM is that citizens should be treated by the state as customers; in other words, the ethos of public service providers should be as close as possible to that of the private sector.

The practice of considering citizens as consumers

In Ireland, the practice of dealing with citizens as customers of government departments and as consumers of public services is driven by the Strategic Management Initiative (SMI), which was launched in 1994. The Comptroller and Auditor General Amendment Act, 1993, introduced a statutory require-ment that departments of state be accountable for the effectiveness and value for money of their work, the intention being that they would thereby focus on service quality from the customers' perspective. Accordingly, particular stan-dards of public service are provided for in legislation. The Public Service Management Act, 1997, requires each government department or office to publish a statement of strategy, the guidelines for which include requiring attention to be paid to improving service delivery, and outlining objectives for improving service delivery systems.

Customer Action Plans

It was from this that the Quality Customer Service (QCS) initiative evolved, and was instrumental in turn in the development of Customer Action Plans (CAPs) for each government department and agency. These CAPs are guided by the twelve principles presented in the appendix to this chapter.

It can be seen that departments are required to develop, promote and imple-ment service delivery plans in a wide range of areas, including access, infor-mation, courtesy, choice, consultation and co-ordination. In developing and embedding the QCS principles in public organisation, the government required that a number of key points be addressed in the CAPs, including: the role of consultation; the opportunities presented by eGovernment; the importance of integration; progress reporting and evaluation; and ensuring QCS issues are addressed in statements of strategy and annual reports (DoF 1997).

The most recent set of CAPs, for 2001 to 2004, are viewed as a serious attempt to generate a customer-oriented ethos and to foster customer-focused practices in the public sector. Ongoing research in the field will contribute to deeper analyses of satisfaction with public services. The CAPs reflect a process of debate, research and consensus-seeking among teams of civil servants as they seek improvements in public service design, development and delivery (see, for example, DETE 1997; DJELR 1997). The discipline of preparing the plans hones the management skills of the participants in a way that enhances their overall competence to address changing demands in a changing social environment. With further iterations, the development process in the public service can clearly increase its capability to provide higher-quality service. In particular, evaluating progress against published performance targets forces a degree of rigour and discipline on proceedings.

'Internal customers'

Indicative of a maturing perspective in applying marketing principles to the public sector is one of the newer ones – that of the internal customer – which ensures that 'staff are recognised as internal customers and that they are properly supported and consulted with regard to service delivery issues'. Treating colleagues as co-producers of services that are ultimately delivered to the public enhances integrative approaches. As an early indication of commitment to this particular aspect of QCS, the *Internal Customer Service Plan 2001–2004* of the Department of Social, Community and Family Affairs is deserving of recognition. Presented as a companion to the CAP, it outlines roles and objectives within the Department, and develops commitments of sections to each other (DSCFA 2000).

The principle of consultation in the process of service design and delivery is fundamental to an open and inclusive process. Among the examples of good practice in this area is Revenue (the Office of the Revenue Commissioners), which is the state tax collection body. Along with such formal mechanisms of consultation as the Tax Administration Liaison Committee and the Small Business Users Panel, Revenue also commissions surveys, customer panels and comment cards to elicit feedback from a range of specialist information groups. Similarly, the Department of Social, Community and Family Affairs has involved itself in a comprehensive consultative process in recent years, engaging with a variety of customers via surveys and panels.

Integrating delivery

For those advocating the QCS approach, the importance of setting specific performance indicators and measuring actual performance against them is paramount. For instance, in its CAP the Office of the Civil Service and Local Appointments Commission (CSLAC) provides explicit targets for its activities, the beneficiaries and delivery dates. The publication of such performance indicators is an approach that puts a degree of pressure on the system, but may also portray a confidence in its ability to make progress. As a commitment to integration, the strategy statement 2002–4 of the CSLAC follows through on this approach by breaking strategy into four critical success areas, which then have four distinct programmes that integrate to support the entire service (CSLAC 2001).

The role of eGovernment initiatives in integrating public service delivery will become increasingly relevant and visible. Of all of the complex service delivery tasks facing government, the integration of services across departments and agencies is especially challenging. The traditional functional and vertical structure of the civil service is in stark contrast to the reality of individual citizens' lives. The ideal of a 'boundary-less' public service organisation, where people are not frustrated by having to undergo several interactions with different government departments in pursuit of a single solution to their problem, may be enhanced by information and communication technology applications.

Irish eGovernment initiatives, for example, will adopt a 'Life Events' approach in attempting to develop integrated service delivery. This approach acknowledges that citizens experience events that require them to draw together the services of diversely structured public sector organisations. So, a family expecting a baby would have to access material on maternity and paternity choices and benefits, workplace entitlements, education, vaccination, registration and so on. Information technology developments should also enable integration of services that would make all these contacts simpler and more accessible. Similarly, events involving change of home or job, retirement and health care are recognised in 'bundled', interdisciplinary solutions to the often complex problems that arise in citizens' real lives.

Measuring quality

There is some inconsistency in the quality of the CAPs of the various departments, however. While many plans are realistic and challenging, a few are plainly less demanding and are lacking in sufficient detail to be entirely credible. One government department's proposal in its CAP to consider the installation of automatically opening doors, while possibly laudable in another context, is not what was intended in this field. As the process diffuses through departments, on the other hand, it seems likely that a greater degree of consistency will be evidenced in and between them. An old saying in management is 'what gets measured gets managed'. So, if executives want to prioritise an issue and ensure that it is paid due attention by staff, they should seek to specify it and confirm that progress will be evaluated. Clarity in the specification is critical for appropriate measurement and progress. The setting of performance criteria is an especially problematic area, however, and it is often easy to present performance indicators that are so vague in either construction or articulation as not to be measurable in any meaningful way. But performance evaluation is fundamental – the CAPs require determined commitment to measurement and assessment if service quality is to improve – and this may be addressed in a number of ways. One obvious solution lies in an improvement in the methods of performance measurement; another approach might be to reduce the breadth of criteria requiring measurement and to focus instead on key measures that would clearly assist in promoting improvement overall.

Choosing the appropriate criteria for measuring progress is notoriously more difficult in the public sector than in private sector corporations. However, the latter have long recognised the essential contribution of local-level operations management and staff in the planning and design of performance measures. This is mainly the consequence of having been witness to the deficiencies of headquarter-domiciled planning teams whose lack of experience at the front line resulted in unworkable plans, with the inevitably limited commitment of those required to implement them. In this case, the involvement of public servants at all levels in developing as well as implementing CAPs is similarly crucial to commitment.

Whatever about the difficulties, it seems clear that the QCS initiative, as principally observed through the CAPs of government departments, has the potential to drive the delivery of improved public services to citizens. Importantly, the very process of service design, development and delivery, informed by best practice in the private sector and other public sector contexts, contributes also to a more competent and professional civil service. As the SMI progresses, future CAPs should become more focused and more effective as organisational learning develops.

The problems of considering citizens as consumers

NPM attempts to import private sector, or free market, ideas and principles into the public service domain. The underlying assumption is that managerial technologies provide better outputs than conventional administrative systems, and that the representation of citizens as consumers aids this. However, important problems arise from casting citizens as customers of government departments and as consumers of public services. In the first instance, the clarity of language and terminology in developing the analogy is problematic. Different historical and political understandings of what it is to be a citizen as distinct from being a consumer also give rise to difficulties, as they open up questions of political culture and meaning. The key differences between 'people acting as citizens' and 'people acting as consumers' require attention if the overall delivery process is to be understood. What must ultimately be resolved is the important paradox of the threat to democratic processes of improved public service delivery.

Problems relating to language and terminology

The familiar rhetoric of NPM is rendered acceptable in large part by the ambiguity and uncertainty in its language and terminology: 'How could anyone not want better service?' It is important to recognise, Fountain notes, that 'rhetoric, metaphor and language powerfully affect cognition and action', thereby giving significant status to such management terms as 'success', 'empowerment', 'action', 'results' and so on (2001: 56). The terms 'consumer', 'customer' and 'client' are also used interchangeably in general discussion. The debate on the subject thus tends to feature the idea of citizens consuming public sector services, and so the citizen-as-consumer theme emerges. As is clear from practice in the Irish Civil Service, the CAPs refer to citizens as customers. Humphreys (1998) provides a usefully consistent and straightforward set of terms that aids in clarifying this, as captured in Table 8.1. Traditionally, the 'bureaucratic paternalism' of civil service administration emphasised a professional model in which politicians and professionals refer to users of public services as *clients* or *client groups*. A 'we know best' attitude to the public prevailed, as politicians and officials shared a common perception of the public interest. In such a relationship, the power lies with the *professional* – the client is perceived as the dependent actor, reliant on the professional person.

Table 8.1 *Relationships between the public and the public service*

Description of member of public	The service relationship is strongly shaped by:
Client	The dominance of the client by the *professional*
Customer	The experience of the customer in using the *organisation*
Consumer	The interest of the consumer in *the product or service* provided
Citizen	The concern of the citizen to influence *public decisions* which affect the quality of life

Source: P. C. Humphreys (1998), *Improving Public Service Delivery*, CPMR Discussion Paper No. 7, Dublin: Institute of Public Administration.

Because of the connotations of impotence on the part of the public, the term *client* is now used less frequently, and it has become more popular to refer to the needs of the *customer*. In developing a customer-oriented or customer-responsive public service, the intention is to provide more satisfactory service as a key organisational value. The emphasis shifts from 'the person' to the 'experience of the customer with the *organisation*'. The notion of the citizen as *consumer* focuses on the relationship of the individual with the actual *product* – be it a good or a service. The consumption of the output of the delivery system is the key issue. In the private sector, consumerism connotes influence over the quality and development of services, but the complexities of public service provision make the concept more difficult to conceive of in that context, and more difficult to apply. Finally, while the public as citizens appears in the political literature, the concept is not commonly addressed explicitly by public management theorists.

Humphreys concludes that: 'If citizens can expect as of right certain tangible standards of service from public bodies, so also must the citizen own the responsibility for ensuring that the system that administers them is guided by objective policies aimed at meeting social rather than personal needs' (1998: 19).

Problems relating to political background

In the contemporary climate, people readily and easily perceive themselves as consumers in the economy and in society. But, with the decline in political engagement, as marked by lower voter turnouts at elections in most liberal democracies in recent years, the notion of citizenship has retreated. Citizenship implies a balance of rights and duties, and the necessity to argue a case and engage with the views of others. As active members of communities, citizens are obliged to defer to the will of the majority, and even to defend views they may not themselves hold dear. Consumers, in contrast, need not be members of a community and do not have to act on its behalf (Gabriel and Lang 1995). They operate in isolation and may make choices, unburdened by social obligation. Historically, then, the two ideas have very different pedigrees.

While the concepts of 'citizen' and 'consumer' are different, what involves them in the convergent discourse in this case is the political background. Gabriel and Lang (1995) describe how political actors attempt to recast each in different directions, depending on the underlying ideology. The political left has generally sought to stretch the idea of the consumer in the direction of citizen, and the right has usually attempted to transform the citizen into a consumer. Having lost faith in the right-wing economists' notion of the 'consumer as hero', the left has sought to enlarge the consumer into a *responsible* consumer, one who thinks ahead and tempers his or her desires by social awareness, and who must occasionally sacrifice personal pleasure to community wellbeing. 'The Right, on the other hand, has sought to incorporate the citizens into its image of the consumer by using the spurious concept of "votes" and "ballots"' (1995: 176). So, citizens 'vote' in the marketplace, which becomes a surrogate for political discourse or engagement. In terms of understanding current complications in dealing with citizens as consumers, a sense of the historical and political background goes some way towards explaining fundamental differences between them. Such perspectives are deep-rooted.

Problems relating to differences between citizens and consumers

Whether or not individuals are consciously aware of their various roles in society, they act as both citizen and consumer simultaneously. Where that situation becomes problematic, both for the person and for the institutions of state, is where there are clashes between them. There is a tension between the market's primary view of the individual as a consumer and the state's view of that same individual as a citizen. Ryan (2001) outlines a number of the problems in this area. First is the distinctly political problem of redefining the nature of the relationship between the government and the public. That is, as citizens come to be regarded mainly as consumers of public services, the relationship between the state and the people becomes one of a passive commercial transaction rather than one of active political engagement. The government and its agents may come to see themselves as independent of their public 'customers'. The public duties and responsibilities of citizens begin to take second place to the rights and complaints of consumers. In a way, this mirrors the separation of public administration and politics so central to NPM, a consequence of which is that government becomes protected from the political demands of society.

The second problem involves the emphasis on the sovereignty of the individual over public welfare. Consumer sovereignty naturally elevates the individual's preferences, whereas public governance must prioritise collective interests. Similarly, collective payment for services in the public domain through taxation requires that the consumers of services are not perceived or treated as more important than other stakeholders. In other words, citizens have a right to be consulted about, say, the provision of higher education even if they are not themselves 'consumers' of it.

The limitations of effectively contrived markets in the public sector constitute the third main problem in the notion of citizens as consumers. There is no competitive dimension to many areas of public service provision, thus making any analogy with markets somewhat suspect. An important difference between the private and public sectors is that customer satisfaction management assumes that customers know their preferences. In respect of complex policy issues, people may not be well informed; and 'experts' may indeed know better than the population at large – something that raises fundamental questions of representation and trusteeship.

Finally, the assumption that markets result in the mutual satisfaction of buyer and supplier is questionable in the public sector, where the preferences of the two often diverge widely. Challenges to the theoretical basis of public goods markets arise because of their differences from private markets. In the public arena, the simplistic assumption of *voluntary* relationships does not hold, as people play the roles of recipients, co-producers, performance supervisors, funders and so on. Ultimately, to put it another way, the market model implies that the production of public services is a technical rather than a political process – as the more traditional view would have it.

Problems related to the paradox of customer service in the public sector

There are dangers in the idea that providing public services can be reduced to production and operations modelling. Notwithstanding the clear improvements to service design and delivery attributable to scientific management techniques, such a view may further reduce the sense that public service delivery is a political process at heart. The term 'running government like a business' suggests that public managers regard citizens as customers to be served, rather than citizens who govern themselves through collective processes.

Public administrators continue to use management tools to make their 'customers' more satisfied with businesslike government. In so doing, however, those managers may become less accountable to the public who are losing control over administration. For instance, in a managerial system, public managers would be able to retain or carry over part of their budget for discretionary spending. This is a 'progressive' situation in management terms, because it enables flexibility to changing conditions, promotes frugality and removes political influence. The assumption is that good administrators are bound always to use public money in the public's interest. However, the strict budgeting associated with the public sector is designed to avoid problems of financial abuse; in other words, to ensure that money is spent exactly as the politicians and electors intended. The issue here is accountability – one that ranks extremely highly in the public service and political arenas.

The design of public service delivery channels is particularly complex. Mass processing approaches often require that bureaucrats retain some minor measure of discretion. But discretion that would be viewed positively in private sector or commercial scenarios might be seen as (and might indeed be applied as) permitting favouritism, and/or the stereotyping of certain groups of citizens. Such solutions to discretionary problems could thus produce outcomes biased on grounds of nationality, gender, class and so on – in which case the paradox arises that the increased empowerment of public servants results in greater problems of delivery and, consequently, reduced levels of service quality to at least some of the customers concerned. The critical gap between public servants and the political process is captured in Fountain's question: 'When public servants are encouraged to "listen to the customer", what arrangements will ensure that they listen to those customers less able to exercise voice, who cannot or do not express their preferences well or clearly, and who may receive poorer quality service if greater discretion is given to frontline personnel?' (2001: 65).

With the separation of politics and administration, politicians may withdraw from direct and frequent involvement in administration, thereby allowing the power of professional bureaucrats to increase. Whether this transition will happen in Ireland more slowly than might be the case elsewhere – if indeed it happens at all – will depend on the decline of what has come to be known as 'clientelism'; for a distinctive feature of Irish political culture has long been the very active role played by politicians as customer or consumer advocates. Various studies have revealed a strong tendency for citizens to channel not just *complaints* about public services but also non-controversial *requests* for a public service, to which they are entitled as of right, through a local Teachta Dála (TD, or Member of Pparliament). Matters of social welfare, housing and medical entitlements dominate the case loads of TDs, and in many cases the TD does little more than transmit the constituent's request to the department or agency concerned.

Clientelism must contribute at least some extent to the improvement of the workings of the state machinery and to ensuring better managerial decisions for the future; and it can hardly be denied that it must also constrain any tendency for the power of the professional bureaucrats involved to increase. However, the evidence from case studies offers a picture of 'brokerage' by politicians that is low key and routine, and major decisions on the allocation of funds are not involved. Rather the politician is like 'a lawyer, who operates not by bribing the judge, but by ensuring that the case is presented better than the citizen would be able to present it' (Gallagher and Komito 1992: 140). We may none the less conclude, in general terms, that greater attention to customer service approaches borrowed from the private sector, in which the citizen is regarded as a customer or consumer, may have negative consequences for democratic processes, and can damage the overall quality of public service in the long run. Market-driven managerialism is primarily based on happy customers rather than involved citizens.

Allied to this perspective is the increase in the application of marketing and market research technologies in public service delivery. Although various research and satisfaction measures do provide opportunities for the public to participate in information and feedback for government agencies, for all their ostensibly empathetic and concerned appearances, it may be that focus groups, surveys and other market research applications actually serve to keep the public at a distance. Market research utilisation may give the appearance of choice, but fail to address the question of real political engagement that results in informed governance. Indeed, it has been argued that the use of market research tools in citizen involvement processes is as much about placation as about information and consultation. The impact initially is on the democratic process, but ultimately on the quality of public services. Notwithstanding the contributions of private sector management technologies to the quality of service delivery in the public sector, there is an onus on researchers in the field to observe the wider consequences.

The prospects for considering citizens as consumers

The public service is a continual subject of criticism. Because public services are generally redistributive, some sections of the community will be prone to view themselves as net contributors and demand greater economy. This outlook is buttressed by the tendency to undervalue general services from which everyone benefits, such as security or infrastructural assets, and to underestimate the costs of additional specific services to oneself, like providing a grant for a local water scheme or keeping open a community hospital. Furthermore, all public services must be rationed in some way – if not through pricing, then by waiting lists and prioritising by public servants such as social workers, hospital doctors and bureaucrats. Inevitably, some individuals or communities will feel that their claims on the public service are being afforded too little priority. NPM has not solved these dilemmas in Ireland any more than elsewhere.

What marks off the NPM critique from others is its focus not alone on the service provided but also on the form of its provision. NPM has also been more persistent than earlier reform movements and has been sustained by a form of neo-liberal economics that has had an influence on how the state itself is perceived globally. Even if the pace of NPM reforms wanes, its impact will be profound. As in other Western states, no Irish political party advocates increased state provision on the scale that once seemed to offer the solution to all major political problems. Hardly conceivable some years ago, for example, toll roads, student loans, public–private partnerships in capital investment, and polluter-pays schemes are all prominent items on the political agenda. Left-wing political parties continue to offer redistributive policies but now eschew direct state provision on a large scale. Their opponents look to facilitating private provision and emphasise personal responsibility. In the catch-phrase of Osborne and Gaebler (1993), the American NPM gurus, the state should be 'steering but not rowing'. It is clear, then, that some element of the citizen as customer will remain a feature of Irish public services. None the less, the older values of *liberté, egalité* and *fraternité* inherited from the French Revolution idea of citizenship are unlikely to be extinguished, even if they need to be reformulated. As an issue in Irish politics today, however, the concept of the 'new citizenship' will retain a powerful appeal.

Appendix: principles guiding Civil Service Customer Action Plans

In their dealings with the public, Civil Service Departments and Public Service offices will act as follows

Quality service standards
Publish a statement which outlines the nature and quality of service which customers can legitimately expect and display it prominently at the point of service delivery.

Equality/diversity
Ensure the rights to equal treatment established by equality legislation, and accommodate diversity, so as to contribute to equality for the groups covered by the legislation (on the grounds of gender, marital status, family status, sexual orientation, religious belief, age, disability, race and membership of the Travelling Community). Identify and work to eliminate barriers to access to services for people experiencing poverty and social exclusion, and for those facing geographic barriers to services.

Physical access
Provide clean, accessible public offices which ensure privacy, comply with occupational and safety standards and facilitate access for people with disabilities and others with specific needs.

Information
Take a proactive approach in providing information that is clear, timely, accurate, is available at all points of contact, and meets the needs of people with disabilities. Ensure that the potential offered by Information Technology is fully availed of and that the information available on public service websites follows the guidelines on web publication. Continue the drive for simplification of rules, regulations, forms, information leaflets and procedures.

Timeliness and courtesy
Deliver services with courtesy and minimum delay, fostering a climate of mutual respect between provider and customer. Give contact names in all communications to ensure ease of ongoing transactions.

Complaints
Maintain a well-publicised, accessible, transparent and simple-to-use system of dealing with complaints about the quality of services provided.

Appeals
Similarly, maintain a formalised, well-publicised, accessible, transparent and simple-to-use system of appeal/review for customers who are dissatisfied with decisions in relation to services.

Consultation and evaluation
Provide a structured approach to meaningful consultation with, and participation by, the customer in relation to the development, delivery, and review of services. Ensure meaningful evaluation of service delivery.

Choice
Provide choice, where feasible, in service delivery including payment methods, location of contact points, opening hours and delivery times. Use available and emerging technologies to ensure maximum access and choice, and quality of delivery.

Official languages equality
Provide services through Irish and/or bilingually and inform customers of their right to choose to be dealt with through one or other of the official languages.

Seirbhísí cáilíochta a sholáthar trí Ghaeilge agus/nó go dátheangach agus custaiméirí a chur ar an eolas faoina gceart an rogha a bheith acu go ndéileálfaí leo trí cheann do na teangacha oifigiúla.

Better co-ordination
Foster a more co-ordinated and integrated approach to delivery of public services.

Internal customer
Ensure staff are recognised as internal customers and that they are properly supported and consulted with regard to service delivery issues.

Source: Government of Ireland (1997), *Principles of Quality Customer Service for Customers and Clients of the Civil Service*, Dublin: Stationery Office.

References

CSLAC (Civil Service and Local Appointments Commission) (2001), *Strategy Statement 2002–2004*, Dublin: Civil Service and Local Appointments Commission.

DETE (Department of Enterprise, Trade and Employment) (1997), *Customer Service Plan*, Dublin: Department of Enterprise, Trade and Employment.

DJELR (Department of Justice, Equality and Law Reform) (1997), *Customer Service Action Plan*, Dublin: Department of Justice, Equality and Law Reform.

DoF (Department of Finance) (1997), *Quality Customer Service Standards*, Dublin: Department of Finance/Stationery Office.

DSCFA (Department of Social, Community and Family Affairs) (2000), *Internal Customer Service Plan 2001–2004*, Dublin: Department of Social, Community and Family Affairs.

Fountain, J. E. (2001), 'Paradoxes of Public Sector Customer Service', *Governance: An International Journal of Policy and Administration*, Vol. 14, No. 1, pp. 55–73.

Gabriel, Y. and Lang, T. (1995), *The Unmanageable Consumer: Contemporary Consumption and its Fragmentation*, London: Sage.

Gallagher, M. and Komito, L. (1992), 'Dáil Deputies and their Constituency Work', in J. Coakley and M. Gallagher (eds), *Politics in the Republic of Ireland*, Galway: PSAI.

Government of Ireland (1997), *Principles of Quality Customer Service for Customers and Clients of the Civil Service*, Dublin: Stationery Office.

Humphries, P. C. (1998), *Improving Public Service Delivery*, CPMR Discussion Paper No. 7, Dublin: Institute of Public Administration.

Osborne, D. and Gaebler, T. (1993), *Reinventing Government: How the Entrepreneurial Spirit is Transforming the Public Sector*, Reading MA: Addison-Wesley.

Ryan, N. (2001) 'Reconstructing Citizens as Consumers: Implications for New Modes of Governance', *Australian Journal of Public Administration*, Vol. 60, No. 3, pp. 104–9.

Further reading

CGS (Co-ordinating Group of Secretaries) (1996), *A Programme of Change for the Irish Civil Service*, Dublin: Co-ordinating Group of Secretaries.

Common, R., Flynn, N. and Mellon, E. (1992), *Managing Public Services: Competition and Decentralisation*, Oxford: Butterworth-Heinemann.

McNamara, T. (ed.) (1995), 'Strategic Management in the Irish Civil Service: a Review Drawing on Experience in New Zealand and Australia', *Administration*, Vol. 43, No. 2, pp. 1–153.

Porter, M. (1990), *The Competitive Advantage of Nations*, New York: Free Press.

Potter, J. (1988), 'Consumerism and the Public Sector: How Well does the Coat Fit?', *Public Administration*, Vol. 66, pp. 49–164.

Smith, P. (1993), 'Outcome-Related Performance Indicators and Organisational Control in the Public Sector', *British Journal of Management*, Vol. 4, pp. 135–51.

Walsh, K. (1995), *Public Services and Market Mechanisms: Competition, Contracting and the New Public Management*, Basingstoke: Macmillan.

9

The challenges of
science and technology policy

Séamus Ó Tuama

Introduction

We live in the age of the technological citizen. This is a period in which science and technology have not only come to play a predominant part in shaping our everyday lives, even to the point of challenging us as citizens in ways previously unimaginable; they are also giving rise to serious problems of regulation and control, or what is today called governance.

This historical turn has been in gestation since the seventeenth-century institutionalisation of science, and of the revolutions in chemistry, biology and physics in the following centuries; but it has taken on the scope, complexity and dynamism we associate with it today only since science and technology became the lead forces in the development of production, particularly after World War II. The most recent phase in the advance of science and technology centres on radical developments in microbiology, microelectronics and microphysics; and the advance is one not just of scale, but also of depth. We see evidence of scale in the ability to explore other planets, to unleash weapons of mass destruction, perhaps even up to the level of planetary annihilation, and to deliver electronic messages around the globe in seconds. Evidence of depth is to be found in the ability to decode the genetic material of an organism, to clone complex mammals and to genetically modify a range of organisms, as well as in the emergence of nanotechnology.[1] That contemporary technology is complex is not in question. Indeed, it is has to be accepted that large technological installations – for instance, a nuclear power plant – cannot be scientifically tested before construction, and that that testing has to await the assembly of the multitude of components. Moreover, systems have become so intricate and their effects so unpredictable that accidents, as Perrow (1999) argues, have become a normal feature of the contemporary world. The rapidity with which complex technology is changing is illustrated by a simple example: the computer used a few decades ago in the lunar module of the United States Apollo space exploration programme had roughly the same capacity as the SIM card used in contemporary cellular or mobile tele-phones.

Advances such as these do not just change our physical reality, but also have an impact on the social and political circumstances in which we exist. The invention of the printing press did not just make printing easier and more efficient, it made books and pamphlets cheaper and more widely available too. The printing press also made possible rapid advances in science by permitting the sharing of information and concepts, and by breaking down barriers to the creation of a scientific community – a group of scientists with common values, common approaches and common methods. As well, printing helped to democ-ratise information, knowledge and culture; it reshaped the way politics was conducted in Europe, and ultimately changed the political order of the conti-nent. At the same time, however, printing also gave rise to questions about the regulation and control of the flow of information.

Today, many compare the advent of the Internet with the invention of the printing press. Only history will be able to judge the accuracy of that compari-son; however, the Internet has had an impact on time-space relations to do with the immediacy and the distance over which the sharing of information and communication can take place, at a level impossible prior to its widespread availability. And in its wake follows a series of problems for the architects of science and technology policy: child pornography, nuclear safety, arms devel-opment, the modification of genetic inheritance and cloning, and (not least) the exclusion of billions from access to this new communications medium.

Concern about issues such as these is not of course confined to Ireland, and this makes necessary a few preliminary points. Firstly, much of the debate and discussion on the governance of science and technology is more vibrant *across* borders than *within* them. The analysis here has, therefore, to balance the uni-versal and the particular context of Ireland. Secondly, the issues raised are impor-tant in terms of cause (problems emanating from science and technology), means (process: democratic engagement and policy formation) and ends (consequences: contingency and risk). I propose to carry the discussion forward on all three fronts. There are none the less certain aspects of the framing and governance of science and technology policy that are particular to Ireland, and will deserve our special attention, among them perceptions of 'expertise', how we deal with issues of public concern, and how we might better approach the broader issues at the heart of the governance of science and technology. In the final section I will also attempt an overview of Irish policy-making, and of the performance of science and technology both as an innovator and as a generator of employment.

The governance of science and technology

Debate about the governance of science and technology increased considerably during the latter half of the twentieth century, and it continues today. While the debate tends to be focused on the definition of the problem of the governance of science and technology and its potential solution, it admits a range of distinct perspectives. Analysis of the debate makes clear that *how* the problem is perceived shapes the proposed solution, but given the differences in perspective it becomes equally apparent that the search for a fixed and final approach to governance and policy formation would be a futile one.

Perrow (1999) presents a compelling commentary on the kinds of risks inherent in complex science and technology systems. He uses phrases like 'normal accidents', and refers to the potential for accidents in design, equipment, procedures, operators, supplies and environment. The notion of 'normal accidents' arises from the fact that accidents are not extraordinary but commonplace. Perrow says 'accidents and, thus, potential catastrophes are inevitable in complex, tightly coupled systems, with lethal possibilities' (1999: 354). Such is the complexity and interdependence of systems that an accident in one system can easily lead to problems in a closely connected one; for instance, a telephone breakdown will affect the electronic information network, which will in turn lead to problems in the financial services sector. It needs to be stressed that while accidents are commonplace this does not mean that they always or necessarily lead to 'lethal possibilities'.

For Zimmerman (1995) too the core issue resides in the very nature of the 'large-scale complex systems' that control science and technology. He claims that these systems generate their own steering functions, and make decisions about risk that once might have been within the remit of the politics of constitutional states; the effect is to grant a core element of governance to 'some of the most significant and powerful institutions of our time' (1995: 86). He believes that a lack of democratic structures to deal with this question allows the technological systems to emerge as *de facto* political systems. Indeed, he makes points about science and technology that are similar to those made by the philosophers John Locke and Jean-Jacques Rousseau about pre-liberal society, seeing a tyranny emerging out of the impotence of the citizen in the face of a weakened polity. The technological complex – the web of people, ideas and structures associated with technology and its development – is free to proceed without an external democratic steering mechanism. The stakes are high, both positively (in terms of potential benefits for society) and negatively (as regards the potential risks for society). The key point is that the problems are not being adequately comprehended by citizens. Zimmerman insists that this imposition of risk on citizens 'without even their tacit consent is undeniably an act of tyranny' (1995: 92).

One attempt to govern science and technology is described as a 'tightly coupled' approach. Proponents of this hold that to be able to deal with the complexity of these systems, it is best to operate in a closed environment – almost in laboratory conditions. Here you try to minimise extraneous factors, minimise interference (including that of public opinion) and apply the best minds to the issues in a controlled and concentrated way. Issues are dealt with sequentially, using the best information and knowledge available, and deploying expertise efficiently and effectively. One should then reach some rational conclusions, which will form the basis of policy advice, enabling movement towards policy formulation and eventually implementation. Bohman (1996) uses the terms 'hypercomplexity' and 'hyperrationality' to frame the identified problem as well as the solution. By hypercomplexity he means the web of interconnected issues; for instance, ecological risk, globalisation, food- and water-supply difficulties, population pressures and worldwide crime. Hyperrationality is another way to describe a tightly coupled decision-making system. The basic idea is to apply maximum effort to solving the problem in a controlled environment, on the assumption that this will be more effective and efficient than public deliberation.

Sclove (1995) is unhappy with the assumptions underlying this type of approach. He argues that technological development needs to be addressed through posing 'appropriate questions'. His contention is that 'technology is implicated in perpetuating anti-democratic power relations and in eroding social contexts for developing and expressing citizenship' (1995: 7). Further, many of the negative and unforeseen consequences of technology have arisen precisely because we have been unable to ask, or did not realise that we should have been asking, questions aimed directly at the social aspects of technology. His conclusions are echoed in the European Commission report *Late Lessons from Early Warnings* (EEA 2001), which lists twelve significant problems related to science and technology that arose because appropriate questions were not asked. The problems identified were related to fisheries, nuclear radiation, benzene, asbestos, polychlorinated biphenyls (PCBs), halocarbon damage to the ozone layer, the link between pre-natal exposure to the synthetic oestrogen diethylotilboestrol (DES) and vaginal cancer, the use of antimicrobials (often referred to as antibiotics) in food production, sulphur dioxide, methyltert-butyl ether (MTBE) as a lead substitute in high octane petrol or gasoline, contamination of the North American Great Lakes, hormone growth promoters, and bovine spongiform encephalopathy (BSE, or 'mad cow disease').

Appropriate questions can be very simple. Is this the best way to solve problem x? Are there alternatives to technology y that may be more appropriate? Should we address problem z first? Perrow (1999) highlights the simple question of 'externalities': what are the associated but sometimes hidden costs of a certain course of action? Taking electricity generation as an example, the cost of externalities like dealing with waste from nuclear plants or the pollution from fossil fuel plants were not anticipated. Had such a question been asked about nuclear plants in the beginning, they might never have been developed (Perrow 1999: 341).

Beck's view of things is that 'progress replaces voting' (1992: 184). He suggests that there is a role reversal between 'the political' and the 'non-political'; while democratic constitutions remain in place 'the political system is being threatened with *disempowerment*' (1992: 187). He anticipates a 'ghostlike' polity, which can no longer make the important decisions on the direction, scope, risk or endangerment of the advances in science and technology that are shaping society. These decisions are being made in a non-political realm, and according to purely techno-economic imperatives.

Democratic engagement and policy formation

Fuller (2000) gives us a useful analytical starting point from which to address democratic engagement. He distinguishes three political perspectives that play a leading role in the debate about the governance of science: communitarianism,[2] liberalism and republicanism. The communitarian perspective, according to him, suffers from problems of 'political correctness' and a tendency to make a direct and uncritical link between research and policy. As regards liberalism, he identifies the central problem as arising from the confusion of the idea of the 'free market' with the idea of 'free inquiry', which has very serious consequences for the scientific community as it impacts, for instance, on the role of the university: is learning to be controlled by markets rather than a spirit of inquiry? For Fuller, the republican approach offers the potential to move beyond the sorts of problems that arise from the other two perspectives. The basis of his claim rests on three fundamental republican precepts:

- that opinion changes for the better may arise from hearing other views;
- that people should not materially fear the consequence of voicing their opinions; and
- that people can recognise a public good over their own individual or group interests.

It hardly needs rehearsing that the ideas discussed here have been in contention in political thought over a considerable period – arguably from Plato and Aristotle, through Rousseau and Immanuel Kant, right up until today.[3] Traditionally, Ireland would have found itself in the communitarian camp; however, more recently that became infused with a stronger sense of liberalism, emerging both from the changing international political climate since the 1970s, and domestically, in particular, through the influence of the Progressive Democrats (PDs), the political party formed in the late 1980s with a neo-liberal economic agenda.

A model of political participation

Using the republican framework provided by Fuller as a basis, we will try to weave a model of political participation that could serve in the Irish context to deal with both opinion and policy formation on science and technology issues. The elements that will be drawn into the model represent not a single unified political canon but a number of different political orientations. In that regard the model is experimental rather than definitive.

Included will be Frankenfeld's (1992) technological citizenship, which, while oriented more towards a liberal perspective than Fuller would have it, provides the outline of a participative rights model that is essential for the operation of a republican approach. We will also introduce discussion of new social movements (Eyerman and Jamison 1991), in tandem with the concept of 'organic government' by Burns (1999), to illustrate the changing political landscape in which this discussion takes place. Strydom (1999) and Jonas (1982) will add a moral, 'responsibility' dimension. And Habermas's (1992) theory of communicative action will provide the outline of some rules of practical engagement.

The republican model proposes engaging the citizen actively and concretely in the decision-making process in a way not circumscribed by traditional notions of democracy, or confined to formal institutions. Frankenfeld (1992) considers how the citizen might gain a greater grip on the process of governing science and technology policy and simultaneously pursue the good life (the central objective of all the great emancipatory ideologies). He proposes what he calls 'Technological Citizenship', as a way of refocusing how we understand citizenship in the liberal democratic tradition to which Ireland belongs. His model would almost certainly require changes to what is effectively the Bill of Rights contained in Bunreacht na hÉireann (the Irish Constitution). He calls for a new social contract with the citizenry, one where four key rights would be incorporated: a right to knowledge or information; a right to participation; guarantees of informed consent; and a limitation on the total amount of endangerment that citizens will be exposed to.

On the face of it, some of these rights already exist, but they are not elaborated or understood in Frankenfeld's terms. A right to knowledge or information would in many cases conflict with liberal intellectual property rights, designed to allow for patenting and the protection of trade secrets. The right to participation would often be at odds with liberal understandings of corporate governance and the role of shareholders vis-à-vis the public – an issue increasingly evident at corporate annual shareholder meetings.

A guarantee of 'informed consent' is at the heart of the dispute at the World Trade Organisation (WTO) between the European Union (EU) and the US on how the presence of genetically modified (GM) ingredients in food should be communicated to consumers. The US Food and Drug Administration does not require food labels to indicate the presence of GM ingredients. The EU, on the other hand, does not have a uniform labelling scheme for GM foods, but is endeavouring to introduce one so as to give consumers the ability to make informed choices. However, at the core of the dispute is an EU moratorium on imports of GM food products, put in place in 1998 in response to consumer fears of the possible health risks. The US says there is no scientific proof that GM foods represent any risk to health, and wishes to have free access to the EU market.

Limiting the total amount of endangerment to personal safety is an incredibly complex issue, even if it seems fundamental that citizens should be protected from danger. Does a 'right' to protection cover the whole cocktail of issues addressed by various social movements, interest groups and lobbying bodies in Ireland in the past? In sum, Frankenfeld's technological citizenship proposes a different power relation between the science and technology complex and ordinary citizens: 'a set of binding, equal rights and obligations that are intended to reconcile technology's unlimited potentials for human benefit and ennoblement with its unlimited potentials for human injury, tyrannization, and degradation' (Frankenfeld 1992: 462).

Changing the relationship between citizens and various power and economic structures has been a concern of social movements in all developed countries. These movements create political contexts in which new issues can be articulated and debated. Eyerman and Jamison point out that these issues do not arise in all contexts and around all issues of contention. These researchers identify the catalysts that lead to the emergence of a social movement as: political opportunity; an issue; and an opportunity for communication about the issue, allowing both articulation and the dissemination of knowledge (1991: 56).

But it is 'cognitive praxis' – a process of collective learning or collective knowledge production – which marks out social movements as key actors on the political stage. Social movements, like the trade unions, the suffragettes, and the Irish language revivalists of the late nineteenth and early twentieth centuries, have always challenged existing knowledge, expertise and political practices, and thus introduce a new dynamic into the public sphere. The 'new social movements' – the women's movement, the environmental movement and the various civil rights movements are among the more prominent of these recently – have all played a significant part in reshaping the way society deals with certain issues. Environmental social movements, for instance, have changed the way ecological issues are understood and discussed. In the process they have challenged scientific certainty and extended the sphere of public interest on many issues; and they have often drawn experts, including scientists, politicians and policy-makers, on to unfamiliar ground. Ireland has seen new social movements engage on science and technology issues like the location of electricity power lines, waste incinerators, mobile phone masts and new roads, as well as blood product contamination, water fluoridation, child immunisation, exhaust emissions, food safety and nuclear waste.

For Burns (1999), this changing political landscape has led to the emergence of a diverse range of new social actors in the process of governance. This in turn poses a serious challenge to parliaments and governments, but it equally offers dynamic possibilities for addressing issues that cannot easily be handled from the centre. In this new context, Burns proposes that attempts at central steering, regulating and monitoring a system like the science and technology complex are 'utopian and destined to fail' (1999: 170). He holds that both governments and parliaments are overloaded by the demands of 'scientification' – the demands posed by the increase in both the number and complexity of issues arising through advances in science and technology. These challenges cannot easily be overcome by constitutional arrangements. He identifies three deficits or deficiencies:

- *representation deficit*: the inability to span the representative challenges of an increasingly diverse and complex world;
- *knowledge and competence deficit*: the incapacity to master the range of technical and specialist knowledge demanded in decision-making; and
- *deficit of commitment or engagement*: a lack of interest in some issues presented for decision on the part of representatives who have a general spectrum of interests.

To this one might add:

- *single interest deficit*: the election of single interest representatives of the type that have joined the Dáil recently (on issues as varied as the availability or otherwise of access to British television stations, downgrading of local hospitals and local economic development); and
- *tied identity deficit*: the espousal of closed regional, ethnic, national and/or religious identities as a primary focus, which would fairly obviously include some candidates and parties presenting for election in both Northern Ireland and the Republic.

'Responsibility' is a key dimension of the model being put forward here. Strydom (1999) proposes that responsibility occupies the space vacated by debates around 'rights' in the early modern period, and by 'justice' in the twentieth century. It also rebalances a deficiency in much discussion on rights in the Anglophone world, where the concept of responsibility or obligation has carried negative connotations. This contrasts, say, with a Kantian view, in which obligation is an inherent and essential dimension of rights theory.

The increased awareness of the role of responsibility is connected to two things: firstly, to the increase in risk and in the uncertainty and unpredictability of life, arising from a complexity of factors, including those arising through science and technology; and secondly, to the ability of social movements to remould traditional ways of dealing with issues, by framing discussion on them in terms of responsibility. Jonas puts this kind of responsibility in context by noting that technology is the exclusive responsibility of humans, but that its capacity to impact on humanity and progressively all other life forms on the planet is ever increasing (1982). For him, responsibility increases with power, and science and technology's capacity for both global and intergenerational damage (that is, the fact that some hazards like nuclear waste and the genetic modification of organisms will persist for many generations) demands a response that is more than ambivalence. Responsibility, then, goes beyond caring purely for the rights of fellow humans, and is also concerned with the exploitation of the planet for the preservation of humanity. Human good must be balanced against the good of all life on the planet.

Understanding of the implications of responsibility is considerably deepened by reference to Strydom's concept of *co*-responsibility. Co-responsibility pertains to individuals as members of a collectivity, based on communication and co-operation, and emerges only through a network of communication at formal and informal levels. Framed like this, responsibility is both a moral imperative and a practical tool for discussion, debate and decision-making. As a practical tool for action it places limits on how both individuals *qua* individuals, and individuals as part of collectivities, may legitimately act. This has implications, for instance, for how individual members of corporate boards or government cabinets articulate positions and make decisions. It also has implications for ordinary people in their day-to-day activities and decision-making, as they too have responsibilities. It puts the idea of a 'whistle-blower' in a different context, since the republican model offers much clearer scope for individual expression of opinion, coupled with protection from the material consequences of expressing a point of view.[4]

Habermas's long-term project of communicative action dovetails with the discussion on responsibility. He proposes a model of communicative discourse or practical discourse, which is different from everyday discourse. Communicative discourse is a reflexive process that is rational, dependable and consistent. He lays down three basic rules that must be followed in order to achieve these goals. They loosely correspond to Aristotle's three-fold distinction between rhetoric, dialectic and logic:

- *rhetoric*: argument is addressed to a universal audience and must be mutually understood; everyone must speak the same natural language; meaning must be clear to both speaker and listener; speakers do not contradict themselves;
- *dialectic*: argument is directed towards attaining rationality; speakers seek agreement; they only articulate and support what they believe; all parties respect these intentions in other participants;
- *logic*: argument here proceeds on the basis that only the force of the better argument should be used to persuade; no external or strategic actions should be deployed; a rational basis is used to establish validity claims.

The model presented in this section attempts to recognise the changing dynamic of political engagement in contemporary society, including concerns about rights to participate and influence decisions, the appreciation of the centrality of responsibility, and the diverging imperatives of risk on one side and the prospects of the good life on the other.

The precautionary principle

Prudence or precaution is a necessary condition for animal survival. One might therefore expect the 'precautionary principle' to play a major part in policy formation in Ireland and elsewhere. Part of the reason that it has not done so relates to the political and cultural construction of the problem being addressed. The precautionary principle draws on a culture of political responsibility, while much of what is called 'progress' or 'development' is seen to be about no more than making rational economic choices. The same dichotomy can be summarised in the following opposing positions:

- *precautionary principle orientation*: evidence of hazard has emerged which is being linked to activity x. It is prudent to desist from activity x, even if cause and effect are not absolutely confirmed. We cannot await conclusive proof, as the consequences may be grave and/or irreversible.
- *economic rational choice orientation*: evidence of hazard has emerged which is being linked to activity x. Scientific evidence of cause and effect is inconclusive or contradictory. While the putative harm could be great, there is certainty that activity x is economically important. It is prudent therefore to continue with activity x until the scientific evidence is absolutely conclusive.

Ireland is a party to several international environmental treaties that incorporate the precautionary principle; however, it has not yet either signed or ratified a number of important agreements, including the path-breaking Convention on the Conservation of Antarctic Marine Living Resources (CCAMLR), an international convention signed in 1982 to protect and conserve the Antarctic marine ecosystem.

Indeed Ireland, as Trouwborst (2002) demonstrates, is not always as assiduous as other EU member states in terms of signing and ratifying such agreements. Nor is it among the countries that have pioneered the integration of the precautionary principle into domestic law. Trouwborst holds that a tight, almost symbiotic link connects the concepts of sustainability (that use of a commodity will not eventually eliminate its availability) and intergenerational equity (concern and responsibility for future generations) with the precautionary principle. He goes on to identify five countries – Iran, India, Brazil, Namibia and Papua New Guinea – that include intergenerational equity in their constitutions; and he reports that up to fifty states, including Ireland's fellow EU member Spain, have recognition within their constitutions of the right to a safe and healthy environment. Although Ireland has had two constitutional referendums on the 'right to life' (whether abortion should be permissible or prohibited), considerable public debate on environmental risk (encompassing a nuclear waste dispute with Britain), and serious public concern about Ireland's neutrality (or involvement in any military alliance), the possible inclusion of the precautionary principle in Bunreacht na hÉireann has not been a matter of political debate.

However, in its submission to the UK public inquiry into the Nirex radioactive waste facilities in Cumbria, the Irish government made explicit appeal to the precautionary principle (DTEC 1996). This opens up four very important policy issues. Firstly, Ireland's case was essentially that Britain had a legal obligation to deal with this issue in keeping with the precautionary principle. The implication is that Ireland (or any sovereign state or, by extension, groups or individuals) should have a right to fair treatment in accordance with the precautionary principle, and that this should be recognised and enforceable under international law. There is of course some distance between making a case and achieving universal applicability, but we ought to see the raising of the issue as an extremely important barometer of the status of the precautionary principle, and a pointer to its possible role in the future. The second policy point arising from this case is that the endorsement of the precautionary principle by the Irish government in its own case should mean recognition of its application not just internationally, but also to environmental policy at home. The third point relates to the onus of proof; it is that the precautionary principle pushes the onus of proof onto the proposers of a facility thought to represent a threat. In other words, the Irish side claimed the facility had the potential to cause serious detrimental impact on the Irish environment; it was up to British Nuclear Fuels Ltd, the custodians of the Nirex plant, to prove it would *not* cause pollution. If they could not do that, then the precautionary principle would hold that the project should not proceed (for further discussion, see EEA 2001). Fourthly, Ireland's deployment of the precautionary principle is an obvious endorsement of the importance of the concept of responsibility in public policy.

Responsibility and rational choice do not make comfortable bedfellows. Ireland, like many Western democracies, is caught in that dilemma. On one side it is being drawn into the international discourse on risk and responsibility, and on the other it is attempting to hold a pragmatic rational-choice position to maximise perceived national interest both politically and economically. That has implications for all areas of policy, not just science and technology – as the debate about the use by the US military of Irish airport facilities at Shannon around the Second Gulf War in 2003 vividly demonstrated. Commentators and politicians expended a lot of words attempting to balance matters of 'principle' (Ireland being an ostensibly neutral country) with 'Ireland's economic interests' (as the location of a huge amount of US industrial investment).

The role of expertise

The idea of expertise and its contribution to the policy-making process has become something of a battleground. As discussed earlier, society has undergone major changes since the middle of the twentieth century, but more especially in the past few decades. Protests against a proposed Electricity Supply Board nuclear power plant at Carnsore Point in County Wexford in the late 1970s confirms the existence of a durable public concern in Ireland about the impact of science and technology, as well as considerable scepticism regarding expertise. Public scepticism has been matched by a growing realisation, even within the scientific community, that much knowledge is 'provisional':

'Scientific expertise is then as much about stating what is unknown, or uncertain with differing degrees of probability, as about setting out commonly agreed and accepted views' (COM(2002) 713: 3).

Confirmation of public thinking on science and technology is available in the 2001 *Eurobarometer* 55.2 (a regular EU-wide social survey), which sought to discover the attitudes of Europeans, including Irish citizens, to science and technology. The full range of findings is too wide to discuss here, but some of them are informative. While a majority of Europeans still have a positive attitude to science and technology, there is scepticism about its capacity to solve a series of specific problems (*Eurobarometer* 2001: Table 18:29). When asked for a measure of their esteem for certain professions, the Irish sample gave a mixed message. They ranked doctors at 69.6 per cent (as against 71.1 per cent in the total sample from all fifteen EU member states); scientists at 22.9 per cent (as against 44.9 per cent); and engineers at 24.3 per cent (as against 29.8 per cent). Not to paint too dismal a picture, among Irish people only sportsmen (at 35 per cent) scored higher than scientists and engineers in a list of ten professions (*Eurobarometer* 2001: Table 26:43).

These findings reflect a context in which the normative basis of scientific knowledge is being contested. The shift in position has been shaped by debates about the nature of facts and the nature of values or norms. Jasanoff suggests a spectrum from a 'traditional' posture to a contemporary one. The three primary positions are:

- *Hard facts – soft values*: scientific knowledge is pure, rational and untainted by non-scientific exigencies.
- *Firm facts – firm values*: scientific knowledge is generated in the context of both internal and external norms. The internal ones refer to the application of scientific method, and the use of 'peer review' (the requirement that research work be subject to anonymous review, challenge and critique before publication); the external ones refer to broader socio-political realities emanating from the public sphere and/or from parts of the scientific community itself.
- *Soft facts – hard values*: scientific knowledge is heavily accented by the political orientation of individual scientists and/or the scientific community. It is merely a 'camouflage for constellations of values and preferences' (Jasanoff 1986: 70).

These help us understand 'expertise' and how it might be used in policy formation. 'Hard facts – soft values' endorses the sort of tightly coupled decision-making model discussed earlier. In this case the views of the experts are all-important, while public opinion has little to contribute. At the other end of the scale, 'soft facts – hard values', represents a position where public opinion is critical, even in the face of strong scientific counter-arguments.

Before looking at cases that indicate the status of expertise in policy discourse in Ireland, we should pursue the question of expertise and its role a little further. A sector of the scientific community representing what Aronowitz (1996) calls 'scientificity' holds itself, together with medicine, as the custodians of enlightenment, reason and rationality. He highlights what we might call the two-way mirror of science and politics. The world of scientificity is behind the mirror. Science gets on with its work, free from the gaze of those in the other room. The scientists engage in the work of science, the accumulation of a rarefied and privileged knowledge. They can also engage in political discussion, as they have the capacity to observe and understand the activities in a room operating on a lower intellectual plane. However, those at the other side of the mirror, because of their lack of expert knowledge, cannot see through the mirror to the world of science. Gieryn (in Cozzens and Gieryn 1990) develops the idea that science engages in what he calls 'boundary issues'. For science this means that the boundary between science and non-science is a barrier of cognitive authority. Only scientists can understand the language and knowledge inside the boundary, while the outer, non-scientific knowledge is of a lower and less important cognitive order.

Latour's *Science in Action* (1987) opened up the study of science, technology and society to a new set of perspectives. These might be placed in two columns. The first column looks at the scientific method, which seeks to understand the accumulation of scientific knowledge as a complex and dynamic process. A narrative of orderly discovery or invention is commonplace, endorsing a notion of incremental building blocks of knowledge, each placed on a neat foundation of similar blocks. But we need to recognise that the accumulation of scientific knowledge is very often tentative and serendipitous and often draws from diverse pools of knowledge and discovery. Our second column, then, places science in the wider context of society. Here we see that it is not distinct from, but a twill in the fabric of, society. Scientists are citizens too.

Lay knowledge and expert knowledge

Fernandez's (2002) report on the combined mumps, measles and rubella (MMR) vaccine, and especially the 2001 *Report on Childhood Immunisation* by the Oireachtas (parliamentary) Joint Committee on Health and Children (OJCHC 2001), offer some insights into how expertise is used to shape policy orientations. Many parents are fearful that rather than being wholly beneficial for their children, MMR immunisation can have serious side effects. This has resulted in dropping rates of uptake for the MMR vaccine, which has in turn raised public health concerns in respect of vulnerable populations. Opinion is polarised between, on one side, MMR proponents, represented primarily by health professionals, scientists and public officials, and, on the other, parents and a minority scientific and health cohort. This is indeed a classic case, where science is unable to prove or disprove an absolute link between the MMR vaccine and some suspected ill-effects, like the onset of autism and immune deficiencies in later life. Doubt persists, no matter how small it may seem from a scientific perspective. In each individual case a parent or guardian must give consent for the vaccine to be administered and take responsibility for the consequences – albeit with the encouragement and assurances of negligible risk by experts. In investigating this issue the Oireachtas Committee invited contributions from both sides of the argument. However, greater weight was given to the 'expert' (hard facts – soft values) view of the proponents than to the 'lay' (soft facts – hard values) perspective of the parents. In essence, the Committee seemed to miss the point: the issue had arisen precisely because the values or norms were strong and the facts weaker – the reverse of the Committees emphasis. The report did nothing to change the concerned parents' view of the MMR vaccine, as it had not addressed their normative concerns, but rather recited again the already available scientific facts.

Water fluoridation is another issue that has polarised opinion. There is an international campaign to stop the fluoridation of public drinking water, and the issue first came to public notice in Ireland in the 1960s when Gladys Ryan challenged the constitutionality of the Health (Fluoridation of Water Supplies) Act, 1960, in Ryan *v.* A.G. [1965] IR 294 (1966). Ryan lost her case at the Supreme Court, but the controversy refused to go away. In recent years the campaign to stop fluoridation gained more momentum and led to the formation of a movement called Ireland's Campaign for Fluoride Free Water (ICFFW). The issue has since been the subject of TV documentaries, newspaper reports and much public debate. The Forum on Fluoridation was established in 2002 to allow an articulation of the issues and to report to the minister for health and children. The ICFFW complained about the composition, procedures and outcome of the Forum (ICFFW 2001), but rather than reducing public concern the Forum seemed to polarise opinion. It too adopted a 'hard facts – soft values' approach, something that was evident in its procedures and is apparent in its final report (FoF 2002).

Appendix 1 of the report provides an insight into the mindset of those sitting on the Forum. It was decided to segregate public (lay) submissions and expert submissions. Submissions from the general public were handled by a subgroup rather than by the Forum itself:

> The only public submissions to the Forum which were not dealt with by the current Sub-Group were those from professional and public bodies and from non-governmental organizations ... such submissions [as] required a higher degree of specific specialist expertise in their assessment were accordingly referred to the appropriate specialist members of the Forum. (FoF 2002: App. 1)

It is clear that the subgroup took great pains to ensure that each public submission was given consideration. However, the central point is that the process placed expert knowledge on a higher plane of importance than the views of the public affected by the policy. Furthermore, in Appendix 17 (Binchy 2002), which deals with ethical issues related to fluoridation, a distinguished academic lawyer makes the assumption of a dichotomy between 'empirical facts' (hard facts) and 'justified' ethical problems (norms). He suggests that if empirical proof should emerge to suggest that fluoride is unsafe, then its use would stop and the problem would disappear. It is clear that the ICFFW is already convinced that this is the case (see ICFFW 2001). Essentially the norms or values are hard in this case, and the facts are weak (or contested).

Where Ireland stands on policy and performance

Irish policy on science and technology is generally utilitarian in nature. It seeks to maximise the economic benefits for the country through inward investment and an orientation towards education for economic goals. Examination of government investment in research and development (R&D) activities indicates a pragmatic distribution of available funds, intended to produce scientists and technologists to work in industry rather than be the innovators of new science and technology.

Unlike many of its EU partners, Ireland does not have a scientific committee advising either the Oireachtas or the government. This means that Ireland is not a member of the European Parliamentary Technology Assessment (EPTA) network, which includes all the institutions that advise parliaments in Europe on the potential social, economic and environmental impacts of new science and new technologies. EPTA has sixteen members: ten member states of the EU together with the European Parliament, the Council of Europe, Switzerland, Norway, the Czech Republic and Flanders. Being outside EPTA, Irish parliamentarians and policy-makers miss opportunities to engage with their equivalents across Europe, and with scientists and interest group representatives in current debates on science and technology policy. Domestically it also means that Irish parliamentarians are disadvantaged in not having the sorts of expertise available to them that their colleagues elsewhere enjoy. Ireland's approach to policy-making has thus been characterised by:

- a primary focus on enhancing competitive advantage rather than addressing fundamental questions about science and technology policy and public engagement;
- the adoption of a wait-and-see approach to policy formulation, taking on policies already in place elsewhere rather than forming these at home; and
- the particularly heavy influence of policy developments in the rest of the Anglophone, English-speaking world.

This contrasts with the situation of Denmark, a country of similar size to Ireland within the EU, which is arguably the world leader in developing new ways of democratically addressing science and technology.

We can see this essentially utilitarian policy unfolding in regard to such indigenous scientific activity as does take place, and in the way Ireland deals with science- and technology-related issues. In 2001, 31.9 per cent of Ireland's total workforce was engaged in the knowledge-intensive services sector, slightly behind the EU average of 32.9 per cent. The medium- and high-technology manufacturing sector accounted for 7.3 per cent of the total workforce, as against an EU-wide average of 7.6 per cent. Together these two sectors account for almost four in every ten workers in the economy. Ireland is by no means the EU leader in either sector, by national or regional comparison. The Stuttgart region of Germany, for instance, has 21 per cent of employees in the medium- and high-technology manufacturing sector, almost three times the level in Ireland, while in Britain, Inner London at 61.1 per cent has nearly twice Ireland's rate of employment in knowledge-intensive services (Eurostat 2002). Science and technology play an increasingly important part in Irish economic activity, but questions can legitimately be posed about its sustainability in a potential economic downturn given relatively low levels of research and innovation.

If we use applications to the European Patents Office in the year 2001 as a barometer of levels of innovation, then Ireland at 327 applications overall, or 86 per million of population, finishes eleventh among EU member states. It fares better in the high-technology sector, coming seventh, at 30.7 patents per million of population; but this is still less than a quarter the rate of EU leader Finland, which is 136.1 per million (Frank 2003). However, there is an apparently promising other side to the picture. The Organisation for Economic Co-operation and Development (OECD) reports that investment in R&D in its member countries has grown at a rate of 4 per cent annually since the mid-1990s. This has been disproportionately driven by the United States, and the EU has averaged only 2.8 per cent growth in the same period. But Ireland goes against the EU trend. Together with Mexico and Iceland, in the 1990s Ireland showed the highest R&D growth rate among the OECD countries, at 13 per cent. This impressive increase has to be seen in the context of remarkable growth in the economy, but also in the light of the low level of R&D activity from which Ireland began. Despite the growth, however, Ireland is still not a member of the elite club of Sweden, Finland and Japan, which all spend more than 3 per cent of annual GDP on R&D (OECD 2001). The latest Eurostat figures for Ireland indicate that only 1.39 per cent of gross domestic product (GDP) was invested in R&D in 1997. When this is further broken down, the contribution of government is only 7 per cent of the total, with higher education providing 19 per cent and business 74 per cent. Yet the shape of this distribution is surprisingly similar to that of world leaders in R&D investment like the USA, Japan, Sweden and Finland. However, Ireland's level of investment against GDP is significantly lower (Eurostat 2001).

Conclusions

Since World War II science and technology have made incredible advances. They have achieved previously unimaginable benefits, together with disbenefits, risks and a barely comprehensible potential to alter life on this planet and even in other parts of our solar system. In this same period the science and technology communities have faced serious internal crises of confidence and challenges to their position as the 'religion of the enlightenment'. The social and political climate has been transformed. The nation state and political institutions have lost some of their lustre, and new social movements have generated new dynamics and challenges. On one side, science and technology systems have assumed a political role; on the other, activists and pressure groups are claiming a greater share in the governance of science and technology.

Needless to say, Ireland does not stand outside of these developments. It too changed dramatically in the course of the twentieth century. Irish society, like the Irish economy, has become more globally oriented and globally influenced, and it has to face many serious science and technology issues. For instance, Ireland cannot avoid taking a position on complex issues like human cloning, stem cell research, and the genetic modification of species. But it must also attend to more mundane issues, like the interaction between the public and science, and the role that Ireland wishes or ought to play in new sciences and technologies. In this chapter I have identified some of these issues, and described how Ireland currently deals with matters of science and technology policy. I have also drawn a road map indicating how these issues might be better addressed, so as to include greater citizen participation, and to ensure an orientation towards responsibility in the policy process

Notes

1 Nanotechnology refers to research and manufacturing where the characteristic dimensions are less than about 1,000 nanometres.
2 Useful website references on communitarianism can be found at www.infed.org/biblio/communitarianism.htm and plato.stanford.edu/entries/communitarianism.
3 Needless to say, republicanism as discussed here is not related to the politics of the Republican Party in the United States, or to republicanism as it is commonly understood in Ireland.
4 A whistle-blower is someone within an organisation who acts autonomously, and without formal knowledge or consent, to alert the public, the media or some external body or group about an activity of her or his organisation which she or he considers to be wrong, illegal or both.

References

Aronowitz, S. (1996), 'The Politics of the Science Wars', in A. Ross (ed.), *Science Wars*, Durham, NC: Duke University Press.
Beck, U. (1992), *Risk Society: Towards a New Modernity*, London: Sage.

Binchy, W. (2002), 'Fluoridation: Ethical Issues', Appendix 17 of *The Forum on Fluoridation*, Dublin: Government Publications Office.

Bohman, J. (1996), *Public Deliberation: Pluralism, Complexity, and Democracy*, Cambridge, MA: MIT Press.

Burns, T. R. (1999) 'The Evolution of Parliaments and Societies in Europe', *European Journal of Social Theory*, Vol. 2, No. 2, pp. 167–94.

COM(2002) 713 *Communication from the Commission on the Collection and Use of Expertise by the Commission: Principles and Guideline – Improving the Knowledge Base for Better Policies*, Brussels: Commission of the European Communities.

Cozzens, S. E. and Gieryn, T. F. (eds) (1990), *Theories of Science in Society*, Bloomington and Indianapolis: Indiana University Press.

DTEC (Department of Transport, Energy, Communications) (1996), 'In the Matter of the Public Inquiry Concerning an Appeal by the United Kingdom NIREX Ltd Concerning the Construction of a Rock Characterisation Facility at Longlands Farm, Gosforth, Cumbria', press statement on behalf of the minister of state at the Department of Transport, Energy, Communications, Dublin, Ireland.

EEA (European Environment Agency) (2001), *Late Lessons from Early Warnings: The Precautionary Principle 1896–2000*, Environment Issue Report No. 22, Luxembourg: European Environment Agency/Office for Official Publications of the European Communities.

Eurobarometer (2001), *Europeans, Science and Technology*, 55.2, Brussels: European Commission.

Eurostat (2001), *Statistics in Focus – Science and Technology*, 06/2001, 'R&D Expenditure and Personnel in Europe in 1999 and 2000', Luxembourg: European Communities.

Eurostat (2002), *Statistics in Focus – Science and Technology*, 04/2002, 'Employment in High Tech and Knowledge Intensive Sectors in the EU Continued to Grow in 2001', Luxembourg: European Communities.

Eyerman, R. and Jamison, A. (1991), *Social Movements: A Cognitive Approach*, Cambridge: Polity.

Fernandez, E. (2002), 'The Controversy over MMR Vaccine in Ireland', case study for the European Network on Scientific Input to Public Policy (ENSIPP) – Second Network Workshop, Fondazione Eni Enrico Mattei, Milan, 3–4 June.

FoF (Forum on Fluoridation) (2002), *Report of the Forum on Fluoridation*, Dublin: Government Publications Office.

Frank, S. (2003), in Eurostat, *Statistics in Focus – Science and Technology*, 'Patent Applications to the EPO Continue on an Upward Trend 1990 to 2001'(Theme 9–4/2003), Luxembourg: European Communities.

Frankenfeld, P. J. (1992), 'Technological Citizenship: A Normative Framework for Risk Studies', *Science, Technology, and Human Values*, Vol. 17, No. 4, pp. 459–84.

Fuller, S. (2000), *The Governance of Science*, Buckingham: Open University Press.

Habermas, J. (1992), *The Theory of Communicative Action (Vol. 2)*, Cambridge: Polity.

ICFFW (Ireland's Campaign for Fluoride Free Water) (2001) http://homepage.eircom .net/~fluoridefree/ Forum%20Analysis.htm.

Jasanoff, S. (1986), *Risk Management and Political Culture*, New York: Russell Sage Foundation.

Jonas, H. (1982), 'Technology as a Subject for Ethics', *Social Research*, Vol. 49, pp. 891–8.

Latour, B. (1987), *Science in Action*, Milton Keynes: Open University Press.

OECD (Orgnisation for Economic Co-operation and Development) (2001), 'Science, Technology and Industry Scoreboard', in *Towards a Knowledge-Based Economy*, Paris: OECD.

OJCHC (Oireachtas Joint Committee on Health and Children) (2001), *Report on Childhood Immunisation*, Dublin: An Comhchoiste um Shláinte Agus Leanuí/OJCHC/ Stationery Office.

Perrow, C. (1999), *Normal Accidents: Living with High-Risk Technologies*, Princeton, NJ: Princeton University Press.

Ryan v. A.G. [1965] IR 294 (1966), *Irish Law Reports 1965*, Dublin: Incorporated Council of Law Reporting for Ireland.

Sclove, R. E. (1995), *Democracy and Technology*, New York: Guilford Press.

Strydom, P. (1999), 'The Challenges of Responsibility for Sociology', *Current Sociology*, Vol. 47, No. 3, pp. 65–82.

Trouwborst, A. (2002), *Evolution and Status of the Precautionary Principle in International Law*, The Hague: Kluwer Law International.

Zimmerman, A. D. (1995), 'Towards a More Democratic Ethic of Technological Governance', *Science, Technology, and Human Values*, Vol. 20, No. 1, pp. 86–107.

10

No racists here? Public opinion, immigrants and the media

Eoin Devereux and Michael Breen

For much of last week, the Southern Health Board's hard-pressed immigration staff spent their time trying to run to ground two completely unfounded rumours which had gained popular currency. One concerned an asylum-seeker who was said to have bought himself a car using a cheque made out in his name by the local authorities. The story was that his children had been subjected to racial insults on the school bus and he had asked for and received money to buy a car so as to shield them from such torments ... The other concerned a Cork woman who was astounded to see that the asylum-seeker in front of her in the supermarket had a trolley laden with sweets, biscuits and other goodies, everything except nutritious food for her children. When the eavesdropper heard the checkout girl suggest she would be better off spending her money on decent food, she was just as astounded to hear the lady reply that it was her child's birthday and the immigration authorities had given her the money to help celebrate it. (Dick Hogan, *Irish Times*, 29 January 2002)

Introduction

According to the Office of the Refugee Applications Commissioners, since 1992 more than 50,000 asylum seekers and refugees have arrived in Ireland. The reversal of traditional outward Irish migration patterns has proven to be politically controversial and the cause of much contention amongst some members of the Irish public. From the outset it is worth remarking that in spite of a modest amount of discussion on asylum seekers and refugees (specifically in relation to the proposal that all asylum seekers and refugees should undergo compulsory health screening), the 2002 general election saw the mainstream political parties in Ireland adopting a position of consensus by avoidance – by largely avoiding the question altogether. This is paralleled in the academic world. With some important exceptions (Gray 1999; MacGreil 1996; Peillon 2000; Lentin and MacVeigh 2002) there has been little interest shown by the

Irish academic community – in research terms at any rate – in the many issues that have affected recent asylum seekers and refugees. There have, however, been two valuable analytical contributions from media commentators: one on the Irish response to the influx (Cullen 2000), and the second a critique of how the media have treated the issues surrounding asylum seekers and refugees (Pollak 1999).

The experience of inward migration to Ireland, after decades of emigration, represents a stark change in social reality. It is imperative that all aspects of this change are analysed from a critical perspective, with particular reference to the shaping of public opinion on this issue. Having defined what asylum seekers and refugees are, adduced some relevant facts and figures, briefly explored theoretical approaches to media coverage, and looked at the historical record of demonisation of the poor and the marginal, this chapter moves to reporting and commenting on survey evidence about Irish attitudes to minorities drawn from the Irish cohort of the 1999/2002 European Values Study (EVS).[1] It rounds this off with some content analysis of media coverage of asylum seekers and refugees as well as of Ireland's own indigenous ethnic minority, the Travelling People. This work draws upon a neo-Marxist theoretical framework, and has been stimulated by a belief in the power of media as a force for influence in the formation of public opinion.[2]

Asylum seekers and refugees: definitions, facts and figures

Within much media and public discourse, the terms 'asylum seeker' and 'refugee' are often used interchangeably and problematically. This has caused considerable confusion. A refugee is a person who fulfils the requirements of Article 1(A) of the 1951 Geneva Convention. A person should be recognised as a 'refugee' where he or she can show a well-founded fear of persecution in his or her country of origin on the grounds of race, religion, nationality, member-ship of a particular social group or political opinion. An asylum seeker is a person seeking refugee status specifically under the criteria stipulated in the 1951 Convention. Asylum seeker status is a temporary one conferred on indi-viduals while the host government determines an individual's right to refugee status. Under the laws currently in force in Ireland, asylum seekers are not per-mitted to engage in paid employment, unlike refugees. The numbers involved worldwide are high (see Table 10.1).

Table 10.2 shows the actual numbers of asylum seekers in Ireland, based on information obtained from the Office of the Refugee Applications Commissioner.[3] While the numbers have increased, when set against an indigenous population of 3.5 million, these figures are still very low.

Table 10.3 is included for comparative purposes. Drawing on 2001 UNHCR estimates, it shows the numbers of asylum seekers and refugees in a number of European countries including Ireland.

Table 10.1 *Refugees worldwide by region, 1 January 2002*[a]

Region	Number
Asia	8,820,700
Europe	4,855,400
Africa	4,173,500
Northern America	1,086,800
Latin American and Caribbean	765,400
Oceania	81,300
Total	19,783,100

Note: [a]Estimated number of persons of concern who fell under the mandate of the United Nations High Commissioner for Refugees, 1 January 2002.

Source: UNHCR (United Nations High Commission for Refugees) (2002), *Refugees by Numbers*, 2002 edition, Geneva: United Nations High Commission for Refugees; also available on the UNHCR website at www.unhcr.org.

Table 10.2 *Numbers making asylum applications in Ireland, 1992–2001*

Year	Number
1992	39
1993	91
1994	362
1995	424
1996	1,179
1997	3,883
1998	4,626
1999	7,724
2000	10,938
2001	10,325

The media and agenda-setting theory

The analysis of media content on refugees and asylum seekers is important for a number of reasons. In the first place, the media are a powerful source of meaning about the social world (Dahlgren 1981; Iyengar and Kinder 1987; Breen 2000). Take, for example, the way in which ethnic minorities are represented; that media coverage tends to view minorities as a 'problem' is confirmed by a large number of studies. Gomes and Williams (1991), for example, examine how the media construct a connection between race and crime. Soubiran-Paillet (1987) investigated the representation of minorities in crime

Table 10.3 *Asylum seekers and refugees of concern to the UNHCR, by chosen country of asylum, 2001*

Country of asylum	Refugees	Asylum seekers	Total population of concern
Portugal	449	–	449
Luxembourg	1,201	–	1,201
Ireland	*3,598*	*10,841*	*14,439*
Spain	6,806	–	6,806
Italy	8,571	–	8,571
Belgium	12,265	664	12,929
Finland	12,728	–	12,728
Norway	50,128	–	50,128
Denmark	73,284	–	73,284
France	131,601	34,551	166,152
Sweden	146,491	17,600	164,091
United Kingdom	148,550	39,400	187,950
Netherlands	152,338	78,550	230,888
Germany	903,000	85,533	988,533

Source: UNHCR (United Nations High Commission for Refugees) (2002), *Refugees by Numbers*, 2002 edition, Geneva, United Nations High Commission for Refugees.

reports in the French and Swiss press. And on ethnic association with negative reporting about crime, see Winkel (1990). Importantly, this kind of media coverage has been found to be of significance in the shaping of public attitudes towards minority groups such as refugees and asylum seekers (Schaffert 1992).

Secondly, while media content does not equate with social reality, it is essential that we examine how media content represents, or more accurately 're-presents', the realities involved in social, economic and political relationships. Given the apparent shrinkage of media content of a more critical nature – owing in no small part to the growing concentration and conglomeration of media ownership in the hands of a few (Bagdikian 2000) – this issue is particularly germane. It is important to determine what or whose version of 'reality' we mainly see or hear about in a media setting.

The Irish people are well served, in the main, by the media and by the high quality of journalism found in radio, television and the broadsheet newspapers. Such media are seen as reliable and trustworthy, and media coverage of events is a measure of their relative importance to Irish society. The public has an expectation, rightly, that the media will report fairly and accurately, without bias, on what is occurring that affects society. Media consumers use media content to exercise a surveillance function on society, relying on the media to tell them those things of import of which the public might otherwise remain ignorant. Such surveillance comes at a price, however: as Cohen puts it, 'the press ... may not be successful in telling people what to think but it is stunningly successful in telling them what to think about' (1963: 13).

Iyengar and Kinder's (1987) work on 'agenda setting' in television news indicates that news coverage affects the mass public's approach to major issues. Their studies show that the people most prone to agenda-setting effects are those who are neither politically active nor strongly affiliated to a political party. Significant non-political news items, then, are relatively easily placed in the public consciousness. The clear consequence is that it is the framers of the news who wield a vast amount of control over how the public views various events and personalities. As well as setting the agenda on public issues, the news media can also set the agenda for themselves, by their repetitious coverage of a single event and their definition of newsworthiness. People, including journalists, cannot pay attention to everything; they are selective. They take short cuts by relying on the most accessible information sources. Frequent repetition of a given story at a national level focuses journalistic attention on that issue. The framing of a news story, therefore, is of critical importance in terms of the ultimate impact of such a story.

Dearing and Rogers subdivide agenda setting into three specific components: media agenda setting, public agenda setting, and policy agenda setting (1996). The first of these results in homogenisation of news content, the second indicates media influence on public opinion, and the third indicates some level of influence on the elites who control public policy. McCombs and Shaw (1993) point out that the metaphor of agenda setting incorporates other communications concepts such as status conferral (the conferring of status by appearance in the media), stereotyping and 'image'. It is precisely these that generate public attitudinal change. Media coverage can set an agenda and can also alter public perceptions of the players in the process, depending on the type of coverage (Brewer and McCombs 1996). The public can only make decisions on the information that it has at its disposal. Iyengar (1991) refers to the 'accessibility of information', which is highly dependent on the pattern of news coverage (1991: 132). While it is clear that other elements enter into the accessibility equation, such as party affiliation, socio-economic status, personal values, religious orientation and cultural perceptions, Iyengar argues that accessibility of information on public affairs is primarily dependent on media content.

Demonising the poor

The practice of demonising certain sections of the poor is not new, and the Irish media are not alone in doing this. For example, in their studies 'Making Claims: News Media and the Welfare State' (1979) and *Images of Welfare* (1982), Golding and Middleton investigated media-generated moral panics about alleged welfare abuse in the UK. During their six-month content analysis study (1979) they found that welfare issues, as such, did not make the news. Significantly, welfare was only considered worthy of coverage when it was connected to other issues such as crime, fraud or sex. A key theme uncovered in their analysis – and developed further in their 1982 study – was that the poor are constructed in a media context as either 'deserving' or 'undeserving'. They examine the case of a man that the British print media dubbed 'King Con' who was found to be engaged in social welfare fraud. What is striking in this case is the extent to which the media emphasised that this was merely the tip of the iceberg, and that welfare fraud was widespread. Media demonisation of certain sections of the underclass has contributed in no small way to legitimising both welfare cutbacks by the state and the furtherance of dominant ideologies about the poor and underclass.

Published research on attitudes to poverty in Ireland (Davis et al. 1984; *Eurobarometer* 1990; MacGreil 1977, 1996) reveals two main kinds of constructions within public discourse: those who deserve support – the 'deserving' or 'God's poor' – and those who do not deserve support – the 'undeserving' or 'Devil's poor'. Research on public beliefs about the causes of poverty reveals that while structural explanations are increasingly offered, explanations that seek to explain poverty in terms of an individual's personal or cultural characteristics remain potent, as the analysis in Table 10.4 shows.

Table 10.4 *Summary of principal findings on public attitudes to poverty in Ireland, 1984–96*

Davis et al. (1984)	*Eurobarometer* (1990)	MacGreil (1997, 1996)
The Irish are strongly fatalistic about causes of poverty. 57% of sample agreed that 'lack of ambition is the root of poverty'. 53% agreed that 'the majority of people on the dole have no interest in getting a job'. 60% believed that 'Itinerants' (Travelling Community) were untrustworthy, careless, excitable and noisy. 23% believed that the unemployed had these characteristics.	Public opinion in Ireland, Denmark and the UK was found to be negative in terms of public beliefs about the poor making it through their poverty. While structural explanations for poverty were strong, ones which blamed individuals for their poverty were also much in evidence: alcoholism/drugs (39%), broken families (33%), too many children (19%), laziness (16%).	The 1977 study points to negative public attitudes to both the Travelling Community and the unemployed. The 1996 study (covering the period 1988–89) reports that negative public attitudes to Travellers have intensified. However, these attitudes were shown to have diminished as regards the unemployed. 11.8% of the sample in 1988–9 agreed that 'The poor person is generally responsible for his/her own poverty.'

The 1999/2000 EVS data does not give any reason to believe that the attitude of blame has changed significantly in respect of those who are without work. As can be seen in Table 10.5, significant numbers of respondents have a negative view of people without work.

Table 10.5 *Respondents' attitudes to work questions, drawn from Irish EVS data, 2000*

Statement	Response
It is humiliating to receive money without having to work for it.	47.6% agree/strongly agree
People who don't work turn lazy.	57.1% agree/strongly agree
Work is a duty towards society.	60.1% agree/strongly agree
People should not have to work if they don't want to.	56.5% disagree/strongly disagree

We know from MacGreil's research on unemployment at the end of the 1980s, when it peaked at 18 per cent, that attitudes softened but without any corresponding softening towards groups like Travellers. At a time of increased prosperity, 30 per cent of Irish respondents in the EVS data suggest that the primary reason for people living in need is 'laziness' or 'lack of willpower'. This specific attitude of blame is statistically correlated with the negative attitudes to work listed above.

That these attitudes are reflected in media coverage is documented in Devereux's (1998) study of the national broadcaster's coverage of poverty, on the Radio Telefís Éireann (RTÉ)1 and Network 2 channels. This combined critical content analysis with an ethnographic approach and examined factual, fictional and fund-raising television; and the particular focus was on the ideological construction of poverty stories. The study concluded that poverty coverage on television is constructed in such a way as not to threaten the status quo. It has, therefore, a significant role to play in the reproduction of dominant ideological discourses about poverty: 'RTÉ's coverage … draws upon the dominant, liberal ideology … in Irish society. Television coverage of poverty is defined by limits which disallow any reference to the unequal social structure (itself a key cause of poverty) and never challenges those who occupy positions of power and domination' (Devereux 1998: 138). We shall return to the question of media influence – in respect of all minority groups – in due course.

Irish attitudes towards immigrants

The Irish data sets drawn from the EVS provide an extremely valuable fund of information on social attitudes in Ireland, and they are the source for all of Tables 10.6 to 10.17. Illustrative of a particularly significant change in attitudes over time is Table 10.6. As part of a series of questions, respondents in each of the three surveys were asked to indicate, from a list of categories of people, the ones they would not want to have as neighbours. The table summarises the data by age of respondent, in relation to immigrants and foreign workers. The differences between 1981 and 1990 are marginal, but those between 1990 and 2000 are notable, with a rise of more than 100 per cent in the numbers of respondents specifically selecting immigrants or foreign workers as undesirable neighbours. The most dramatic increase is seen in the case of the selections by 25–34-year-olds: from 1.3 per cent in 1981 to 8.6 per cent in 2000. We should note that this change is marked by yearly rises in the number of applications for asylum, a rise in the number of work permits issued to foreign nationals (from 18,000 in 2000, to 34,335 in 2002), and increased media coverage – some of it negative and misinformed.

Table 10.6 *Numbers and percentages of all respondents mentioning immigrants and foreign workers as unwanted neighbours, by age category, by year, 1981–2000*[a]

Age categories of respondent	Mentioned by		
	1981	1990	2000
18–24	14	3	14
	4.0%	2.0%	8.9%
25–34	3	5	18
	1.3%	2.8%	8.6%
35–44	11	6	24
	6.4%	3.0%	11.3%
45–64	21	24	41
	7.6%	8.0%	14.7%
65+	17	13	25
	9.3%	7.7%	16.8%
Totals	66	51	122
	5.4%	5.1%	12.1%

Note: [a] In this and all subsequent tables, the numbers and percentages refer only to those respondents who answered the question; the respondent numbers therefore vary.
Source: EVS Irish data, 1981, 1990, 1999/2000.

It is important to place the figure of 12.1 per cent that appears in the last cell of Table 10.6 in a wider context, by comparing it with other 'unwanted neighbour' mentions. The summary data for all categories mentioned by respondents is given in Table 10.7. The level of intolerance expressed as regards immigrants and foreign workers is on a par with that expressed in respect of Muslims (13.6 per cent), people of a different race (12.4 per cent) and Jews (11.1 per cent). However, it is significantly less than the level of intolerance of drug addicts (65.7 per cent), people with a criminal record (56.3 per cent) and Travellers (50.1 per cent).

In Table 10.8 we see the selections made by respondents from various suggested responses as to how Ireland might react to people from less developed

Table 10.7 *Summary data for unwanted neighbour mentions: numbers and percentages of respondents mentioning in each category, 1999/2000*

Mention category	Number of mentions	%
Criminal record	1004	56.3
Different race	1007	12.4
Left-wing extremists	1008	33.3
Heavy drinkers	1007	36.4
Right-wing extremists	1007	32.2
Large families	1007	9.4
Emotionally unstable people	1006	25.1
Muslims	1007	13.6
Immigrants and foreign workers	1007	12.1
People with AIDS	1006	23.0
Drug addicts	1006	65.7
Homosexuals	1008	27.4
Jews	1007	11.1
Gypsies	1007	24.4
Travellers/Itinerants	1008	50.1

Source: EVS Irish data, 1999/2000.

Table 10.8 *Numbers and percentages of respondents' attitudes to the immigration of people from less developed countries, by age categories, 1999/2000*

Age categories of respondent	Anyone can come who wants to	Can come when jobs are available	Strict limits on the number of foreigners	Prohibit people coming to Ireland from other countries	Totals
18–24	11	73	67	3	154
	7.1%	47.4%	43.5%	1.9%	100.0%
25–34	20	90	94	1	205
	9.8%	43.9%	45.9%	0.5%	100.0%
35–44	13	103	83	10	209
	6.2%	49.3%	39.7%	4.8%	100.0%
45–64	27	133	111	10	281
	9.6%	47.3%	39.5%	3.6%	100.0%
65+	12	64	67	4	147
	8.2%	43.5%	45.6%	2.7%	100.0%
Totals	83	463	422	28	996
	8.3%	46.5%	42.4%	2.8%	100.0%

Source: EVS Irish data, 1999/2000.

countries who wished to come to Ireland. The numbers advocating absolutist policies are relatively small in all age categories, with 8.3 per cent of all respondents advocating a completely open frontier policy and just 2.8 per cent advocating a total prohibition on inward migration. The remainder are relatively evenly balanced between those who are willing to allow immigration when jobs are available (46.5 per cent) and those who wish to see strict limits on the numbers of foreigners (42.4 per cent).

Table 10.9 indicates that there is a slender majority, across all age groups, in favour of inward migrants maintaining their own customs and traditions rather than having to adopt the customs of the host country. This attitude of acceptance of other traditions is most marked amongst the youngest age cohort, at 62.5 per cent, as against the 37.5 per cent who think that inward migrants should adopt local customs. Table 10.10 compares the responses seen in Tables 10.8 and 10.9 in a cross-tabulation comparison. The chi square statistic for this cross-tabulation was non-significant, indicating that there is no relationship between the two sets of attitudes; in other words, there is no reason to believe that those who are opposed to immigration are any more likely to impose indigenous customs on inward migrants than are those in favour of immigration.

Table 10.9 *Numbers and percentages of respondents' attitudes to immigrants' customs, by age categories, 1999/2000*

Age categories of respondent	Should maintain own distinct customs and traditions	Should adopt the customs of Ireland	Totals
18–24	85	51	136
	62.5%	37.5%	100.0%
25–34	106	71	177
	59.9%	40.1%	100.0%
35–44	101	79	180
	56.1%	43.9%	100.0%
45–64	132	116	248
	53.2%	46.8%	100.0%
65+	72	55	127
	56.7%	43.3%	100.0%
Totals	496	372	867
	57.1%	42.9%	100.0%

Source: EVS Irish data, 1999/2000.

Turning to general levels of concern for others, the 1999/2000 EVS sought to discover how concerned respondents were about various categories and groups in society. Tables 10.11, 10.12 and 10.13 provide the answers from the

Table 10.10 *Cross-tabulation of attitudes to immigration with attitudes to immigrants' customs: respondent numbers, 1999/2000*

Immigrants	People from less developed countries				Totals
	Anyone can come who wants to	Can come when jobs are available	Strict limits on the number of foreigners	Prohibit people coming to Ireland from other countries	
Should maintain own distinct customs and traditions	40	244	199	10	493
Should adopt the customs of Ireland	27	161	169	12	369
Totals	67	405	368	22	862

Source: EVS Irish data, 1999/2000.

Table 10.11 *Cross-tabulation of concern for immediate family with age categories: respondent numbers and percentages, 1999/2000*

Concerned for immediate family?	Age categories of respondents					Totals
	18–24	25–34	35–44	45–64	65+	
Very much	95 60.9%	138 66.7%	148 70.5%	203 73.0%	104 72.2%	688 69.1%
Much	26 16.7%	26 12.6%	26 12.4%	26 9.4%	18 12.5%	122 12.3%
To a certain extent	9 5.8%	11 5.3%	11 5.2%	17 6.1%	6 4.2%	54 5.4%
Not so much	13 8.3%	16 7.7%	12 5.7%	17 6.1%	6 4.2%	64 6.4%
Not at all	13 8.3%	16 7.7%	13 6.2%	15 5.4%	10 6.9%	67 6.7%
Totals	156 100.0%	207 100.0%	210 100.0%	278 100.0%	144 100.0%	995 100.0%

Source: EVS Irish data, 1999/2000.

Table 10.12 *Cross-tabulation of concern for human kind with age categories: respondent numbers and percentages, 1999/2000*

Concerned for human kind?	Age categories of respondents					Totals
	18–24	25–34	35–44	45–64	65+	
Very much	11	29	34	52	25	151
	7.1%	14.1%	16.3%	18.8%	17.0%	15.2%
Much	26	41	43	42	33	185
	16.8%	20.0%	20.7%	15.2%	22.4%	18.7%
To a certain extent	80	95	75	107	53	410
	51.6%	46.3%	36.1%	38.8%	36.1%	41.4%
Not so much	31	29	45	58	28	191
	20.0%	14.1%	21.6%	21.0%	19.0%	19.3%
Not at all	7	11	11	17	8	54
	4.5%	5.4%	5.3%	6.2%	5.4%	5.4%
Totals	155	205	208	276	147	991
	100.0%	100.0%	100.0%	100.0%	100.0%	100.0%

Source: EVS Irish data, 1999/2000.

Table 10.13 *Cross-tabulation of concern for immigrants with age categories: respondent numbers and percentages, 1999/2000*

Concerned for immigrants?	Age categories of respondents					Totals
	18–24	25–34	35–44	45–64	65+	
Very much	5	19	26	35	19	104
	3.2%	9.3%	12.4%	12.5%	12.9%	10.4%
Much	17	43	40	42	27	169
	10.8%	21.0%	19.0%	15.1%	18.4%	16.9%
To a certain extent	84	94	77	117	58	430
	53.5%	45.9%	36.7%	41.9%	39.5%	43.1%
Not so much	44	41	50	71	35	241
	28.0%	20.0%	23.8%	25.4%	23.8%	24.1%
Not at all	7	8	17	14	8	54
	4.5%	3.9%	8.1%	5.0%	5.4%	5.4%
Totals	157	205	210	279	147	998
	100.0%	100.0%	100.0%	100.0%	100.0%	100.0%

Source: EVS irish data, 1999/2000.

Irish data, broken down by age categories, in response to questions about concern for immediate family, human kind and immigrants respectively.

There is an interesting contrast across the levels of concern expressed for 'human kind' and 'immigrants' when compared to that expressed for 'immediate family'. Fully 81.4 per cent of respondents stated that they were 'very much concerned' or 'much concerned' with immediate family, compared to 33.9 per cent for human kind and 27.3 per cent for immigrants. On the opposite end of the scale only 13.1 per cent of respondents stated that they were 'not so much concerned' or 'not at all concerned' with immediate family compared to 24.7 per cent with human kind and 29.5 per cent with immigrants.

The next four tables give the data on Irish respondents' answers to questions about willingness to help specific categories of people: sick and disabled (Table 10.14); elderly (Table 10.15); neighbours (Table 10.16); and immigrants (Table 10.17).

Table 10.14 *Cross-tabulation of willingness to help the sick and disabled with age categories: respondent numbers and percentages, 1999/2000*

Willing to help the sick and disabled?	Age categories of respondents					Totals
	18–24	25–34	35–44	45–64	65+	
Absolutely yes	33	59	76	102	47	317
	21.2%	28.5%	36.2%	36.4%	32.0%	31.7%
Yes	91	99	98	137	72	497
	58.3%	47.8%	46.7%	48.9%	49.0%	49.7%
Maybe yes/ maybe no	31	43	31	36	21	162
	19.9%	20.8%	14.8%	12.9%	14.3%	16.2%
No	1	3	4	5	7	20
	0.6%	1.4%	1.9%	1.8%	4.8%	2.0%
Absolutely no	–	3	1	–	–	4
		1.4%	0.5%			0.4%
Totals	156	207	210	280	147	1000
	100.0%	100.0%	100.0%	100.0%	100.0%	100.0%

Source: EVS Irish data, 1999/2000.

Again, there is a marked contrast across the levels of willingness to help people. Some 81.4 per cent of respondents stated 'absolutely yes' or 'yes' when asked about willingness to help sick and disabled people, compared to 80.7 per cent giving the same response for the elderly, 72.3 per cent for neighbours, but only 34.2 per cent for immigrants. Likewise, only 2.4 per cent responded 'absolutely no' or 'no' when asked about sick and disabled people, compared with 2.1 per cent as regards the elderly, 3.8 per cent as regards neighbours, but

Table 10.15 *Cross-tabulation of willingness to help the elderly with age categories: respondent numbers and percentages, 1999/2000*

Willing to help the elderly?	Age categories of respondents					Totals
	18–24	25–34	35–44	45–64	65+	
Absolutely yes	34	50	73	94	46	297
	21.7%	24.2%	34.8%	33.5%	31.1%	29.6%
Yes	91	110	99	140	73	513
	58.0%	53.1%	47.1%	49.8%	49.3%	51.1%
Maybe yes/ maybe no	32	44	35	40	21	172
	20.4%	21.3%	16.7%	14.2%	14.2%	17.1%
No	–	–	3	7	8	18
			1.4%	2.5%	5.4%	1.8%
Absolutely no	–	3	–	–	–	3
		1.4%				0.3%
Totals	157	207	210	281	148	1003
	100.0%	100.0%	100.0%	100.0%	100.0%	100.0%

Source: EVS Irish data, 1999/2000.

Table 10.16 *Cross-tabulation of willingness to help neighbours with age categories: respondent numbers and percentages, 1999/2000*

Willing to help people in the neighbourhood?	Age categories of respondents					Totals
	18–24	25–34	35–44	45–64	65+	
Absolutely yes	23	31	54	77	31	216
	14.7%	15.0%	25.6%	27.3%	21.2%	21.6%
Yes	81	107	107	143	70	508
	51.9%	51.9%	50.7%	50.7%	47.9%	50.7%
Maybe yes/ maybe no	45	59	43	53	39	239
	28.8%	28.6%	20.4%	18.8%	26.7%	23.9%
No	7	6	7	9	6	35
	4.5%	2.9%	3.3%	3.2%	4.1%	3.5%
Absolutely no	–	3	–	–	–	3
		1.5%				0.3%
Totals	156	206	211	282	146	1001
	100.0%	100.0%	100.0%	100.0%	100.0%	100.0%

Source: EVS Irish data, 1999/2000.

Table 10.17 *Cross-tabulation of willingness to help immigrants with age categories: respondent numbers and percentages, 1999/2000*

Willing to help immigrants?	Age categories of respondents					Totals
	18–24	25–34	35–44	45–64	65+	
Absolutely yes	5	9	22	28	13	77
	3.2%	4.4%	10.5%	10.2%	8.8%	7.8%
Yes	46	52	55	76	33	262
	29.3%	25.4%	26.3%	27.6%	22.4%	26.4%
Maybe yes/ maybe no	71	114	91	130	74	480
	45.2%	55.6%	43.5%	47.3%	50.3%	48.3%
No	35	24	39	40	25	163
	22.3%	11.7%	18.7%	14.5%	17.0%	16.4%
Absolutely no	–	6	2	1	2	11
		2.9%	1.0%	0.4%	1.4%	1.1%
Totals	157	205	209	275	147	993
	100.0%	100.0%	100.0%	100.0%	100.0%	100.0%

Source: EVS Irish data, 1999/2000.

17.5 per cent as regards immigrants. The ambivalent middle group, responding 'maybe yes/maybe no', came to 16.2 per cent for sick and disabled, 17.1 per cent for the elderly, 23.9 per cent for neighbours and 48.3 per cent for immigrants.

Media coverage of refugees, asylum seekers and travellers

We now return to the possible influence of the media on the public attitudes. The content analysis that follows is by no means exhaustive, but it does provide pointers to some influences on the formation of Irish public opinion about minority groups of all kinds. What is immediately clear is that the changing circumstances of the Irish economy from 1996 to 2000, together with the development of the Celtic Tiger economy (see Chapter 1), have in fact resulted in indigenous poverty effectively disappearing from the media, only to be replaced by a 'new poor' – immigrants, refugees and asylum seekers. This is typified by a series of newspaper articles with particularly sensationalist headlines, as documented by Pollak (1999). The appendix to this chapter gives some typical headlines over the last few years.

The stories at the beginning of this chapter, quoted in Hogan's critical piece in the *Irish Times*, are not untypical either, and are in wide circulation; in October 2002, in the run-up to the second referendum on the Nice Treaty, they surfaced a number of times. Indeed, the Minister for Social and Family Affairs was so concerned that she directed officials in her department to make inquiries at a number of Health Boards around the country, to follow up allegations that some asylum seekers were in receipt of special grants for the purchase of cars. On 16 September 2002 the *Irish Mirror* ran a story about refugees buying cars with government cheques: 'Free Cars for Refugees: Cash Grants Buy BMWs', ran the headline. The thrust of the article was that refugees were using monies obtained for assistance to purchase second-hand cars 'including BMWs and Toyotas'. The article 'revealed' that one refugee site was 'full of second-hand cars'. One politician was quoted as stating: 'it does not set a good example and is sure to infuriate other young people in this country who cannot afford to buy a car'.

An *Irish Mirror* editorial on the same day denounced the 'money grabbing con artists' who were 'cruising around Ireland' and condemned the government for the legislative loophole that facilitated these 'rogue refugees'. The next day the same paper ran a further story entitled 'Probe into Car Scandal', in which it announced a government inquiry had resulted from the previous day's story. An inquiry did take place, as indicated above, with the minister subsequently announcing that 'no evidence has been found to support such allegations'. This announcement went unreported by the *Irish Mirror.*

It is evident that these mythical stories continue to circulate, despite official denials and denunciations. And there are three possible explanations for this. The first is that what we are seeing is a simple manifestation of visibility whereby refugees, specifically those whose country of origin is clearly not Ireland, are seen to be driving cars; this is followed by a leap to a conclusion that is very wide of the mark. As we have already noted, there are in fact in excess of 34,000 foreign nationals with legal permits to work in Ireland, and it may be that these are confused in the minds of some people with refugees or asylum seekers. Secondly, there is a possibility that some people who have received legitimate assistance from the government have decided that the best use to be made of some of this is the purchase of a second-hand car. That in no way negates their right to support – indeed there are shades here of historical refusals to help the poor because they might spend the money on alcohol. Thirdly, what we could be seeing is a manifestation in the media of national xenophobia, by which cultural stereotypes and caricatures are perpetuated. This latter explanation is supported by a simple review of the headlines quoted in the appendix to this chapter. It is also supported by the experience of Travellers in Ireland, and specifically by media coverage of this group down the years.

Travellers generally see themselves as Irish people with a separate identity, culture and history. They constitute between 0.5 and 1.0 per cent of the national population. Aspiring to a nomadic lifestyle, they remain for the most part a marginalised group in society. This marginalisation is often reflected in the media representation of them, and there is a long history of representing Travellers as 'a problem' (Devereux 1998). (Until its funding ceased in

November 2002, the *Citizen Traveller* campaign attempted to counter misrepre-
sentations of Travellers in the media, through a billboard and radio advertising
campaign.) In 2002, as Ireland was becoming increasingly culturally and eth-
nically diverse, there was a depressing example of public attitudes towards
Travelling People: all of the existing children in a national (primary) school in
Galway were withdrawn by their parents and moved to a different school
because three Traveller children had been enrolled. So by the beginning of the
2002/3 academic year, only the Traveller children were on the rolls, putting the
very future of the school in doubt. The issue of negative attitudes towards
Travellers cannot be laid entirely at the door of the mass media, of course, and
can also be said to reflect a form of national xenophobia.

Turning our attention finally to an important broadsheet newspaper, a
search by the authors of twelve months (November 2000–October 2001) coverage by the *Irish Times* of refugees, asylum seekers and Travellers yielded a
total of 264 stories in which these groups were mentioned in headlines. This
data is given in Table 10.18. It deserves to be emphasised that a clear distinction was generally made in the *Irish Times* coverage between refugees and
asylum seekers, and most of the information provided was in the form of
straight news stories.

Table 10.18 *Number of stories in the* Irish Times *in various categories, November
2000–October 2001*

Character of coverage	Headline focus[a]			
	Refugees and asylum seekers	Refugees	Asylum seekers	Travellers
Lead stories	(0) 0	(1) 1	(0) 0	(0) 2
Letters	(0) 1	(0) 4	(0) 7	(0) 7
Features	(0) 0	(2) 3	(1) 4	(0) 3
News	(0) 3	(45) 70	(21) 64	(1) 77

Note: [a]Numbers in brackets refer to the number of stories in each category that focused on that
same category in an overseas rather than a home setting.

It is interesting to note that stories about Travellers accounted for almost 30
per cent overall. When these stories are analysed, a definite pattern emerges, as
seen in the sample in Table 10.19. In the case of stories about Travellers, those
which report Traveller behaviour in a negative fashion (for example, Traveller-
on-Traveller violence, Traveller encampments) seem to get greater coverage
than those about Travellers which highlight the problematic conditions under
which most Travellers live (e.g. lack of serviced halting sites, high Traveller
mortality rates, Traveller experience of bias).

Much of this coverage ignores poverty, or it focuses on marginal issues
rather than ones related to the economic and social systems. Indeed, immi-

Table 10.19 *Story headlines and word count in the* Irish Times, *November 2000–October 2001*

Story headlines	Word count
International Day Against Racism	1133
Travellers' Encounter Compared to *Braveheart*	582
Travellers Seek Money to Leave Industrial Estate	576
Travellers Camp at Gates of Sailing Club	486
6,000 Travellers Still Live on Unserviced Sites	97
German Nazis Stab Refugees	64
Travellers Live Shorter Lives	54
Anti-Traveller Bias Plan Launched	45

grants, refugees, asylum seekers and Traveller groups have virtually been conflated into one category representing the 'new poor' in Irish society; and they are now covered as the 'Devil's poor' were in the past.

Conclusions

Despite an overall picture of tolerance, or at worst equivocation, in public attitudes to immigrants emerging from the evidence adduced here, the picture is none the less a depressing one. As for the role of the information media in such attitude formation, following van Dijk (1988, 1990, 1998a, 1998b), this chapter has stressed that media content plays a central role in shaping public discourse and beliefs about 'race' and ethnicity. So despite the obvious limitations of the content analysis offered above, and the consequent inability to draw direct links between media coverage of immigrants and the formation of public attitudes about them, there is enough in the data to give rise to concern.

The realities of recent inward migration into Ireland are as follows: in order to meet labour shortages, the Irish state has actively encouraged foreign nationals to seek employment here under a permit system; the numbers of refugees and asylum seekers coming to Ireland are comparatively low; and there is a high rejection rate for those seeking refugee status. The authors would argue that in many instances the Irish media fail to reflect these complexities. Moreover, much media coverage continues to represent and reproduce the dominant view of immigration as a 'threat' to Irish society – that the Irish state is being or is about to be 'overwhelmed' by a 'flood' of immigrants. Such arguments were indeed openly used most recently by a minority of those who opposed to Irish ratification of the EU's Nice Treaty. The problematising of immigrants (in terms of crime or welfare fraud, for example) within Irish media discourse conforms to the wider tendency of the mainstream media always to demonise the most marginalised in society.

What is needed to counter this is an increase in awareness of the kind of findings presented here – among the public in general and powerful elites in particular – so as to ensure that public policy and public discourse are informed by hard fact rather than impression, rumour and hearsay.

Appendix: some Irish newspaper headlines about refugees and asylum seekers

5000 Refugees Flooding into Ireland
Floodgates Open as a New Army of Poor Floods the Country
Gardaí Increasingly Worried About Refugees in Street Crime and Prostitution
A New Determined Style of Beggar
Demand for Curb on Tide of 'Refugees'
Refugee Children in Care to Top 1,500
Refugee Children Sold as Sex Slaves
Mother's Anguish as Junkie Daughter Marries Nigerian Refugee for £5,000 in Asylum Scam
Blitz on Refugees' Sham Marriages
Refugee Rip-Off is Revealed
Government Crackdown on Bogus Asylum-Seeker Advisers
Refugees Flooding Maternity Hospitals
Refugee Rapist on the Rampage
Tax-Payers Face Bills of £20m+
Crackdown on 2000 Sponger Refugees
Inmates Lobby to Stay in Jail as Refugees Fill Up Hotels
Refugee Flood to Spark Homes Crisis
Alert on Bogus Refugee Weddings
Refugee Tried to Bite Me to Death

Source: Based on A. Pollak, 'An Invitation to Racism? Irish Daily Newspaper Coverage of the Refugee Issue', in D. Kiberd (ed.), *Media in Ireland: The Search for Ethical Journalism*, Dublin: Open Air; E. Devereux and M. Breen (2001), 'Blind, Deaf and Dumb: The Media, the Middle-Class and the Representation of Poverty', Paper to EFACIS Conference 'Ireland and Europe at Times of Reorientation and Re-imagining', University of Arhus.

Notes

1   The European Values Study is a large-scale, cross-national and longitudinal survey research programme on basic human values, initiated by the European Value Systems Study Group in the late 1970s. It is now carried on by a foundation, and is commonly described as the EVS (see www.europeanvalues.nl).
2   While the authors acknowledge the power of the audience in interpreting texts according to the polysemic paradigm (Fiske 1987), we also believe that encoded meanings are particularly significant and influential, capable of setting agendas and shaping public discourses (McCombs and Shaw 1972, 1993; Kitzinger 1990; Deacon et al. 1999).

3   Information from the Office of the Refugee Applications Commissioner can be found
    via the eGovernment website at www.oasis.gov.ie.

References

Bagdikian, B. H. (2000), *The Media Monopoly*, sixth edition, Boston, MA: Beacon Press.

Breen, M. J. (2000), 'When Size Does Matter: How Church Size Determines Media
    Coverage of Religion', in J. Thierstein and Y. R. Kamalipour (eds), *Religion, Law and
    Freedom*, Westport, CT: Praeger.

Brewer, M. and McCombs, M. (1996), 'Setting the Community Agenda', *Journalism and
    Mass Communication Quarterly*, Vol. 73, No. 1, pp. 7–16.

Cohen, B. (1963), *The Press and Foreign Policy*, Princeton, NJ: Princeton University
    Press.

Cullen, P. (2000), *Refugees and Asylum Seekers in Ireland*, Cork: Cork University Press.

Dahlgren, P. (1981), 'TV News and the Suppression of Reflexivity', in E. Katz and T.
    Szecsko (eds), *Mass Media and Social Change*, London: Sage.

Davis, E. E., Grube, J. W. and Morgan, M. (1984), *Attitudes to Poverty and Related Social
    Issues in Ireland*, Paper No. 17, Dublin: Economic and Social Research Institute.

Deacon, D., Fenton, N. and Bryman, A. (1999), 'From Inception to Reception: The
    Natural History of a News Item', *Media, Culture and Society*, Vol. 21, pp. 22–31.

Dearing, J. W. and Rogers, E. M. (1996), *Agenda-Setting*, Thousand Oaks, CA: Sage.

Devereux, E. (1998), *Devils and Angels: Television, Ideology and the Coverage of Poverty*,
    Luton: John Libbey Media.

Devereux, E. and Breen, M. (2001), 'Blind, Deaf and Dumb: The Media, the Middle-Class
    and the Representation of Poverty', Paper to EFACIS Conference 'Ireland and Europe
    at Times of Reorientation and Re-imagining', University of Arhus.

Eurobarometer (1990), *The Social Situation in the European Union*, 54.2, Luxembourg:
    Office for Official Publications of the European Communities.

Fiske, J. (1987), *Television Culture*, London: Methuen.

Golding, P. and Middleton, S. (1979), 'Making Claims: News Media and the Welfare
    State', *Media, Culture and Society*, Vol. 1, pp. 5–21.

Golding, P. and Middleton, S. (1982), *Images of Welfare, Press and Public Attitudes to
    Poverty*, Oxford: Blackwell.

Gomes, R. C. and Williams, L. F. (1991), 'Race and Crime: The Role of the Media in
    Perpetuating Racism and Classism in America', *Urban League Review*, Vol. 14, No. 1.

Gray, B. (1999), 'Steering a Course Somewhere Between Hegemonic Discourses of
    Irishness', in R. Lentin (ed.), *The Expanding Nation: Towards a Multi-Ethnic Ireland*,
    Dublin: Trinity College.

Iyengar, S. (1991), *Is Anyone Responsible? How Television Frames Political Issues*, Chicago:
    University of Chicago Press.

Iyengar, S. and Kinder, D. R. (1987), *News that Matters: Television and American Opinion*,
    Chicago: University of Chicago Press.

Kitzinger, J. (1990), 'Audience Understandings of AIDS Media Messages: A Discussion of
    Methods', *Sociology of Health and Illness*, Vol. 12, No. 3, pp. 25–46.

Lentin, R. and McVeigh, R. (eds) (2002), *Racism and Anti-Racism in Ireland*, Belfast:
    Beyond the Pale.

McCombs, M. and Shaw, D. (1972). 'The Agenda-Setting Function of Mass Media', *Public Opinion Quarterly*, Vol. 36, pp. 176–185.

McCombs, M. and Shaw, D. (1993), 'The Evolution of Agenda-Setting Research: Twenty-Five Years in the Marketplace of Ideas', *Journal of Communication*, Vol. 43, No. 2, pp. 58–67.

MacGreil, M. (1977), *Prejudice and Tolerance in Ireland*, Dublin: College of Industrial Relations.

MacGreil, M. (1996), *Prejudice in Ireland Revisited*, Maynooth: St Patrick's College.

Peillon, M. (2000), 'Strangers in Our Midst', in E. Slater and M. Peillon (eds), *Memories of the Present*, Dublin: Institute of Public Administration.

Pollak, A. (1999), 'An Invitation to Racism? Irish Daily Newspaper Coverage of the Refugee Issue', in D. Kiberd (ed.), *Media in Ireland: The Search for Ethical Journalism*, Dublin: Open Air.

Schaffert, R. W. (1992), *Media Coverage and Political Terrorists: A Quantitative Analysis*, New York: Praeger.

Soubiran-Paillet, F. (1987), 'Presse et delinquance ou comment lire entre les lignes', *Criminologie*, Vol. 20, No. 1.

van Dijk, T. A. (1988), *News Analysis: Case Studies of International and National News in the Press*, Hillsdale, NJ: Lawrence Erlbaum.

van Dijk, T. A. (1990), *Racism and the Press*, London: Routledge.

van Dijk, T. A. (1998a), *Ideology: A Multidisciplinary Approach*, London: Sage.

van Dijk, T. A. (1998b), 'Opinions and Ideologies in the Press', in A. Bell and P. Garrett (eds), *Approaches to Media Discourse*, Oxford: Blackwell.

UNHCR (United Nations High Commission for Refugees) (2002), *Refugees by Numbers*, 2002 edition, Geneva: United Nations High Commission for Refugees; also available on the UNHCR website at www.unhcr.org.

Winkel, F. W. (1990), 'Crime Reporting in Newspapers: An Exploratory Study of the Effects of Ethnic References in Crime News', *Social Behavior*, Vol. 5, No. 2, pp. 87–101.

11

Parity democracy:
gender and political participation

Kathleen Long

Introduction

In any democratic system of government representation of the people, in all their varied subcategories, can be located in two areas of political practice: *representation of members* within the decision-making arena of governmental structures, and *consideration of interests* within the decision-making process and public policy sphere.[1] Historically, however, all groupings of citizens within a democracy have not been represented in its institutions, and recent representation of minority groups still cannot be defined as adequate. In early 2003, Ireland stood tied for sixtieth place in the world as regards the percentage of women members in its national Parliament, with only 13.3 per cent of parliamentarians in the Dáil (the lower house) being women, and 16.7 per cent in the Seanad (the upper house). This chapter examines the reasons why the numbers are not more balanced, and analyses some of the major barriers in liberal democracies to *parity democracy*, which Galligan defines as 'the goal of equal participation by women and men in all aspects of decision-making in a society' (1999: 295).

A framework for examining Ireland's parity democracy

The political science literature on gender, together with the writings of Ware (1996) on political parties, combine to produce a structure for examining the distinct barriers to parity democracy. In what follows we will examine the *sociological* barriers of the influence of cultural values and social norms, the *institutional* barriers of political parties (especially in candidate selection and recruitment) and the electoral system, and the *competitive* barriers of the influence of money/resources and corruption.[2]

Galligan and Wilford (1999) have provided a tool, in their categorisation of political party policies on action to ensure women's representation, that can be transposed to analyse these structured categories. These researchers created four 'engendered' categories in which to place party perspectives on women, on a continuum from low to high positive action. *Reinforcement* affirms traditional roles. *Neutrality* sees women as a part of the government process, but only in quasi-equal terms with men by focusing on merit and gender-neutral policies and approaches. *Recognition* values women's separate involvement in political thought and practice, promoting voluntary actions that strive to lift the participation of women up to the male norm. Finally, *facilitation* recognises cultural and systemic barriers and can incorporate quotas, educational programmes, political training and other interventionist strategies to work positively for equality.

Sociological barriers: the influence of cultural values

Randall and Smyth (1987) focused on the negative cultural attitudes of Irish society, from the earliest stages of socialization. As they say, 'Irish women have until the very recent past been subject to a particularly intense, if complex, process of socialization, through the agency of family, school, and the Church, into an acceptance of an extremely traditional division of labour between the sexes and its implications for women's political role' (1987: 200). Three of the most influential cultural factors, and the ones which will be focused on here, are the images of the traditional Irish family, the impact of the republican movement, and the influence of the Roman Catholic Church.

The traditional Irish family

A discussion of the traditional notion of the family in the Irish context can begin with an examination of Bunreacht na hÉireann – the Constitution of Ireland – which was created and ratified in 1937. There are two subarticles, 41.2.1 and 41.2.2, which help to contextualise this vision of the Irish family. The first asserts that: 'In particular the state recognizes that by her life within the home woman gives to the state the support without which the common good cannot be achieved.' The second subarticle says that: 'The state shall therefore endeavour to ensure that mothers shall not be obliged by economic necessity to engage in labour to the neglect of their duties in the home.' Connelly (1999) notes the importance of the wording of these articles: 'The message conveyed by the use of such language and the ascription of particular historical and social roles to women and men is that power and status in Irish public life are the preserve of the male' (1999: 19).[3]

It could be argued that these two sections of Bunreacht na hÉireann have helped to create, promulgate and perpetuate a cultural belief that affects the way many people think about women's involvement in all areas of public life. At the very simplest, these phrases can be understood to affirm that women's most important place is at home, managing the household and children. At the most complex, the existence of these articles sends messages undermining the value of women's leadership in other areas of social and community life; for by their very involvement in those areas, women could be thought of as neglecting their 'primary duties' of hearth and home.

Various feminists, academics and government officials have taken this section of the constitution as the starting point for their fight for equality for women. The Second Commission on the Status of Women (SCSW), in their report to the government in 1993, recommended the deletion of article 41.2.2 (SCSW 1993: 27) Later the Review Group on the Constitution suggested amendment of the section, and there was additional support for amending it in some agreed form from both the All-Party Oireachtas Committee on the Constitution and the Commission on the Family. The Review Group's revised, gender-neutral Article 41.2 read: 'The State recognises that home and family life give society a support without which the common good cannot be achieved. The State shall endeavour to support persons caring for others in the home' (SCSW 1999: 7). There was also a more controversial proposal in 1999 for an equal rights or anti-discrimination amendment. However, no action has been taken by the government on any of these recommendations.

The Roman Catholic Church must also be mentioned with relation to the dissemination of an image of the traditional Irish family. The Church supported the notion of an Irish model of the family from the beginning, and formulated its opinion on various state policies with the 'natural family' at the forefront of its considerations. This influence was evident in respect of such issues as the Health Act, 1947, and the Mother and Child Scheme of 1951, as well as the debates surrounding divorce, adoption and contraception. One marked demonstration of this emphasis on family can be seen in the text from the Bishop's Committee on Adoption in 1952, which states: 'The Church regards the natural family as the ideal unit of family life and, therefore, must oppose any measure in an Adoption Bill that would tend to substitute an artificial for a natural family' (quoted in Whyte 1980: 276).

The impact of the republican movement

The early years of the twentieth century were a socially and politically volatile period in Irish history. It was a time for the shaping of a distinctive 'Irish identity'. Gardiner (1993) highlights women's involvement during this turbulent time, stating that 'Irish women experienced a double incentive to political mobilization – as [both] suffragists and freedom fighters – in the early years of the century' (1993: 46). As the political reality unfolded, however, nationalism became the stronger of the two movements, forcing the women's movement to take a back seat. One consequence was that the primacy of the familial role for Irish women was maintained in the creation of the Irish Free State. Ward argues that 'with no organisation to give priority to women's needs, post-partition

Ireland was able to implement, with little resistance, highly reactionary policies in relation to women, whose domestic role within the family became endowed with almost sacramental qualities' (quoted in Daly 1997:104).

After Fianna Fáil won the election of 1932, they continued the policies restricting women's rights begun by the Cumann na nGaedheal government, which 'effectively censored information on birth control, banned divorce, and virtually excluded women from jury service in criminal and civil cases' (Shannon 1997: 262). Fianna Fáil also implemented measures of their own which had a deleterious impact on the lives of women. For example, the infamous 'marriage bar' required most women employed in teaching, the civil service, local authorities, health boards and most businesses to resign their positions upon marriage. Statistics show that between 1922 and 1977 only 24 of the total of 650 Teachtaí Dála (TDs, or Members of Parliament) elected to the lower house were women (Shannon 1997: 262). It should be noted, moreover, that these figures include many women who were elected on the basis of their connections through family relationship with a male revolutionary or politician (Manning 1979: 94–5).

The influence of the Roman Catholic Church

A third factor that has a tremendous influence over Irish culture is the Roman Catholic Church, the primary religious institution in the country. As O'Connor (1998) states, 'Within Ireland, the institutional church is a social and cultural reality. Even today, its influence on various aspects of social life, such as the educational system, is very considerable. Much of the dynamic for change in Irish society at this point in time, can be understood as arising from a tension between church and state' (1998: 27). The granting in the 1937 Constitution of a 'special position' to the 'Holy Catholic Apostolic and Roman Church as the guardian of the Faith professed by the great majority of the citizens' had a cultural impact;[4] for it 'reflected and reinforced Roman Catholic social teaching in endorsing the family as the primary unit of society ... [and] defining womanhood in terms of motherhood' (O'Connor 1998: 63). The special status also allowed for a continued spreading of the influence of the Church, which for women was seen as 'extremely narrow and rigid': 'The central importance of the family and of women's role as child-bearers and home-makers, the indissolubility of marriage, total opposition to all forms of artificial contraception and above all abortion, all these are essential precepts of the Church's teaching' (Randall and Smyth 1987: 197). The authority of the leaders of the Catholic Church was widely accepted culturally, and it could be argued that the Church has only diminished in its role as the sole moral voice for the people of Ireland in the latter half of the twentieth century. According to Randall and Smyth, 'A complex of forces such as economic change, urbanisation, tourism, EEC membership and perhaps most of all the development of Irish television, have gradually worked to undermine its hold' (1987: 197–8).

Due to the influence of the women's movement in Ireland and the nation's integration into the European Union (EU), the overarching trends in Irish culture in respect of family, state and Church are changing. This movement, however, is a slow one. Wilcox found that 'Irish women are among the most supportive of general gender equality, of equality in politics and increased numbers of women in the legislatures, and of the goal of radically transforming society ... yet they are the least likely to favour equality in the family and among the least likely to trust women in non-traditional professions' (Wilcox 1991: 529). More research is needed in this area to measure current levels of such attitudes, but it is clear that cultural influences in Ireland – especially historical ones concerning the image of the family, the nationalist movement and the Catholic Church – retain a strong grip on the everyday lives of the people in Ireland, subconsciously or otherwise.

Influence of social norms: the media

The second piece of the sociological puzzle under examination is the media as the promoter of social norms. Although the Irish media are historically seen as one of the main promoters of 'liberal' ideas, the various media themselves suffer from a lack of women in positions of power and decision-making. There are in fact some common themes across national boundaries in research on the media. Political scientists have found that the media's coverage of women fails not in *commission* but in *omission*, in that the media do not generally deal with women's influence in areas other than what might be traditionally regarded as 'women's topics', like family, health and education. There is also an unbalanced focus on the shared concerns of women and what they accomplish together, without focusing on the individual achievements of women politicians.

There has been no published research on the influence of the Irish media in promulgating social norms or cultural values as regards women in politics. However, Galligan highlights the importance of the media in framing the debate when she notes that: 'In Ireland today, the story of the relationship between women and public policy is told through the media' (1998: 1). Following a discussion of topics such as the election of Mary Robinson to the Irish presidency, and that of Mary McAleese who succeeded her, as well as abortion cases and the infected blood tragedy,[5] Galligan theorises at length about a new perception of women being portrayed in the media. But for her answer as to why this has occurred, she looks not to the activity of the media but to growing feminist activism in many areas of Irish life.

A conclusion on sociological barriers

Taking account of the notion of the traditional Irish family, the impact of the republican movement, and the influence of the Roman Catholic Church, it can be argued that Irish society has acted in a manner that *reinforces* the traditional roles of women – in politics as in other spheres of human activity. Support for this conclusion can be found in several quarters: in the failure to change those articles in Bunreacht na hÉireann supporting the primary role of a woman as wife and mother; in the primacy of nationalism as the leading social movement since the foundation of the state; and in the persistence of the moral voice of the Roman Catholic Church, at both the conscious and subconscious levels.

As for the influence of the Irish media, they tend to avoid the superficial, such as the clothing and general appearance of female candidates; and they also avoid the tendency to 'gender frame' every debate (see Norris 1997). In part this might be attributed to the power of political parties in the Irish system, since media coverage of politicians focuses mainly on their message as a member of a particular *party*. On the other hand, there have been few newspaper articles or television programmes that specifically buttress or support the notion of parity democracy; rather, editorials and features act in an ostensibly *neutral* manner, highlighting the merit and experience of the candidates concerned. The influence of the media can thus fairly be characterised as neutral.

Institutional barriers to the representation of women

Political parties and candidate selection elsewhere

In Europe generally, political parties are the 'gatekeepers' of political life, by virtue of their processes of candidate recruitment and selection. Ireland is no different. Therefore, it is within parties that any changes in pursuit of gender equality must occur. At this party organisational level, actions can be grouped into three main areas of strategic action. A *rhetorical* strategy is one that begins with the party leaders, where they 'talk the talk' about the importance of women's involvement in all areas of party politics, but this generally does not involve real movement towards equality. A strategy of *positive action* (or affirmative action) is one that includes special training for women candidates and, sometimes, financial assistance. The final strategy is known as *positive discrimination*. It calls for mandatory quotas for the numbers of women in party positions and candidate selection. These quotas, which are regarded by some as reverse discrimination, can take many forms, including temporary quotas, and quotas that are negotiable in number (Lovenduski 1993: 8–11). The political parties of Europe implement these strategies in various ways, and in order to place Irish practice in context it is useful to look at a few examples.

In terms of level of representation, the best results for women in Europe – indeed in the world – have come from the Nordic countries. The case of Sweden, ranked first, with women making up 45.3 per cent of parliamentary members, demonstrates the success of positive discrimination. Cross-party female politicians did not demand formal quotas in Swedish political parties, but made parties set a goal of 40 per cent representation for *each* sex. Denmark is ranked second in the world, with women making up 38 per cent of members of its Parliament. The Danish parties adopted voluntary quotas, which were temporary in nature. Because the numbers of women in elected office did increase as a result, quotas were abandoned in 1996. Norway, which ranks fifth at 36.4 per cent representation of women, also established quotas in the mid-1970s. By the 1979 local elections, women made up one third of all elected local representatives.

Germany is a split case, with some parties employing positive discrimination through quotas, and others choosing the path of positive action. Germany is currently ranked tenth in the world, with 32.2 per cent women in the lower house and 24.6 per cent in the upper house. In Belgium, the system of party lists was the major barrier to parity. In order to combat this, the government passed legislation in 1994, known as the Smet-Tobback Law, which required that a maximum of two thirds of a party list be of one gender. Some Belgium political parties operate quotas, and since 1999 there has been a requirement to alternate candidates on the basis of gender on the party lists. Taken together these actions have brought about improvements, albeit slowly; in the Belgian Senate 28.2 per cent of members are women, and in the Chamber of Representatives the figure is 23.3 per cent.

The political parties of France have historically been staunchly opposed to positive action or discrimination to promote gender parity, and have thus left change in the hands of government. The French constitution was amended in July 1999, and a 'parity law' was passed in June 2000. This is the first such law in any country, is applicable to most elections, and requires that 50 per cent of candidates (with a margin of one either way) be of each gender. The legislation is backed up by a system of fines, and has already made a significant impact in elections for local councillors and Members of the European Parliament (MEPs); further real progress should be measurable in the next few election cycles.

Italy's political system has notoriously been plagued by corruption at various levels – something which might keep many people, both men and women, away from the world of politics. In terms of the political parties, the major players have different strategies in relation to women candidates, some of which are grounded in traditional family roles; some of which are highly influenced by the Catholic Church; and none of which incorporates positive action or positive discrimination techniques. Overall, Italy ranks seventy-fourth in the world in the representation of women, with only 9.8 per cent in the lower house of Parliament and 7.8 per cent in the upper house.

Political parties and candidate selection in Ireland

A governmental commission, the Commission on the Status of Women, was established in 1972 to examine the lives of Irish women in all their aspects, including political life. At that time, the Commission made a specific call for parties 'to make a greater effort to include women in party structures and as candidates for election' (Galligan and Wilford 1999: 152). This gentle request was met with little action by the political parties, and it was effectively repeated in more forceful terms by the SCSW in 1993. It called for a positive action programme that would include, for example, minimum quotas of women candidates in each party, family friendly policies, adequate timing between selection and election day, and reserved seats for women on national executives/executive committees (SCSW 1993: 220–1). The government published two follow-up progress reports in 1996 and 1999, but once again very little action was taken.

More recently, the Department of Justice, Equality and Law Reform (DJELR) commissioned two reports by the National Women's Council (NWC), entitled *Politics Needs More Women: What the Irish Political System Must Do* (2002a) and *Irish Politics: Jobs for the Boys* (2002b). Before offering recommendations, these reports examined the current situation as regards women's representation, the possible role of the government and political parties, and electoral system models elsewhere in the EU. The second report, *Jobs for the Boys*, compiled after the spring 2002 general election, highlights a lowly 1 per cent improvement in the number of women elected to the Dáil in the preceding ten years, as well as no change as regards local elections, where the number of women representatives remained at 15 per cent over the same period. The report also notes that a staggering 45 per cent of current female TDs come from dynastic 'political' families, where male members (fathers, husbands, uncles, grandfathers) had laid the groundwork for name recognition as well as providing the political networks which allowed these women to overcome certain barriers. The report goes on to identify some factors which the NWC believes act as barriers to women's participation in national politics in Ireland, including: the socialisation process; incumbency (having won an elected position, the occupant becomes less likely to be defeated next time round); underrepresentation of women in traditional entry points such as law or business; an absence of child care support; a lack of family friendly policies; and family unfriendly working hours. Needless to say, many of these barriers are experienced by women in other areas of the world of work, and they all demand the attention of the government.

In the *Irish Politics: Jobs for the Boys* report the NWC recommends radical action by the government and political parties. It applauds the successful use of quotas in other European nations, the influence of supportive governments, and the enactment of equality laws. It calls for further legislation, similar to that in France, which requires a 40:60 per cent gender ratio among candidates of each political party – for both national and local elections – in order to be entitled to receive 50 per cent of their election funding. The quota would be temporary, and could be removed once women reached 40 per cent representation, as in the case of Denmark. The report further calls on the government to provide resources and support to the women's community sector in order to facilitate greater political involvement; to establish a national support structure for women in decision-making; to re-establish an Oireachtas (government) committee for women's affairs; and to make the Dáil more family friendly, with shorter sitting hours but longer parliamentary sessions.

Against the background of all these recommendations from governmental commissions and of experience elsewhere, we can now examine the practice of each Irish political party – including their own words in election manifestos, and the outcome of the 2002 general election – to determine if they are acting in a manner of *reinforcement, neutrality, recognition* or *facilitation* in pursuit of progressive parity democracy.

The parties and parity democracy: Fianna Fáil

Since the formation of the party in 1926, Fianna Fáil has held a central position in Irish political life, and has gained an average of 40 per cent of voters' first preference support in elections for more than seventy years. In working for parity democracy, however, Fianna Fáil has not contributed much, due perhaps, in great measure, to its historical foundations. For while he was successful in harnessing support for Fianna Fáil from all sections of the electorate, 'de Valera's paternalism and restricted view of the role of women found reflection within the party organisation' (Galligan and Wilford 1999: 154).

Of the modern party, Galligan says: 'The continued pattern of women's absence from power within Fianna Fáil can largely be attributed to the persistence of the view within the party that women provide the support services for the election of male candidates' (1998: 161). Certainly the party leadership has consistently used only a rhetorical strategy in promoting gender parity. A slight change in attitude has come about fairly recently, however, as evidenced in the 1997 election manifesto, *People Before Politics* (Fianna Fáil 1997). On the issue of the representation of women within the party ranks, Fianna Fáil declared its strong support for the 'establishment of quotas and targets for women as a medium term strategy' (Galligan 1999: 157). In response to the SCSW, the party spoke of instructing constituency executives to guarantee a gender balance on slates of candidates, holding early selection conventions to build local profiles, providing training programmes, and reserving four out of fifteen seats on the National Executive for women.

The 2002 manifesto, *A Lot Done, More to Do* (Fianna Fáil 2002), seemed to forget a great many of the promises of the 1997 version. Only one section mentions gender issues; entitled 'Gender Equality', it states, in a very unspecific manner, that

> We believe that the key lesson of the last few decades on work on equality is that activity cannot be concentrated in one area, nor can progress be achieved primarily through distinct programmes. It is through the effective mainstreaming of equality policy that real progress can be achieved. At the same time, serious and sustained targeting on specific issues continues to be required. (Fianna Fáil 2002: 82)

No mention is made of any need to act in a proactive manner – whether as a party or as part of government – to further parity democracy in Ireland. Fianna Fáil thus still lies at the more traditional end of the spectrum. It is especially unfortunate to note that it actually regressed in the 2002 election cycle, moving the party backwards into a policy combining aspects of *reinforcement* and *neutrality*.

The parties and parity democracy: Fine Gael

Gathering 20 to 25 per cent of the popular support of the people of Ireland, Fine Gael has been slightly better than Fianna Fáil in terms of progressive attitudes and policies for women, the leadership of Garret FitzGerald being evident in some of the modernisation. The first wave in the 1980s was a slow one and traditional patterns asserted themselves, with women finding local leadership positions more often as secretary and treasurer than as chair. A Fine Gael Women's Group, founded in 1985 to support and encourage women within the party, led to a second wave of modernisation in the 1990s that included an emphasis on recruitment and training. Their positive action strategy also contained a voluntary 33 per cent quota for women candidates, especially for local elections; but the party generally has a theoretical leaning in favour of targets rather than quotas for female candidates. Fine Gael does not reserve seats for women on Executive Council, but insists that it none the less achieves a good gender balance.

Another aspect of this positive action strategy was the appointment of 'a gender proofing' front bench member. Like Fianna Fáil, Fine Gael favours more family friendly practices in the Oireachtas, as well as a government supported crèche. It is also Fine Gael's 'intention' to arrange selection conventions with enough time to ensure all candidates can develop a high profile. However, these examples of word choice – 'favour', 'intention' – demonstrate the lack of forcefulness and specifics needed to guarantee a truly progressive policy.

The 1997 Fine Gael election manifesto, entitled *Securing a Safer Society* (Fine Gael 1997), included only a few references to women's influence on public policy, most of which were related to women as victims of crime, thus demonstrating rather traditional and protectionist tendencies. The 2002 manifesto, *Towards a Better Quality of Life* (Fine Gael 2002), makes no mention of issues of gender, let alone gender parity in representative government. Overall, the Fine Gael party rests at the conservative end of a gender-recognition category. Like Fianna Fáil, Fine Gael demonstrated negligible prioritising of the issue during the 2002 election, and has indeed slipped slightly backwards into a policy practice of gender *neutrality*.

The parties and parity democracy: the Progressive Democrats

A splinter party created in 1985 mainly from the ranks of Fianna Fáil, the Progressive Democrats (PDs) stand close to the forefront in equality of representation, even though – remarkably – they deny any commitment to gender equality. Possible reasons for the successful record of the PDs can perhaps be related to its recent establishment and its current strong female leader, Mary Harney. There were fewer institutional connections between the PDs and the traditions and leaders of the past, and with the legacies of Irish nationalism, the Catholic Church and traditional notions of the family. The co-founder, party leader and Tánaiste (Deputy Prime Minister) plainly contributes to the aura of equality within the party; and many women party members see Harney as a role model who naturally makes the party more supportive of women's participation in decision-making.

Regarding overt public policy efforts for the equality of women, the PDs profess a strong conviction against positive action. Their 1997 manifesto, *A New Deal* (PDs 1997), contained three sentences regarding women and a vague and general commitment to the notion of equality. Unlike other parties, the PDs did not respond to a formal request from the author for information about the implementation of the recommendations of the SCSW. Their 2002 Manifesto, *Value for Your Vote* (PDs 2002), suggested a slight shift, however, from an ideology of complete gender *neutrality* to one demonstrating some *recognition* of gender. It included a section entitled 'Women in Leadership', which began with the statement 'The Progressive Democrats believe that our democracy is unfinished while so few women are participating in political life and leadership.' Quoting the then overall statistics on Dáil membership, they boasted that one third of PD candidates for the 2002 election were women, as well as half their Dáil members. The PDs also called for the removal of the dual mandate (permitting people to be members of the Dáil and a local authority at the same time – see Chapter 4), which, it has been argued, might allow and even encourage more women candidates. While it could have been said after the 1997 general election that the only woman-led party had the worst record for recognising the importance of gender, with the 2002 manifesto the tide evidently washed gently up into the area between *neutrality* and gender *recognition*. In order to place itself firmly in the latter category, however, the PDs will have to enter a world of promotional strategies and special policies; and they show very few signs of doing so.

The parties and parity democracy: the Labour Party

As the main left-wing party in Ireland, the Labour Party leads in working for greater women's representation within its party structures. The party's historical grounding in an ideology of equality regardless of class allowed for the earliest incorporation of gender equality issues into party policy in the late 1960s. Even in this case, however, progress was slow, with the first positive action programme by a political party that included the use of a limited quota system arriving only in 1984.

A larger step forward came with the creation of a Gender Quota Committee in 1989, which established a formula in 1991 for the involvement of more women in party decision-making; this required the immediate adoption of a minimum 20 per cent gender quota, and a commitment to increase that progressively to 40 per cent. This was a clear move in the direction of parity democracy, and by the local elections of 1998, over 30 per cent of Labour candidates were women. The Labour nominee, Mary Robinson, won the 1990 presidential election, and became the first female President of the Republic of Ireland.

In their 1997 election manifesto, *Making the Vital Difference* (Labour 1997), the Labour Party included numerous specific ideas geared towards enhancing political equality. These included amending Article 41.2 of the constitution and introducing a family leave policy. The party's 2002 manifesto, *Ambitious for Ireland* (Labour 2002), mentioned a number of gender-related topics. The first was the need for a continued push for constitutional change: 'We propose that the outdated provisions on women in the home would be replaced by a gender-neutral provision on the role of family members and carers who work in the home.' As regards representation in government, under the heading 'Equality and Law Reform', the manifesto said that 'the lamentable record of the outgoing administration in relation to gender equality will be rectified by new legislation to require 40% gender balance in appointments to state boards'. Like the PDs, they called for a lifting of the dual mandate. Although there was no direct appeal for quotas or a parity law, the Labour Party continued on its *recognition* pathway to parity democracy – somewhat lacking in specifics but staying on message.

The parties and parity democracy: the Green Party

This rather young and very small party, established in 1991, held only two seats in the Dáil after the 1997 election, but won six seats in the 2002 election. As a declared party of the left, it professes a strong belief in gender equality within party ranks, and can be categorised as *facilitatory* in its quest for parity democracy. The party constitution of 1997 includes five articles related to gender balance, among them one that requires a 40 per cent quota for committee members and candidates. During party meetings and conventions, a crèche is available for all party members, and the party supports increased family friendly policies for the Dáil.

The Green Party 2002 manifesto, *Meeting the Challenges, Seizing the Opportunities* (Green Party 2002), was the only one to discuss a party position on parity democracy at great length, and with specific promises. Under the section 'Maintaining Our Communities', the Greens aver that 'Ireland can only benefit from a true gender balance in all aspects of life. We also believe that equality must encompass increasing life choices for all, enabling all individuals to pursue fulfilling careers and lifestyles' (Green Party 2002). On political representation, they stand closely allied with the reports of the NWC, calling for better child care, half of any party's funding being contingent on a 40:60 gender balance among election candidates, and greater gender equity in governmental appointments. In March 2003 the Greens departed from their previous support of the dual mandate, and called for a referendum on the issue instead. Overall, however, the Greens are at the forefront of the fight for parity democracy, yet their limited electoral status hampers their effectiveness in sparking change.

The parties and parity democracy: Sinn Féin

In the 2002 election, Sinn Féin increased its number of Dáil seats from one to five. In its campaign, the party took up the banner for gender equality in representation. The party's leader, Gerry Adams, in a speech in April 2002, addressed the party's election theme – *Building an Ireland of Equals* (Sinn Féin 2002) – which later became the title of the election manifesto. The party even issued a separate leaflet entitled 'Women in an Ireland of Equals', which called for the creation of new structures to facilitate fuller political involvement for women. It fell short of specific recommendations for implementation of these structures, but supported the NWC proposal for a 40:60 gender quota on management boards, and called for an outside body to monitor the implementation of the National Plan for Women. Sinn Féin can therefore fairly be described as falling into the *recognition* category.

The electoral system

The other institutional factor that needs to be analysed is the electoral system. The Irish electoral system is one of proportional representation by means of a single transferable vote (PR[STV]). This system is very different to a simple plurality, one member per constituency, 'first-past-the-post' system, where an elector casts a single vote for one person only, and the candidate with the most votes, even if they do not amount to a majority of those cast, is the winner. PR(STV), by contrast, operates in multi-member constituencies, and electors vote for the candidates in order of their preference, marking the ballot paper '1', '2', '3' etc. Using a complicated counting system, there are no wasted votes and the effect is to produce a result reasonably proportional to the wishes of the voters.[6] A great deal of research exists about the impact of electoral systems on the representation of women in national parliaments.[7] Norris says that in terms of the fairness of the outcome, PR(STV) 'falls somewhere in the middle' (1999: 117). Party lists (where electors do not vote for individuals but for lists of candidates drawn up by the political parties) seem to benefit women more because the parties are likely to ensure that the lists are balanced and representative, because there is more scope for affirmative action, and because of greater opportunity for party competition. We may conclude none the less that PR(STV), as a reasonably fair electoral system, serves to facilitate equal gender representation and does not act as a serious barrier to women's representation.

A conclusion on institutional barriers

Overall, in terms of their approach, Irish political parties fall somewhere in between the proactivity of the Nordic countries and the dismal case of Italy, and could be said to have a rather neutral outlook. The ones with the most influence – Fianna Fáil and Fine Gael – remain near the conservative end of the spectrum, a fact played out in the 2002 election: Fianna Fáil returned a lower number of women than in the previous Dáil (just under 9 per cent), while Fine Gael has its smallest percentage of women TDs in twenty-five years (6 per cent). On the other hand, the PDs achieved gender parity, while one third of the Labour Party's TDs are women. Detracting from the progressiveness that this implies, it must be noted that the actual number of women in the Dáil is still pitifully small. As for the electoral system, as we have noted above, it can be categorised as *facilitating* gender parity, but only if political parties use the possibilities to a greater degree by ensuring more women candidates.

Competitive barriers to the representation of women in Ireland

Influence of money/resources

Political systems in Europe are dominated by political parties, and competition between them is strongly influenced by the funding that they receive and, more particularly, how resources are distributed to candidates. However, no studies have been done on the influence of funding on the campaigns of women politicians in Ireland. In particular, research is needed on whether there are any differences in the ways that parties support women and men financially, as well as the timing of the funding (e.g. do parties allocate appropriate resources to women to build the necessary local base, as per the recommendations of the SCSW and the NWC?). One reason for the lack of research might be that the entire campaign process in Ireland is rather short, and there is thus more academic focus on such issues as manifestos, before the election, and the formation of coalition governments, after the election.

Limits on campaign spending are dictated by the Electoral Act of 1997 and the Electoral Amendment Act of 1998. Limits for total permitted spending by candidates in a general election for the Dáil are low, particularly as compared to campaigns in the United States. The maximum expenditure limit per candidate for the largest constituency size of five seats is little more than €26,000. Candidates and parties also simply do not have the opportunity to spend as much money as in the US because of the shortness of the campaigns.

In the case of Ireland, then, money or the lack of it has not historically disadvantaged women. It might be argued, however, that women entering the political arena generally begin at a financial disadvantage, and thus need compensating support from their parties in order to contest successfully. One of the more obvious reasons for this is the lack of pay equity that still exists in the modern Irish experience – and indeed that of most countries around the world. As McNamara and Mooney note, 'Even young Irish women who have had equal access to education and training earn just 86% of average male earnings. The average Irish woman earns 73% of average male hourly earnings' (2000: 14).

Since most female candidates are supported by a party, it must be concluded that in the Irish case, money and resources are neutral in effect. As of now, with the strict national campaign laws and funding regulations, this competitive factor can be rated as *facilitatory* for women seeking elected office. This might change in upcoming elections, however, with an increasing number of independent candidates who must fundraise outside of political party circles.

Corruption

Collins and O'Shea (2000) chronicle the causes, consequences and reality of corruption within the Irish political system. While this work is highly informative and groundbreaking, there is insufficient information available from it to enable analysis of whether corruption is a barrier or otherwise to women's involvement in politics in Ireland. By some accounts, the existence of corruption in current political systems is seen as an advantage for women, for the linkage between corruption and the present status of parliaments as predominately male institutions allows women to be seen as 'outsiders' untouched by the wickedness of the past. Moreover, there are instances where women have proven in reality to be less corrupt in politics. Indeed Collins and O'Shea report on a summary by Transparency International (2000), which asserts that 'Higher levels of women's participation in public life are associated with lower levels of corruption. Corruption is less severe where women comprise a larger share of parliamentary seats ... [Further,] higher rates of female participation in government are associated with lower levels of corruption' (2000: 64). However, we clearly cannot offer any judgement on this score in respect of Ireland – for the time being at least.

A conclusion on competitive barriers

It is fairly clear that the factors of money and resources, as well as the existence of corruption, do not seem to have a large impact on the levels of gender parity within the Irish political system. In other words, none of these factors seems – outwardly at any rate – to advantage or disadvantage women as against men. The only phenomenon likely to influence that picture in the near future would be a further increase in the number of independent, non-party candidates and the consequential need for personal fundraising. For now, these competitive barriers must be rated as *facilitatory* in respect of money and resources and *neutral* as regards corruption.

The most influential factors?

Out of all this analysis of the sociological, institutional and competitive influences on gender parity in political representation in Ireland, some factors stand out as being of the greatest importance. For reasons detailed above, cultural values and political parties act as the two most significant barriers to women reaching parity in elected representation, *reinforcing* traditional roles for women or retaining a *neutral* stance towards increasing gender parity. While these are obviously not the only barriers to parity democracy, they are highly influential ones. Figure 11.1 illustrates the six main factors analysed in this chapter, breaking down political parties into leading parties and smaller parties.

Figure 11.1 *Rating of factors influencing levels of women in political office in Ireland*

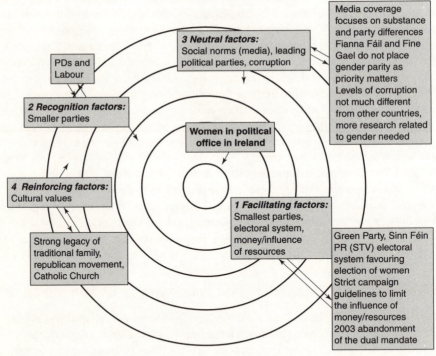

Source: Adapted from political party model by A. Appleton and A. G. Mazur (1993), 'Transformation or Modernization: The Rhetoric and Reality of Gender and Party Politics in France', in J. Lovenduski and P. Norris (ed), *Gender and Party Politics*, London: Sage, p. 96.

A comparison with the United States

Most of the comparators referred to in this chapter have been in Europe, and it would be useful finally to contrast the situation in Ireland with that in the US, which is only slightly ahead of Ireland in the world ranking of female participation, with 14.3 per cent women members in the House of Representatives and 13 per cent in the Senate. In the US, the media and the electoral system serve as the strongest of the factors that militate against gender parity in political representation. In the world of media relations, much emphasis is placed on the skill of female candidates in juggling family and career, but this stress will no doubt lessen in the coming years. As more women enter the political field, and more men accept equal responsibility in the affairs of home and family, gender framing and stereotyping will cease to be newsworthy. As for the electoral system, little change is on the horizon. A reform of the electoral system seemed likely after the 2000 presidential election, which exposed the inadequacies of voting through the electoral college. That reform movement has since lost its momentum, however, and it would need a remarkable spark to ignite a change of the electoral system into one more conducive to the representation of minority groups – a system such as PR or the party list.

On the other hand, it is important to acknowledge again the power of incumbency as a strong barrier to parity in representation, especially in the US. As Darcy et al. have observed, 'it appears that while voter discrimination now plays at best a small part in keeping women out of office, the impact of incumbency and low turnover for many offices is a major explanation' (1994: 90–1). This factor emerges as key in many of the works analysing the 2002 election, especially when taken with redistricting (the redrawing of constituency boundaries) due to census results.

Looking outward: learning from others

The lessons that Ireland could learn from the European countries cited earlier are fairly clear, particularly as regards positive action and positive discrimination. However, comparison with the US is also of some interest. Although both Ireland and the US are Western liberal democracies, each is influenced by very different sociological, institutional and competitive factors. Indeed, in respect of the first two categories, they differ fundamentally: cultural values for Ireland, versus media for the United States; political parties for Ireland, versus election laws and procedures for the United States. It is through pairings like this that each country can gain knowledge to improve its own democracy.[8]

The area in which Ireland could very specifically learn from the US is in managing the cultural shift from traditional notions of the family to redefined roles for both men and women. This does not mean that there can be a smooth and simple transition; but the success of American businesses in working to shatter the 'glass ceiling' that prevents the advancement of women in management bears close examination. As regards the institutional aspects, Ireland suffers from a lack of a political party leadership in keeping gender parity high on the agenda. Following the release of the November 2002 report of the NWC, only one party leader, Pat Rabbitte of Labour, asserted the need for proactive movement towards parity within his own party. And although not much can be learned from the mainstream US political parties, something can be gleaned from individuals. With the much less structured party system in the US, candidates rely heavily on garnering personal donations and support for each individual campaign. Perhaps the message here is that women in Ireland might be better served by standing outside the party system; they should rather tap into grassroots sources of support, financial and otherwise, using the networks and techniques deployed by the female candidates of all parties in the US as models.

Studies of American politics find that female politicians are not any less 'electable' than men,[9] and the same is sure to be true in Ireland. In the light of this, the looming reality of women's leadership in elected office is an inevitable and exciting development. Gender parity is the first step to better democracy, which in turn promises better nations and better lives for all. Borrowing from the 2002 election manifesto of Fianna Fáil, 'Lots done, more to do.'

Notes

1 Theorists who focus on issues of representation include Phillips (1991), Lovenduski and Norris (1991), O'Connor (1998) and Mansbridge (1999).

2 One major barrier to the equal representation of women recognised in international literature, 'incumbency', will be referred to only briefly in this chapter due to the limits of the available statistical data in Ireland.

3 This 'special position' section was removed from the constitution by referendum in 1972.

4 Recent writings about the decrease in levels of Church power include Clancy (1991), MacGreil (1991), and Hornsby-Smith and Whelan (1994). It is important to note, as well, that the research for this chapter was completed before the impact of the sexual and paedophile scandals of the Roman Catholic Church was fully recognised and analysed in both Ireland and the United States in 2002.

5 Blood products supplied in the 1970s and 1980s by the state blood transfusion service were found to be contaminated with the hepatitis C virus.

6 For a fuller description of the STV electoral system, see Collins and Cradden (2001: Ch. 2).

7 This cross-national research on electoral systems and their influence on female candidates includes the work of Rule and Zimmerman (1992), Darcy (1992), Norris (1994, 1999), Lijphart (1994) and Matland (1998).

8 As a US citizen, the present writer believes that the United States could learn much from the example of Irish democracy.

9 The recent work of Susan Carroll (2001) provides a stellar examination of the issue of women's representation in the United States from multiple angles.

References

Appleton, A. and Mazur, A. G. (1993), 'Transformation or Modernization: The Rhetoric and Reality of Gender and Party Politics in France', in J. Lovenduski and P. Norris (eds), *Gender and Party Politics*, London: Sage.

Carroll, S. (ed.) (2001), *The Impact of Women in Public Office*, Bloomington: Indiana University Press.

Clancy, P. (1991), 'Irish Nuptuality and Fertility Patterns in Transition', in G. Kiely and V. Richardson (eds), *Family Policy: European Perspectives*, Dublin: Family Studies Centre.

Collins, N. and Cradden, T. (2001), *Irish Politics Today*, Manchester: Manchester University Press.

Collins, N. and O'Shea, M. (2000), *Understanding Corruption in Irish Politics*, Cork: Cork University Press.

Connelly, A. (1999), 'Women and the Constitution of Ireland', in Y. Galligan, E. Ward and R. Wilford (eds), *Contesting Politics: Women in Ireland, North and South*, Boulder, CO: Westview Press.

Daly, M. E. (1997), 'Oh, Kathleen Ni Houlihan, Your Way's a Thorny Way! The Condition of Women in Twentieth-Century Ireland', in A. Bradley and M. Gialanella Valiulis (eds), *Gender and Sexuality in Modern Ireland*, Amherst: University of Massachusetts Press.

Darcy, R. (1992), 'Electoral Barriers to Women', in W. Rule and J. Zimmerman (eds), *United States Electoral Systems: Their Impact on Women and Minorities*, New York: Praeger.

Darcy, R., Welch, S. and Clark, J. (1994), 'Women, Elections, and Representation', in M. Githens, P. Norris and J. Lovenduski (eds), *Different Roles, Different Voices: Women and Politics in the United States and Europe*, New York: HarperCollins.

DJELR (Department of Justice, Equality and Law Reform) (2001), *Draft 1: National Plan for Women 2001–2005*, www.justice.ie.

Fianna Fáil (1997), *People Before Politics: Fianna Fáil Manifesto 1997*, Dublin: Fianna Fáil.

Fianna Fáil (2002), *A Lot Done, More to Do: Fianna Fáil Manifesto 2002*, Dublin: Fianna Fáil.

Fine Gael (1997), *Securing a Safer Society*, Election Manifesto, Dublin: Fine Gael.

Fine Gael (2002), *Towards a Better Quality of Life*, Election Manifesto, Dublin: Fine Gael.

Galligan, Y. (1998), *Women and Politics in Contemporary Ireland: From the Margins to the Mainstream*, London: Pinter.

Galligan, Y. (1999), 'Women in Politics', in J. Coakley and M. Gallagher (eds), *Politics in the Republic of Ireland*, London: Routledge.

Galligan, Y. and Wilford, R. (1999), 'Gender and Party Politics in the Republic of Ireland', in Y. Galligan, E. Ward and R. Wilford (eds), *Contesting Politics: Women in Ireland, North and South*, Boulder, CO: Westview Press.

Gardiner, F. (1993), 'Political Interest and Participation of Irish Women 1922–1992: The Unfinished Revolution', in A. Smyth (ed.), *Irish Women's Studies Reader*, Dublin: Attic Press.

Green Party (2002), *Manifesto 2002: Meeting the Challenges, Seizing the Opportunities*, Dublin: Green Party.

Hornsby-Smith, M. P. and Whelan, C. T. (1994), 'Religious and Moral Values', in C. Whelan (ed.), *Values and Social Change in Ireland*, Dublin: Gill and Macmillan.

Labour (1997), *Making the Vital Difference: Manifesto 1997*, Dublin: Labour Party.

Labour (2002), *Ambitious for Ireland: Manifesto 2002*, Dublin: Labour Party.

Lijphart, A. (1994), *Electoral Systems and Party Systems*, Oxford: Oxford University Press.

Lovenduski, J. (1993), 'Introduction: The Dynamics of Gender and Party', in J. Lovenduski and P. Norris (eds), *Gender and Party Politics*, London: Sage.

Lovenduski, J. and Norris, P. (1991), 'Party Rules and Women's Representation: Reforming the Labour Party Selection Process,' in *British Elections and Parties Yearbook, 1991*, Hemel Hempstead: Harvester Wheatsheaf.

Lovenduski, J. and Randall, V. (1993), *Contemporary Feminist Politics: Women and Power in Britain*, Oxford: Oxford University Press.

MacGreil, M. (1991), *Religious Practice and Attitudes in Ireland*, Maynooth: Survey Research Unit.

McNamara, M. and Mooney, P. (2002), *Women in Parliament: Ireland, 1918–2000*, Dublin: Wolfhound Press.

Manning, M. (1979), 'Women in Irish National and Local Politics 1922–1977', in M. MacCurtain and D. O Corráin (eds), *Women in Irish Society: The Historical Dimension*, Dublin: Arlen House.

Mansbridge, J. (1999), 'Should Blacks Represent Blacks and Women Represent Women? A Contingent "Yes"', *Journal of Politics*, Vol. 61, No. 3, pp. 628–54.

Matland, R. E. (1998), 'Enhancing Women's Political Participation: Legislative Recruitment and Electoral Systems', in A. Karam (ed.), *Women in Parliament: Beyond Numbers*, Stockholm: IDEA.

Norris, P. (1994), 'The Impact of the Electoral System on the Election of Women to National Legislatures', in M. Githens, P. Norris and J. Lovenduski (eds), *Different Roles, Different Voices: Women and Politics in the United States and Europe*, New York: HarperCollins.

Norris, P. (ed.) (1997), *Women, Media, and Politics*, New York: Oxford University Press.

Norris, P. (1999), 'Women's Representation and Electoral Systems', in R. Rose (ed.), *Encyclopedia of Electoral Systems*, Washington, DC: CQ Press.

NWC (National Women's Council of Ireland) (2002a), *Politics Needs More Women: What the Irish Political System Must Do*, www.nwci.ie.

NWC (National Women's Council of Ireland) (2002b), *Irish Politics: Jobs for the Boys!*, www.nwci.ie.

O'Connor, P. (1998), *Emerging Voices: Women in Contemporary Irish Society*, Dublin: Institute of Public Administration.

Phillips, A. (1991), *Engendering Democracy*, Cambridge: Polity.

PDs (Progressive Democratics) (1997), *Manifesto 1997: A New Deal*, Dublin: Progressive Democrat Party.

PDs (Progressive Democrats) (2002), *Manifesto 2002: Value for Your Vote*, Dublin: Progressive Democrat Party.

Randall, V. and Smyth, A. (1987), 'Bishops and Bailiwicks: Obstacles to Women's Political Participation in Ireland', *Economic and Social Review*, Vol. 18, No. 3, pp. 189–214.

Rule, W. and Zimmerman, J. (1992), *United States Electoral Systems: Their Impact on Women and Minorities*, New York: Praeger.

SCSW (Second Commission on the Status of Women) (1993), *Second Commission on the Status of Women: Report to the Government*, Dublin: Stationery Office.

SCSW (Second Commission on the Status of Women) (1996), *Second Progress Report of* the Monitoring Committee on the Implementation of the Recommendations of the Second Commission on the Status of Women, Dublin: Stationery Office.

SCSW (Second Commission on the Status of Women) (1999), *Third Progress Report on the Implementation of the Recommendations of the Second Commission on the Status of Women*, Dublin: Brunswick Press.

Shannon, C. (1997), 'The Changing Face of Cathleen ni Houlihan: Women and Politics in Ireland, 1960–1996', in A. Bradley and M. Gialanella Valiulis (eds), *Gender and Sexuality in Modern Ireland*, Amherst: University of Massachusetts Press.

Sinn Féin (2002), *Building an Ireland of Equals*, Dublin: Sinn Féin.

Transparency International (2000), *Year 2000 Corruption Perceptions Index*, Berlin: Transparency International.

Ware, A. (1996), *Political Parties and Party Systems*, New York: Oxford University Press.

Whyte, J. H. (1980), *Church and State in Modern Ireland: 1923–1979*, Dublin: Gill and Macmillan.

Wilcox, C. (1991), 'The Causes and Consequences of Feminist Consciousness among Western European Women', *Comparative Political Studies*, Vol. 23, No. 4, pp. 519–45.

Websites

www.fiannafail.ie
www.finegael.ie
www.gov.ie/poc (Standards in Public Office Commission)
www.greenparty.ie
www.ipu.org (Inter-Parliamentary Union)
www.justice.ie (Department of Justice, Equality and Law Reform)
www.labour.ie
www.nwci.ie (National Women's Council of Ireland)
www.progressivedemocrats.ie
www.qub.ac.uk/cawp (Center for the Advancement of Women in Politics)
www.sinnfein.ie

Further reading

Clift, E. and Brazaitis, T. (2000), *Madam President: Shattering the Last Glass Ceiling*, New York: Scribner.

Galligan, Y. (2001), 'The Politics of Women's Representation in Northern Ireland and the Republic of Ireland', John Henry Whyte Memorial Lecture, 22 November, Belfast: Centre for Advancement of Women in Politics.

Sapiro, V. (1981), 'When are Interests Interesting?', *American Political Science Review*, Vol. 75, pp. 701–16.

Thomas, S. and Wilcox, C. (eds) (1998), *Women and Elective Office: Past, Present, and Future*, New York: Oxford University Press.

Index